THE SOUL
—OF A—
LEADER

THE SOUL
— OF A —
LEADER

*Character, Conviction, and Ten Lessons
in Political Greatness*

Waller R. Newell

HARPER

An Imprint of HarperCollins*Publishers*
www.harpercollins.com

HarperCollins books may be purchased for educational, business, or sales promotional use. For information, please write: Special Markets Department, Harper-Collins Publishers, 10 East 53rd Street, New York, NY 10022.

FIRST EDITION

Designed by Renato Stanisic

Library of Congress Cataloging-in-Publication Data

Newell, Waller R.

The soul of a leader : character, conviction, and ten lessons in political greatness / by Waller R. Newell.—1st ed.
  p. cm.
ISBN: 978-0-06-123854-3

1. Presidents—United States—History. 2. Elections—United States—History. 3. Leadership—History. 4. Democracy—History. I. Title.
JK511.N49 2009
352'.23—dc22   2008036432

09 10 11 12 13 OV/RRD 10 9 8 7 6 5 4 3 2 1

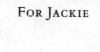

FOR JACKIE

Contents

INTRODUCTION

What Are We
Looking for in a Leader?

W hat are we looking for in a leader? In 2008, as the American presidential election race heated up, the theme of *leadership* was on everyone's lips. Each candidate claimed that he possessed the capacity for leadership, that magical quality of personality, character, conviction, and vision that transcends mere policy debates and forges a new path for the country as a whole. While this is true in every election, it was especially true in the 2008 election. Why? Because, for the first time in half a century, there was no sitting president or vice president to take the field. In the primaries, all of the candidates in both major parties were relatively untested for national office, even if they had backgrounds in Congress or as governors. Because each candidate needed to find a way of bringing himself or herself to the public on a truly national level, the contenders had to make leadership *the* fundamental issue. Each claimed this charismatic quality as a way of getting out in front of the pack, of galvanizing the electorate at an emotional as well as a rational level.

The importance of staking this claim to leadership is compounded by the widespread feeling, already effectively evoked by Senator Barack Obama, that we are not just witnessing a change in the direction of the presidency, but a *generational* change. The torch is being passed from a generation shaped by the Vietnam War to one shaped by 9/11 and the war in Iraq—in the same way that the previous generation received the torch from their predecessors, who had been shaped by World War II and the cold war. Yet if anything is safe to predict, it is that the new generation with which Senator Obama identifies himself will be faced by the same kinds of threats on a similar scale of war, terrorism, famine, and genocidal violence as those that so sorely tested the baby boomers in recent years and the Greatest Generation before them. How will the new generation of leaders respond? What will inspire them? What precedents will they follow? It is important that we reopen a series of traditional questions whose contemporary relevance is more compelling than ever. What is the special quality of leadership that sets the great ones—a Lincoln, a Churchill, an FDR—apart? What can history teach us about prudent, principled, and courageous statecraft? Our theme is nothing less than the *soul* of a leader and the lessons of political greatness.

To repeat our original question: What are we looking for in a leader? In recent years, political junkies of all stripes may have indulged in a period of addiction to the television series *The West Wing*. The actor Martin Sheen, who played Democratic president Josiah Bartlett, was cheered when he appeared at the 2004 Democratic Convention as if he really were the president, or what was wanted in a president. It is easy to see why: President Bartlett's character was a compendium of qualities that, while probably impossible to combine in any single candidate in real life, answer to powerful traditions and longings in the American electorate. A native of New Hampshire and former governor of that state, he was descended from a patrician Yankee family whose ancestors included a signer of the Declaration of Independence, evoking a familiar northeastern pedigree of authority we identify with Franklin Roosevelt and the later aspirations of the Kennedys to the status of proper Bostonians. Yet while he attended the predictable prep school in the wooded setting, instead of proceeding to an Ivy League college, the fictional Bartlett broke ranks and attended Notre Dame—connecting him to the brawny industrial and agricultural heartland of the Midwest, another powerhouse constituency in presidential politics. Improbably, given his *Mayflower* pedigree, although not impossibly, he was Roman Catholic, not the more typical Protestant. This gave him a more populist, urban ethnic edge—his backslapping, anecdote-spinning manner was more Irish than WASP, more like JFK than, say, McGeorge Bundy. He was a loving family man, always desirable in a president. His wife, Abigail, was a nationally reputable thoracic surgeon, but with a touch of Dixie, both sexy and mothering, like a synthesis of Hillary and Lady Bird Johnson. He came from a dysfunctional family background, having been abused by his father. Finally, answering the public's desire that their presidents be in some way intellectually distinguished and a cut above the average, he rather improbably combined with this mélange of Yankee, Catholic, and midwestern roots no less than a Nobel Prize in economics! He was a dramatic digest of the qualities David Halberstam called, in reference to the Kennedy administration, "the best and the brightest," an amalgam of the most attractive presidents of both parties since World War II.

When compared with such fictional ideals, it's hardly surprising that few of the candidates who emerged in the real 2008 race measured up. Instinctively, the public senses that each candidate has both attractive and unattractive or dubious qualities. Among the Republicans, Mitt Romney was handsome and personable, a family man, the son of a popular Michigan governor and a successful former governor himself of Massachusetts who introduced a public health-care system that many believe could serve as a model for the whole nation. Yet he made an unseemly number of flip-flops, reversing previous liberal views about abortion rights and stem cell research in order to court social-issue conservatives, which smacks of insincerity and a lack of conviction. Rudy Giuliani, a hero of 9/11 while mayor of New York, momentarily defied expectations by becoming a leading candidate in a party where southern or Sunbelt origins and a strong pro-life stance were thought to be indispensable. However, while he did not reverse himself as often or as blatantly as Romney, and refused to say he supports the criminalization of abortion or the reversal of *Roe v. Wade*, he said he was content with whatever the Supreme Court rules, pledging only to appoint strict constructionist judges. It was a prudent middle ground, but it did not convey strong conviction in the same way as his unflinching support of the war on terrorism. The nominee, John McCain, was a war hero of astonishing courage, a steadfast supporter of the war in Iraq, and a man who has always compelled respect for refusing to toe the party line when it conflicted with his best judgment (over, for instance, campaign finance reform); yet he has also stumbled by appearing to waffle over gay marriage.

The candidates on the Democratic side also earned mixed reviews from their party's base. Hillary Clinton gained much respect for her hard work as a senator, the command of issues she shared with her husband, the former president, and her refusal to don sackcloth and ashes over her vote in favor of toppling Saddam Hussein by military invasion. Yet her uncomfortable waffling on that issue—she would not apologize for her vote then, but if she had to do it again, she would not, and she favors repealing the legislation now—together with her still widely perceived qualities of shrillness, naked ambition, and a queenly disdain for criticism preserved the air of distrust that surrounded her. That uneasiness was compounded by the flaccid quality of her speeches, a string of generalities that seemed designed to prevent her from committing herself to any specific view ahead of time, and by her cringe-making attempts to "loosen up" in public by telling rather heavy-handed jokes about her problems with Bill and then informing the press frostily that it was now time to laugh.

The party's nominee, Barack Obama, is articulate and exudes a natural grace in public perhaps not seen since John F. Kennedy. Many have seen a real magic in the man when he speaks, especially among people under the age of forty. He has likened himself to JFK, so far the youngest man ever to be elected president, in part as a way of deflecting criticism about a lack of previous experience that he implies was true of Kennedy as well. It is true that both men ran for president with scanty congressional track records, and that Kennedy's youthful vigor compensated for his lack of legislative nuts-and-bolts experience. But it is not an entirely accurate parallel. Despite his own comparative political inexperience, JFK did serve for three terms in the House of Repre-

sentatives and was twice elected to the Senate, whereas Obama has yet
to complete a single term. More important, JFK, unlike Obama, was a
bona fide war hero, shaped, like the rest of his generation, by the great
struggle against the enemies of democracy led by Franklin Roosevelt
and Winston Churchill. Moreover, he was a voracious student of history going back to his Harvard days, while Obama has shown few signs
of historical appetite. Above all, JFK came from a powerful political dynasty whose founder, his father, Joseph P. Kennedy, an S.E.C. chairman
and ambassador to Britain under Franklin Roosevelt, was tied to a formidable Democratic political machine in Boston. JFK grew up in an atmosphere saturated with the expectation of public service. By contrast,
Senator Obama, while vastly more affable and at ease in public than
Hillary, is mainly a candidate of abstract nouns—peace, hope, change,
the future—that leave one in doubt about a strong sense of purpose or
the grit of his inner personality. He is in a sense a princely candidate,
offering the public the gift of his own graciousness and optimism, while
remaining mostly an enigma when it comes to how he would govern.

All of the candidates so far on either side, then, have attractive
qualities and troubling ones. None of them adds up to a Jed Bartlett.
Has anyone ever? That is one of the issues we will explore in this
book. Some, I'll suggest, have come close to matching the complete
set of ideal qualities we all seem instinctively to yearn for, while others
have striven for them but failed in ways both saddening and instructive. The rising generation of leadership contenders will find that they,
too, like all past aspirants to high office, will have to aim for the height
and avoid the pitfalls, and this will in turn require them to search for
the soul of a leader in themselves.

Has the Meaning of Leadership Changed?

A skeptic might ask at this point: Can history—even recent history, let
alone going back to the time-tested lessons of Churchill, Lincoln, or
Pericles—really provide guidance for the requirements of leadership
in the rising generation? Has not the meaning of leadership changed
so fundamentally as to make past lessons outmoded?

There are reasons for entertaining this possibility, reasons that are widely recognized by even casual students of the culture. Leadership has certainly been demystified. Saturation media coverage through the growth of cable television, the Internet, and the blogosphere has made it difficult for leaders to preserve their mystique, an aura of dignity, and separation from the public at large. No personal problem or ailment can be concealed for long from the press. Gone forever are the days when Franklin Roosevelt's polio could be kept secret, with a pliant press corps cooperating by interviewing him seated in his open car, or when JFK could cajole reporters with a wink and a manly nudge to cover up his trysts. Media saturation makes every president almost too familiar a presence, and that creates a false sense of intimacy, leading to the pop culture craving fed by Barbara Walters, Larry King, or Oprah Winfrey to make leaders reveal their "true" selves before millions on television. It has almost become a ritual that they must cry or otherwise emote about their marital problems in order to prove that they are "real" people like other Americans. Even the redoubtable Margaret Thatcher had to produce tears for Barbara Walters to show that she, too, was an ordinary housewife and mom between bouts of union busting and sinking the *Belgrado*.

The magic of leadership has also been eroded by a widespread and well-documented cynicism among Americans about the motives of politicians. Global political movements like the peace movement of the 1980s and the environmentalist movement rekindling itself today appear to transcend narrow national boundaries in their appeal to international idealism, making the concerns of ordinary American politics seem parochial and self-interested. Moreover, the potency and glamour of leadership once associated with presidents like Roosevelt and Kennedy have to some extent been siphoned off by celebrity leaders like the pop star Bono or the late Princess of Wales, whose gossamer realm of international media celebrity corresponds to seemingly borderless issues like the alleged ravages of economic globalization.

Of course there is nothing new about international causes and alliances, whether it be the crusade to abolish slavery in the nineteenth century, where Britain led the way, or the great military alliances of the two world wars. For that matter, the American Founding Fathers appealed to what Jefferson termed "the opinions of mankind" in Enlightenment Europe for support. But in these instances, while the cause may have been transnational, it was individual nation-states that took the lead. Global politics means something rather different. Starting with the peace movement of the 1980s and recurring in the antiglobalization and environmentalist movements of today, many people feel that they belong primarily to a "new civil society" of progressive young people united by their idealism, and only secondarily to nation-states. They believe, moreover, that they are the catalyst for change, with nation-states playing catch-up or frequently retarding progress by sticking to the old-fashioned politics of international tension, the arms race, and the struggle for economic superiority. In its most utopian version, the global politics movement believes that the continued existence of the nation-state, with its retrograde values of patriotism, profit, and exclusiveness, is the primary obstacle to world peace and saving the earth from the ravages of technological exploitation. At the same time, however, an appeal must still be made to the leaders of powerful nations to get on board.

Increasingly, celebrities have come forward to act as leaders for this alleged new global civil society. Internationally known, they already transcend borders, whether it be the late Princess of Wales's activism against land mines and on behalf of AIDS victims or the entertainers Bono and Angelina Jolie on the eradication of poverty. In the case of Al Gore, we have the interesting new variation of someone who previously held high national office becoming a world celebrity *after* leaving conventional politics, achieving a second lease on political life by joining the international Celebritariat of socially conscious movie stars, rock groups, and talk show hosts. While the national leaders at the G-8 summit in June 2007 were preoccupied with traditional great power tensions—principally Russia's saber rattling to counter what it saw as American poaching on its sphere of influence through building a missile shield installation in the Czech Republic—Bono and the singer-activist Bob Geldof complained loudly that these old-fashioned issues had been a gigantic "distraction" from the real issues.

Nevertheless, while these celebrities have great influence (if not always great knowledge) and are even courted by presidents and prime ministers, ultimately it is the latter who must be persuaded and who must take action. It is too early to tell, while the new century is still young, where the trend toward global politics will lead and how much further national leadership elites will be displaced by its self-proclaimed celebrity leaders. My own guess is that, for the foreseeable future at least, it is the leaders of the great nation-states who will continue to call the shots, although they will be unable to resist the pressure from the new spirit of global citizenship. (The lifelong anticommunist Ronald Reagan ended his presidency by proposing unprecedentedly deep cuts in both American and Soviet nuclear arsenals, and pressure from the peace movement at home certainly played a role.) But that means, at the end of the day, that statecraft of the traditional kind will remain of paramount importance—and be influenced, as always, by the psychology of leadership.

Compounding the demystification of traditional national politics and a general cynicism about the motives of elected officials is an emphasis, beginning in the 1970s and intensifying every year since then, on seeing politics purely as a game, a technique for winning, divorced from a substantive debate about good and bad policy, just and unjust aims, virtue as opposed to vice, and a sound character as opposed to a flawed one. What we witness now is politics as *process*—a flurry of communication skills, spin, and focus groups. The media often treat politics like a spectator sport, and the public absorbs this cynical view. Recent presidential races have exposed candidates, including Al Gore and John Kerry, as more or less openly casting about for some short-term trick, knack, or hook—a different hairstyle, a new tie color—as if this might turn the tide. The slow build of a Nixon or even a Clinton, evolving their views through long years of previous public service and debate, seems more and more a thing of the past. Further contributing to this cynical take on politics as a game of media saturation and image manipulation are the staggering amounts of money now needed to run, each presidential race eclipsing the seemingly unsurpassable level of loot from the last one.

The influence of the commercial media, including the entertainment media, on presidential and congressional races during the past twenty years has been a hotly debated partisan issue. Democrats point to the growth of "soft money" vehicles on the Republican side during the 1980s, including political action committees with their own cable programs and the rise of publicly licensed broadcasters like Fox that have a consistently pro-conservative slant. For their part, Republicans complain that the vast majority of journalists, including broadcast anchorpersons, are Democrats, and that the bulk of Hollywood movies and television series contain a more or less openly anti-conservative bias. They also bristle at the political activism of movie and rock stars who, they argue, use their celebrity status to promote various leftish causes on *Jay Leno* or *Letterman* while hawking a new CD or film.

In my view, both sides have very powerful media resources that largely balance each other, but of different sorts. On the one hand, the influential filmmaker Jonathan Demme can release a remake of *The Manchurian Candidate* on the eve of the 2004 election that updates the villains from the Communist Chinese to a sinister American vice presidential candidate with Haliburton-like ties, converting the film to a multimillion-dollar paid political announcement against the Bush administration. On the other hand, conservative pundits like Rush Limbaugh and Bill O'Reilly reach millions of devoted followers every week on airwaves licensed by the federal government. Moreover, both parties are quickly discovering that the world of traditional political advertising and other kinds of media, including film and the blogosphere, are merging rapidly. Not only are increasing amounts of campaign funds being raised online, but political ads are now being produced on desktop computers by political activists not necessarily affiliated with or approved by official campaign organizations and sent directly onto the Internet, bypassing the usual apparatus of focus groups and campaign advisors. Three young men in their twenties from upstate New York (one of whom was working at a Red Lobster) recently created an online movie called *Loose Change* that debates whether the Bush administration carried out the 9/11 attacks itself or merely allowed them to happen in order to have an excuse to launch unjust wars. At least ten million people viewed that movie online before the last midterm elections, in which the Republicans lost both houses of Congress, and the young men were approached by several major Hollywood studios about a big-budget Hollywood remake of their homemade Internet video. Who could deny that the opportunities for increased awareness and debate offered by these new technologies also offer increased potential for abuse? There is no point wishing them away—they're here to stay.

There is a nostalgic tendency among people of my baby boomer generation on both the left and the right to idealize the media of the Edward R. Murrow days as somehow more sober, more responsible, than reporters of today. There is some truth to this. But it is important to bear in mind that, throughout history, politicians and parties have *always* sought to spend money to shape public opinion and thereby advance both their material interests and their political convictions, and they have stopped at nothing to do this. Politicians in late republican Rome like Pompey and Caesar shamelessly lavished money and offices on their partisan supporters while blackening the reputations of their foes. Augustus Caesar was a mastermind at seducing artists like Vergil with fat stipends in order to ensure that their poems would serve as propaganda for his numberless professed virtues. During the French and Russian revolutions, broadsheets alleging the most scandalous acts of sexual debauchery by the reigning empresses were all over the streets. If the American press did achieve a certain sobriety and objectivity during the Pax Americana of the fifties, that had certainly not been true in the past. Throughout the nineteenth century, newspapers regularly engaged in outrageous character assassination. Andrew Jackson was accused in the press of being married to an adultress and bigamist. John Quincy Adams was lambasted for taking on the airs of a "European potentate" by purchasing a pool table for the White House.

We may well need to rethink our inherited distinctions between such categories as politician, interest group, celebrity, and journalist. They are all tending to merge. But that, as I have just suggested, is in a sense a return behind a fairly recent interval of sobriety to what has in fact been the main tendency throughout political history—the unconstrained pursuit of influence through the organization of like-minded opinion, heavily larded by money and partisan muckraking. When we realize that, in embracing this brave new world of merging boundaries and Internet communication, we are in a sense only returning to what has been true all along, albeit with powerful new technological means, it is less disturbing—indeed, it can be a source of excitement and new energies.

Michael Moore and George Clooney are not merely filmmakers and celebrities who also happen to have leftward partisan political leanings. They are in effect *leaders* of important constituencies within the left, organizing opinion *through* their creative work as artists in the same way that in the past would have been done by political action committees, and, further back still, local party organizations and urban political "machines." Michael Moore is in a way the William Randolph Hearst of today, extending his sharply partisan message by film rather than by print, but like Hearst making a bundle of money in the process and accumulating enormous influence and star power among some core constituencies of the Democratic Party. He had an undeniable impact on the Republican defeat during the midterm elections by rallying the antiwar base of the party, and he continues to exert that influence now, extended more recently to the scandal of American health care. Politicians started becoming celebrities as far back as FDR, and certainly by the time of JFK, who was in many ways a Hollywood figure. In more recent years, the reverse has been happening—celebrities are becoming politicians, whether outright like Ronald Reagan and Arnold Schwarzenegger, or indirectly, as shapers of public opinion. Moore or Clooney (well, certainly Clooney) could probably run for public office if an appealing opportunity presented itself. But they may well prefer the reach of their influence through film and the media to the ardors of campaigning and the need for habitual caution in public speech. The same is true of the daytime television guru Oprah Winfrey, whose campaign appearances for Barack Obama pushed the distinction between media celebrity and political power broker to the breaking point.

Career officeholders, as well as the serious print media for national politics, sometimes flatter themselves that celebrities who run for office will embarrass themselves because they lack the experience of "professional" politicians. But this expectation has been repeatedly contradicted by events. Think of Ronald Reagan, whose complex and evolving political personality we will consider at some length in Part One. Whatever his failings, they certainly did not include withering under the assault of candidates more narrowly confined to political careers like Jimmy Carter and Walter Mondale, whom Reagan trounced at the polls. Many pundits were licking their chops over how Arnold Schwarzenegger would inevitably be exposed as a fraud when career politicians like the incumbent governor of California Gray Davis cut him to ribbons in the television debates over hard policy. In reality, Schwarzenegger displayed every bit as much evident competence as they did on the issues, and considerably more in his ability to fashion the issues into a broad message that appealed to average voters. That he could fashion an accessible rhetoric on hard policy issues was no doubt connected to his acting skills, a skill set any career politician would envy and spend a good deal of effort trying to acquire.

Of course, it is undeniable that my point about not being unduly concerned about the blurring of lines between celebrity and politician could be taken too far. Ronald Reagan's rise was aided by his movie career, where he almost always played the all-American good guy embodied by his candidacy. But on his way to the White House he also put in a long public speaking career on conservative issues and two terms as governor of America's richest and most populous state. By contrast, Fred Dalton Thompson, to whom many were looking to revive the Reagan magic, began as a prosecutor, moved on to playing authoritative conservative roles in movies, then won a Senate seat, which he left partway through his second term so as to once again play an authoritative conservative character on *Law & Order*. This is a case where, whatever his merits may prove to be, his media persona is indistinguishable from his political persona—indeed, he used politics as a springboard to great success in the entertainment media, whereas Reagan did the reverse.

Another recent variation, perhaps the oddest of all to date, has been Al Gore. As already noted, he became a celebrity through his advocacy of environmentalism after having already served in high office as senator and vice president, and having been his party's nominee in 2000 for the presidency, perhaps suggesting that, whereas before celebrity might have been a stepping-stone to high office, now high office might lead to becoming a celebrity afterward over a new set of policy issues—although he may use this recent celebrity status to return to national politics yet again.

Still, while the merging of politics and fame may be perplexing or even troubling, it is pointless to criticize celebrities for using their influence to propagate a partisan political message. For Michael Moore, his power as a filmmaker and his power to shape opinion are indistinguishable, and how can he be criticized for it? The answer is not to carp about his alleged abuse of his fame and wealth, but to rebut the message of his films rigorously if one takes issue with them. It is understandable that one sometimes feels irritation with celebrities for using fame gained in another sphere, like pop music or movies, to speak out on public policy when, absent that fame, they would command no more attention than the average person. But how are they different, in using their influence and wealth this way, from newspaper barons like Rupert Murdoch or, indeed, any newspaper editorialist who may have no recognized expertise or credentials in the topic under discussion? These are all ways in which the First Amendment enables us to organize the opinion of like-minded partisans in order to do what we think is right in politics.

It is well to remember that the concept of the mainstream press as the "fourth estate" has no unique constitutional status apart from the freedom of speech guaranteed to everyone. It merely captures how the mainstream print and electronic media attempt to set themselves apart from other opinion makers. In First Amendment terms, there is no difference between Seymour Hersh and Bono, between Charlton Heston and Anthony Lewis, between David Frum and Angelina Jolie, just as there is no difference between the *New York Times*, a political action cable channel, a blog, or a corporate newsletter. All are engaged in organizing like-minded opinion, often with a dividend of large financial profit, whether for themselves, their businesses, their causes, or all three. And, whatever we may think of their views, these opinion makers—stars, tycoons, filmmakers, columnists—have every right to do this. It is the views themselves that matter, not who holds or is entitled to hold them. For instance, in my opinion Michael Moore is dead wrong about Republican foreign policy, but not because he is a filmmaker—because he is wrong.

Character Counts

Although much about the political process has changed in the past twenty years, the fundamentals remain the same. Character counts. The challenges of war and peace, of justice at home and abroad, arise continually anew. Despite the oceans of money and the vast new technological means for communication, the public will ultimately take the measure of the men and women running and ask themselves: Who is the most honest? The most courageous? Who has thought the most carefully about what government needs to do? Bill Clinton is reported to have limited his advice to the former First Lady as the 2008 primaries got under way to this: Stick to a few clear and consistent themes. You can adjust your tactics, but not these basic issues. People see through flip-flops and inconsistencies, and those candidates generally lose. As the only full two-term Democratic president since Franklin Roosevelt, Clinton was more than entitled to an opinion. As we will see, this capacity for flexible tactics in the service of an unchanging long-range purpose is one of the hallmarks of great political leadership throughout history, from Periclean Athens down to the American founding and the modern titans, including Lincoln, Churchill, and FDR.

Major leaders have *always* been celebrities, and they have always attracted mass adulation as well as envy. The Greek historian Xenophon, in his idealized portrait of Cyrus the Great, the founder of the Persian Empire that almost snuffed out Greece, reports that Cyrus was the first great leader to enhance his height and appearance artificially. Beginning with Augustus Caesar, the physical appearance of all Roman emperors was flagrantly improved in their official public sculpture, and not merely out of vanity. These busts and statues, distributed throughout the public squares and buildings of every city in the empire, were meant to show how the emperor embodied in his person the best aspirations of the Roman government for promoting peace, order, law, liberal education, prosperity, and moral virtue. In principle, it was no different from the burnishing, airbrushing, and soft-focus photography in promotional videos for the candidates of today, captured as they walk pensively along a beach, looking suitably grave or benign by turns, hair and complexion plumped and plucked. Statesmen, moreover, have always had speechwriters and spin doctors to shape their messages to the public. Pericles was a close friend of the famous teacher of rhetoric Protagoras. Vergil and other artists like Horace enhanced the virtues of the Emperor Augustus and his divine mission to bring peace and civilization to the world. Coins and temple inscriptions communicated the main "talking points" of each new emperor's administration to every city in the Roman Empire.

Moreover, it has always been recognized that certain leaders stand out from the rest, sometimes for their extraordinary energy and ardor in serving the common good, sometimes (unfortunately) for an ability to dazzle and overwhelm that can serve darker ambitions for exclusive domination, power, and glory. The nineteenth-century German sociologist Max Weber called this *charisma*, a term derived from ancient Greek to describe leaders like Oedipus the Tyrant in Sophocles' drama, leaders who, through their unusually great public services, achieve a kind of godlike celebrity and adulation—more so if, like Oedipus, they have obtained their power illegitimately by murder and usurpation and therefore must work extra hard to prove that they deserve it on their merits. Without making an ethical judgment, at a gut level most students of history and current events can distinguish these potentially charismatic figures—not always or necessarily benevolent, but larger than life, compelling, or unusual—from more ordinary leaders. Contrast, say, Napoleon Bonaparte with the Duke of Wellington. Or Franklin Roosevelt with Dwight D. Eisenhower. Or Richard Nixon with Gerald Ford. Or Margaret Thatcher with Ted Heath. Solid and competent leaders versus more brilliant, contentious, aggressive figures, either hated or adored. Indeed—as we shall see—sometimes the greatest servants of the common good have shared certain darker qualities with its greatest abusers.

The Crucible of War

Before turning to that dilemma, however, another constant in great leadership past and present must be mentioned first. If there is a single factor that prevents politics from collapsing entirely into a carousel of process, gamesmanship, and communication skills, and requires old-fashioned virtues of the kind demonstrated historically by great leaders, it is international affairs and the threat of war. When war and terrorism loom, it doesn't matter whether you wear earth tones or a red power tie. War is the crucible of leadership, whether we like it or not, and it's not going away. Time and again, as we will see in this book, American presidents who come to power bent on emphasizing issues of domestic politics, opportunity, and justice for their own people find themselves pulled into international conflict—it is a common thread from Pericles down to Thomas Jefferson, Theodore and Franklin Roosevelt, JFK and LBJ, Jimmy Carter, Bill Clinton, and Bush senior and junior. Usually the conflicts are between the United States and another country. In Lincoln's case, of course, his main political mission was dealing with an internal war that threatened to destroy the still-young American republic.

Nations that have openly pursued conquest and empire, such as France and Britain, have somewhat less difficulty making room for martial glory in their self-understanding. Britons still sing "Rule Britannia" in lusty tones at the soccer match, though their empire is long gone. The honor guard of the president of France with its magnificent uniforms recalls the Emperor Napoleon's elite cavalry corps, the Imperial Guard. But Americans find it particularly distasteful and morally queasy to think that leadership in wartime is the chief test of greatness (although some presidents, like FDR and Nixon, have played the role not merely willingly but with a good deal of private excitement and gusto). Americans tend to believe that it is natural for human beings to pursue their individual freedom and prosperity in peace, and that everyone around the world would do the same if left alone and allowed to do so. They tend to see war as a distortion introduced into human affairs by an unscrupulous few, or by religious or ideological fanaticism, or as an act of desperation bred by poverty and a hopeless future. If only we could communicate with our would-be foes, many Americans are convinced, or help alleviate their poverty, everyone would come to their senses and choose the fruits of peace. The idea that Americans want peace with all nations, and have no unjust ambitions abroad, runs back to the very foundation of the republic. As Thomas Jefferson put it in his *Notes on the State of Virginia*:

It should be our endeavor to cultivate the peace and friendship of every nation, even of that which has injured us most [Great Britain], when we shall have carried our point against her. Our interest will be to throw open the doors of commerce, and to knock off all its shackles, giving perfect freedom to all persons for the vent of whatever they may choose to bring into our ports, and asking the same in theirs. Never was so much false arithmetic employed on any subject, as that which has been employed to persuade nations that it is in their interest to go to war.

Perhaps it would be best of all, Jefferson continues, if America isolated herself from Europe and the rest of the world so as to minimize the danger of being drawn into wars:

This I hope will be our wisdom. And, perhaps, to remove as much as possible the occasions of making war, it might be better for us to abandon the ocean altogether, that being the element whereon we shall be principally exposed to jostle with other nations.

It can be difficult for Americans to accept that anger, aggression, religious zeal, honor seeking, and a lust for domination may be irreducible dimensions of human nature. They may exist alongside other equally natural desires for personal comfort and security, or a leaning toward tolerance and justice in dealing with others. But they may sometimes burst those boundaries, and they will never be eradicated from the human soul. Again and again, the United States, a major power in the world for the past century, has been compelled to assume a role in such international conflicts, and often the role of world leader.

We witness the same trend repeatedly. A president comes to power bent on being less absorbed in foreign policy than his predecessor, determined to focus instead on solving America's own problems, and ends up being lured or compelled to become embroiled in international affairs himself. Lyndon Johnson inherited the White House with no other aim than to help the disadvantaged at home; instead, he was almost entirely consumed by the debacle in Vietnam. Jimmy Carter came to the White House determined to withdraw from what he saw as the morass of Kissingerian realpolitik and obsession with being a world power to restore American decency at home; in the end, his most important achievement was brokering the Camp David Accords making peace between Israel and Egypt. Bill Clinton's 1992 campaign, captured in his staff's in-house slogan "It's the economy, stupid!" marked his desire to turn away from the late Reagan administration's ever more sweeping forays into international grand strategy and enact domestic reforms to benefit the American people. But Clinton, too, proved unable to resist the power of the presidency to levy war (intervening in Kosovo) and make peace (brokering the failed negotiations between Israel and Arafat). Finally, George W. Bush took office aiming to focus on "compassionate conservatism" at home, including the promotion of faith-based organizations to take over some roles of the welfare state and rescuing the pension system, and was widely perceived as a neo-isolationist. Instead, his entire presidency was defined by 9/11 and his entire political capital used up by his wars in Iraq and Afghanistan.

Some of the newer generation of aspiring leaders like Barack Obama have shown a likely sincere, and typically American, optimism that the dangers of international tension and terrorism are fading, that a new generation will be better at communicating with potential foes and making peace, that once the dreadful error of the Bush administration's war in Iraq is reversed we can all return to concentrating on "hope" for the American future at home. But it will not be that way. Whoever wins the 2008 presidential election, whether he wishes it or not, will be pulled into world affairs and very likely into the use of military force abroad. Whatever else may change about the new generation of leadership, this fact will not. A President Obama may come to office proclaiming that we must turn inward and heal our wounds at home; yet by the end of his time in office, he will have been pulled, with lesser or greater reluctance, into various foreign hot spots—the Israeli-Palestinian conflict, genocide and famine in Africa, the instability of Pakistan, the saber rattling of Russia, North Korean and Iranian nuclear mischief making, China's menacing of Taiwan and tug-of-war with Japan over the Senkaku Islands, and any number of others.

Because this can be predicted to happen with about as much certainty as anything in politics, we need to be thinking ahead of time about which candidates seem best equipped for this role, because, like it or not, the successful one will be bound to assume it. Whether it is to be president McCain or Obama, as I write these lines in the summer of 2008, both will face the same ongoing world crisis. As a new generation succeeds the old, whether led by the eloquent young man or by the grizzled veteran, the challenges will be the same. In normal times, democracies can rely on the strength of their institutions to make up for a lack of brilliance and boldness in their leaders. As we will see at length in Part Two, the American founders were keenly aware of this and counted it a strength of the new republic that institutions mattered more than statesmen of genius like those produced by the ancient republics of Greece and Rome. They knew from Thucydides and the other ancient authorities on statecraft that some of these, like Pericles, were genuinely dedicated public servants, but that others hid behind their talents a desire to dominate and even tyrannize over their fellow citizens.

However, grave crises require exceptional leaders—especially so grave a crisis as war. We also first learn this from Thucydides, who saw how Athenian expansionism and the superpower struggle with

Sparta gave a brilliant but unscrupulous adventurer like Alcibiades the opportunity to thrust himself to the head of Athenian politics in a way not possible under normal peacetime conditions. Since Alcibiades, the West has witnessed a steady stream of men who relish the stress and glory of military and international affairs, whether for good or ill or a mixture of motives—Napoleon, Lincoln, Churchill, FDR, JFK, Nixon—and who, by amassing the authority to wield armed might, begin to be perceived by some of their fellow citizens as overbearing and even a threat to their liberties. A precise evaluation of their motives must, as we will see in this book, vary from case to case, but the tension remains throughout. War, which cannot be avoided at all times, is a catalyst for extraordinary ambition at home.

There was a tendency during the later Bush years among political partisans, including some of the candidates in the presidential primaries, to act as though America's perceived low standing in the world stemmed solely from the president's failures of policy in Iraq, and that his replacement by a new president would in and of itself restore America's prestige. But the new president will face many of the same crisis spots, because they do not originate in American policy alone, and because hostility toward the United States is often a matter of a deeply principled hostility toward the Enlightenment and its secular values, which America, the Athens and democratic empire of today, most fully embodies.

The war on terrorism will therefore resume the moment the new president takes the oath of office. If Iran continues on its path toward nuclear weapons, the crunch in relations with America will involve the new president very quickly, and talking to Iran's leaders will not be sufficient to remove those weapons. Only then will we know how serious Iran is about acting on the most apocalyptic strain of its rhetoric, the destruction of Israel to spark a nuclear Armageddon leading to the Last Days. These tensions may well only increase in the coming years, as will the Israeli-Palestinian conflict and the possibility of another war with Hezbollah, intensified by Iran's continued subversion of Lebanon's internal affairs through its proxies Hezbollah and Syria.

Even if—and it is a very big if—American forces are able to withdraw from Iraq without leaving civil strife in their wake, a likely outcome there is a de facto Shiite majority regime or independent Shiite statelet with its own links to Iran. Finally, less noticed but very real, the military situation of American and NATO forces in Afghanistan remains precarious, with the Taliban showing an unexpected capacity for resurgence and making a comeback as a regional governing authority in some places.

Looming behind these strategic issues is their root cause, the utopian vision of jihadist and terrorist ideology itself, the successor to the totalitarian worldviews of communism and fascism that embroiled America in several wars in the past century. Distortions of genuine religion, all of the jihadist movements, from Hezbollah to Hamas, the Taliban and the most radical reaches of the Iranian mullocracy, share a uniform blueprint for what they will do once they achieve or increase their power—a collectivist utopia that abolishes civil liberties, the rights of women, freedom of expression, and the "corruption" of secular democracy. Regardless of whether they are Sunni or Shia, and of whether they may be in conflict with each other on other issues, all of these variants of fundamentalism hold this utopian vision in common. In Iraq, for instance, while older clerics like Ali al-Sistani have been more moderate and traditional, the young firebrands drawn to Muqtada al-Sadr are followers of the Khomeinist vision of a radical Islamist republic in recent years reenergized by Mahmoud Ahmadinejad. In Iran itself, some leadership elements have embraced a renewed revolutionary fervor, making further inroads on freedom of the press and other civil liberties in the name of returning to the purity of Khomeini's vision. Even in relatively pro-Western regimes such as Egypt, Saudi Arabia, and Pakistan, jihadist movements wait in the wings, eager to sweep away what they see as corrupt un-Islamic governments and institute the return to the pure origins of the faith.

While jihadist ideology is doubtless in part a reaction to the despair of poverty, it is not reducible to it. And it will therefore not necessarily fade away as Western-style prosperity reaches the non-Western world, as Senator Obama seemed to suggest in his first major foreign policy speech, "The War We Need to Win," an overly optimistic line of reasoning that, as I have suggested, has deep roots in the American view of international relations. Jihadism has its own self-generated, principled critique of and rejection of liberal democracy and the West. Many of its leading figures come from backgrounds of professional status and wealth. Improvements in the standard of living will not quench their ardor for conflict, because it derives from a love of struggle and a spiritual critique of their chief enemies, America and Israel. They will not be talked out of these views or bought off.

Both candidates should realize this, and should be ready to educate the American people in these complex and unappealing realities. While mere talking and hope are not the answer, neither is "a hundred years" of occupying Iraq. The right balance of diplomacy and the capacity for force is indispensable for meeting the future we face now, as it has been in every era of mankind since the Peloponnesian War. The Bush administration's failure to educate the American people in these realities was one of its chief flaws, squandering an initial surge of support for the military action against Saddam Hussein by failing to link that action with the general war on terror, and especially failing to enlighten the citizenry about the worldview of the terrorist foe and why no single military victory will make it go away. Will President Obama or McCain be up to this grave test of a leader's ability to shape and educate public opinion about hostile forces beyond its borders, a hallmark of their greatest predecessors, including FDR and Churchill?

If history proves anything, it is that war is sometimes unavoidable for a peace-loving nation. Moreover, it may be better to strike preemptively than wait to be attacked and risk defeat, or at any rate a far more destructive war later. The attempt to appease Hitler's aggression in the 1930s only emboldened him, gave him time to arm, and made him much harder to defeat later on. That is why pacifism is often a chief cause of military conflict. As we will see in Part One, that lesson was seared into the souls of British and American leaders during World War II and the cold war—sometimes for better, sometimes for worse—and it persists down to the present in the neoconservatives' crusade to topple Saddam Hussein and its frequently lamentable aftermath. On the other hand, going to war always undermines a society and its political system internally—even when the result is victory. As we will see in Part Three, the hubris of Athenian expansion led to the calamity of its misguided attempt to conquer Sicily, the Vietnam War of the West's first democratic empire, which in turn led to crisis and collapse at home. Avoiding war can be dangerous, and going to war almost always is. Steering the ship of state between the Scylla and Charybdis of unworldly pacifism and hubristic bellicosity is the hardest and sometimes the grandest task of an American president.

Authoritarian regimes are particularly vulnerable to the aftershock of launching wars, because their internal structures, being based on oppression, are brittle and contain much seething discontent that can erupt at the first sign that the government is tottering through defeat or stalemate in battle. Imperial Russia's attempt to prove its military might by foolishly taking on Japan—which delivered a crippling defeat to the czar's fleet—exposed the autocracy's weakness and helped lead to the revolution of 1905, a dress rehearsal for 1917. The czar's equally foolish order to mobilize in 1914 to make a gesture of support on behalf of Slavic Serbia against the Austro-Hungarian empire and Germany dragged Russia into a war that brought down the Romanov dynasty and delivered the Bolsheviks to power. Strikingly, the successor to the czarist autocracy, the Soviet empire, repeated this pattern of foreign adventurism prompting collapse at home. Hoping to inject the comatose Soviet system with new revolutionary fervor, Leonid Brezhnev invaded Afghanistan in 1979—the first direct land invasion by the Red Army since the end of World War II. This attempt at reviving "the proletariat in arms" was a military disaster that caused huge resentment as the body bags came home, and delivered the final kick at the rotting door of the Soviet system, paving the way for Mikhail Gorbachev and the regime's eventual demise.

Modern democracies have tended to be more resilient at handling the domestic shocks of war, but they, too, suffer. American domestic politics were deeply divided by the Spanish-American War, a blend of imperial aggression and a wish to liberate the decrepit Spanish empire's remaining New World colonial possessions, and by the war in Vietnam, which drove two presidents from office and left American cities in flames and university campuses scarred by riots. The United Kingdom, by draining her blood and treasure to save Europe from the Nazi threat, emerged victorious but exhausted, soon to be shorn of her empire. In this there is a cold lesson for aspiring statesmen: You will pay a price if you go to war, and you will pay a price if you do not. Knowing which way it is likely to go is perhaps the single greatest test of a leader's intelligence, intuition, grasp of world affairs, insight into history, and feel for human motivation, both at home and on the part of the possible foes abroad.

Personality and Conflict

This book explores the personalities of exemplary leaders in the context of the great swirl of events in which their talents were summoned forth. The challenge is to uncover the lessons about leadership that these outstanding personalities learned through the conflicts and controversies of their own eras, and the great issues of war and peace that were imposed upon them. War in particular is a major theme uniting the discussion of all the leaders, for a leader's ability to weigh the threat of war, the desirability of maintaining peace, and the need to defend one's country or one's allies turns out to be among the most important tests of leadership, and the one that calls upon leaders to make the most of their talents, their stamina, their patience, and their ability to inspire others.

As a result, I have planned this book around three major segments. In Part One, we will turn to past leaders for inspiration and insight as we set about meeting these new challenges in the present. I discuss the saga of the modern American presidency from JFK to George W. Bush, a saga rooted in Vietnam, which in turn harkened back to the cold war, World War II, and the lessons that American leaders drew from these conflicts. The discussion is framed in terms of a generation about to depart the historical stage. Many people have the sense that we are approaching the end of an era and about to turn leadership over to a new generation. I will explore how the parade of leaders from Kennedy to Bush has now run its course, leading to the emergence of a new and as yet largely unformed generation of leaders with a still uncertain relationship to that earlier heritage.

Part Two takes us further back in time and widens the canvas to include Europe as well as America. The focus here is on the emergence of Abraham Lincoln as the greatest American leader of the nineteenth century. But I also consider him in light of the impact made on his generation by an extraordinary European leader, Napoleon Bonaparte—an impact acknowledged by Lincoln himself, along with Ralph Waldo Emerson and many others—and in light of the Founding Fathers' complex and conflicted views on political honor and the qualities needed to serve the common good in a democracy. In this connection, we look back further, to consider statesmen of the ancient world, such as Brutus and Cato, who provided important inspiration for Washington, Hamilton, and the other founders.

Continuing that exploration of the ancient republics, in Part Three we travel even further back in time to the first Western democracy, Periclean Athens, and the vivid range of leadership personalities that emerged from the first superpower conflict, the long struggle between Athens and Sparta. This set of precedents has been consulted and invoked repeatedly by leaders down to the modern era, providing a unifying motif for our investigation of the soul of a leader. Churchill and JFK viewed the struggle against Nazi and Soviet despotism as the modern counterpart to Athens's defense of Greece against the Persian Empire. Alexander Hamilton reflected soberly on ancient Athens in arguing that the new American democracy would avoid its pitfalls. Lincoln's Gettysburg Address is often compared to Pericles' Funeral Oration—both models of inspirational rhetoric in which honor for the fallen in combat is used as a way of encouraging a democracy to live up to its own noblest values. The way back is the way forward: In order to get to the roots of Western thinking about leadership, we must push back from our current understanding until we reach the most time-tested allegories of leadership behavior in Thucydides.

My aim is to stimulate a discussion about the enduring qualities of leadership, looking back to the West's first democracy and its struggles with the moral dilemmas of its own empire for a reminder that the challenges facing leaders today, and the qualities demanded of them, have remained constant from ancient times to the present. I conclude with a modest effort to codify ten secrets of leadership, intended to provoke reflection on the preceding three parts, and on the challenges of tomorrow.

The Virtue That Dare Not Speak Its Name?

Before embarking on our search for the soul of a leader, however, let us pause over the most perplexing question in our preliminary reflections on statecraft, and one that will loom large in the reflections to follow—the question of honor, specifically the pursuit of honor through preeminent public service.

Describing the worldview of our educated elites, the sociologist Peter Berger observes:

> Honor occupies about the same place in contemporary usage as chastity. An individual asserting it hardly invites admiration, and one who claims to have lost it is an object of amusement rather than sympathy. Both concepts have an unambiguously outdated status in the *Weltanschauung* of modernity. Especially intellectuals, by definition in the vanguard of modernity, are about as likely to admit to honor as to be found out as chaste. At best, honor and chastity are seen as ideological leftovers in the consciousness of obsolete classes, such as military officers or ethnic grandmothers.

Virtually no politician today, and certainly no presidential candidate, would openly admit to being motivated by a desire to derive public honor from achieving high office. At most, they might speak of "the privilege to serve," their obligation "to give something back in return for the blessings my family and I have enjoyed." These are admirable sentiments. And I would not advise any of the current candidates to reveal their infatuation with Peter the Great or Charlemagne. Any campaign strategist who did so would be axed early in the primary season. When it comes to plumbing the psyche of a leader, however, a love of honor—acknowledged or not—cannot be divorced from our assessment. It strains credulity when we reflect on human nature to imagine a man or woman expending the ferocious energy it takes to achieve high office without feeling a sense of inner dignity and superior merit, bestowed on them by their fellow citizens. The Kennedys were perhaps the last American political dynasts who reveled openly in the majesty of the White House, with Jackie Kennedy evoking the atmosphere of a monarchical court, replete with regular visits from the greatest artists and thinkers of the time. The family's well-known penchant for rough-and-tumble games of touch football was often cited as evidence that Kennedys "love to win." ("He was the world's worst loser," Kenny O'Donnell wrote of his boss, John F. Kennedy. "Even in small things, a race against a traffic light, he hated to be beaten.") Still, few aspirants to the American presidency would dare express their love of honor openly—and some may indeed genuinely not feel it. In our time, the love of victory in competition for high office has been almost entirely deflected to the world of pop culture, sports, and the business world. While we rather starchily deny that a decent politician could be motivated by anything other than pure disinterested public service, we enjoy the guilty pleasure of vicarious identification with Don Corleone, whose calm sagacity in crime recalled a great Renaissance prince, or with the cheerfully ruthless Tony Soprano, who seemed able to emerge from his ruminative funks long enough to crush would-be usurpers rather than cede his power.

Even as victory and prestige as acceptable motivations for distinction in public life have become largely taboo, store shelves are filled with business books with titles like *Machiavelli in the Boardroom* or *The Management Maxims of Genghis Khan*. The principles of cunning, subtlety, indirection, forging of alliances, and punishment of enemies that once were staples of the literature on statecraft are now restricted to the private realm of moneymaking. Here, it seems, we can permit ourselves to think about realpolitik in a way that has been airbrushed from our discourse about public life. Yet we are bound to pay a price for driving underground, into subpolitical realms like the corporate world, a realistic and fully rounded understanding of ambition and honor seeking that ought equally to take center stage in the analysis of politics and leadership. Sometimes the Machiavellian business books reach ludicrous extremes. The author of *Cola Wars*, for example, compares a standoff between rival cola manufacturers to the steely brinkmanship between JFK and Nikita Khrushchev during the Cuban Missile Crisis. The comparison is intended quite seriously, without a trace of irony. On one hand, we can be relieved that most of the truly absorbing battles for mastery in American life take place at the level of colas rather than with tanks in the streets over control of the state. On the other, to deny that politicians *are* motivated by a desire for prestige—and that they need this incentive to achieve power even when their policies are entirely devoted to the common good—risks impoverishing our understanding of the psychology of leadership and reducing our public professions of why we seek office to hypocritical cant.

It is well to remember that this fastidiousness about admitting to ambition on behalf of the common good is of relatively recent origin. It was said of Charles de Gaulle by the socialist poet Alexis Leger: "It is not winning he likes, it is conquering." Theodore Roosevelt wrote and spoke openly about the manly satisfactions to be found in competition and victory, including in public life. "I wish to preach, not the doctrine of ignoble ease," he liked to thunder, "but the doctrine of the strenuous life, the life of toil and effort, of labor and strife; to preach that highest form of success which comes, not to the man who desires mere easy peace, but to the man who does not shrink from danger, from hardship, or from bitter toil, and who out of these wins the splendid ultimate triumph." For TR, fighting to win high office in order to do good was only one part of a wide panoply of manly striving for superior achievement that animated every walk of American life, an extension of the settlers' taming of the frontier in an epic struggle that purged the weak of spirit from the body politic. As Vice President Thomas Marshall observed of TR, "Death had to take him sleeping, for if Roosevelt had been awake, there would have been a fight."

As we will see in Part Two, Abraham Lincoln was remarkably preoccupied with the role of honor in democratic politics, and with his own irrepressible longing for the admiration of his fellow citizens. As he wrote in a rare confession of ambition (to the intimate friend of his youth, Joshua Speed) referring to the afterlife of the most glorious heroes of the ancient Greek and Roman world: "I have no doubt it is the peculiar misfortune of both you and me to dream dreams of Elysium far exceeding all that anything earthly can realize." In an early speech that we will explore at length, he vividly evoked the psychology of the greatest and most ambitious rulers, such as Alexander the Great, Julius Caesar, and Napoleon, "the tribe of the eagle," and makes it clear that their lust for distinction, while it can be dangerous, can also be a motive for distinguished service to the republic, and at any rate, human nature remaining constant, is with us today as much as it was in ancient times.

The key to understanding the traditional outlook on honor is to bear in mind that it is not a question of whether it is good or bad to seek honor. The central question is whether one seeks honor for the right purposes—serving the common good and helping others—or for purposes of self-enrichment, a monopoly on power and prestige and, in the worst instance, outright tyranny. As far back as Plato, Aristotle, and Cicero, this tradition has been maintained and preserved, inspiring ambitious young men to achieve a balance in their souls between active and contemplative virtues. In the active realm, they must display courage on behalf of their country when called upon in war, and (on a higher plane) display the moral and intellectual qualities required for deliberative and responsible citizenship. A higher calling still is the life of the mind and the cultivation of the soul's longing for immortality through cultural refinement, intellectual breadth, and religious faith—the core traditional meaning of liberal education in the West. A good leader needs a fully enriched, fully developed soul, and this is achieved through the most expansive exercise of our moral and intellectual faculties for self-improvement and serving the common good.

. . . .

IN THIS MODEL of human nature, the lower sphere of the active virtues is the route to the higher sphere of self-development and reflection. Those moral and intellectual virtues cultivated through public service are precisely the qualities of soul that prepare one inwardly for the life of the mind: the same prudence, moderation, sense of justice, and deliberation required by statesmanship are needed at a higher level for liberal studies. Plato describes this balance through the analogy of the chariot of the soul riding through the heavens. The charioteer represents the intellect, the two powerful horses represent physical lust and glory seeking. The charioteer of the intellect must rein in and guide these potentially unruly horses and prevent them from crashing the chariot in its celestial journey across the heavens as they plunge downward into their respective vices. Yet equally important is that the power of those horses, harnessed and redirected from vice toward virtue, is needed to energize the life of the mind. For the charioteer can't steer the chariot through the heavens without drawing on the power of those mighty steeds. In this way, the allegory teaches that mind and passions must form a harmonious whole. There can be no hard division between the active life and the contemplative life, between crude and barbaric rulers and detached, ineffectual thinkers.

Instead, this tradition encourages us to see the civic virtues as the necessary route to the intellectual and cultural virtues, such that those devoted to the life of the mind are *also* vigorous and responsible citizens. Another classical expression of this balance, and one of the most influential during the Renaissance and the Enlightenment, is Cicero's *Dream of Scipio*. As a statesman, Cicero defended the constitution of Rome against the despotic ambitions of Caesar. In the *Dream of Scipio*, he presents the earlier Roman statesman and general Scipio Africanus the Younger as the ideal Roman. A brilliant success in public life and on the battlefield, Scipio reserves his greatest respect for the life of the mind. A man is not only to be vigorous in serving the common good, but refined, moderate, gracious, and learned. These qualities, the very opposite of demagogues like the talented but unscrupulous Caesar, were "everything that entitles a man to praise."

It should be said, of course, that our reservations about revealing our ambitions for public honor are also grounded solidly in Western thought, much of it springing mainly from Christianity. St. Augustine, for example, offers a withering castigation of the entire classical preoccupation with worldly honor through serving the common good typified by Plato and Cicero: "Is it reasonable and wise," he asks, "to glory in the extent and greatness of the [Roman] Empire when you can in no way prove that there is any real happiness in men perpetually living amid the horrors of war, perpetually wading in blood? . . . In the absence of justice, what is sovereignty but organized brigandage?" Compared with the eternal reward that awaits a devout Christian in the hereafter, all worldly honor is cheap tinsel, reduced to an empty shell of vainglory and selfish power seeking. Given America's history as a country with a deep Christian heritage, it is no surprise that a secular version of this discomfort with glory seeking should persist in American political life. In a sense, the Enlightenment project of modern secular democracy compounded the already ingrained Christian distrust of political honor seeking. For the Enlightenment's stress on equality, individualism, personal well-being, and commercial enterprise—all central to the vision of the Founding Fathers—also appeared to cast a shadow on the thrusting ambitions of Lincoln's "tribe of the eagle" through martial glory and the battle for supreme status in the state. Modern America takes a page from Voltaire, urging man to "cultivate his garden" through the arts of peaceful commerce rather than the old aristocratic code of dueling and triumph in war.

Yet we forget that many Renaissance humanists and Enlightenment thinkers, including their Christian participants, still saw a positive role for honor through serving the common good, not seeing it as necessarily violating either Christian faith or the rights of man. Such Renaissance humanists as Erasmus, Castiglione, Vergerius, and Pico della Mirandola all invoked the classical models in urging a blend of ancient honor seeking of the kind extolled by Plato and Cicero and Christian humility in serving God and mankind. As we will see in greater detail in Part Two, this attempt to combine ancient traditions of aristocratic honor seeking through serving the common good with more recent Christian and modern values of human equality undulates throughout the American founding and straight down to the present. Washington, Jefferson, Madison, Hamilton, and the other founders, often steeped in classical learning, were absorbed by the question of how much the pursuit of manly honor could be permitted as a legitimate motive for serving the new American republic, and at what point it courted the danger of corrupting one into becoming a demagogue or tyrant. They sought strenuously to follow the positive examples of heroes of the Roman republic like Cato and Brutus, and to avoid imitating the usurpers Catiline and Julius Caesar, who used democratic rhetoric to seduce the mob. The same preoccupation resurfaces in Lincoln's speech about "the tribe of the eagle," and in his contemporary Emerson's avowal that "it is natural to believe in great men."

This brings us to the most disturbing problem of all: What if the psychological traits of aggressiveness and victory seeking that might lead to tyranny are among the *same* traits displayed by true statesmen? This was among the chief worries of Washington and Lincoln. Where do you draw the line? How can a leader know when he has crossed over into a longing for preeminent power, disguised from others and perhaps even from himself as a noble longing to excel in serving the people? This problem will come up again and again in our investigation of the soul of a leader.

The central question that will guide this exploration is not one of distinguishing between selfish honor and selfless public service. Rather, it is a matter of distinguishing between selfish and tyrannically inclined honor seeking and the healthy and estimable pursuit of honor through justly serving the common good. Important and successful leaders are neither pure realists nor pure idealists. In order to achieve a just end, they must acquire political power, or be reduced to ineffectual moralizing from the sidelines. In order to do this, they need to be pragmatic, even Machiavellian in some ways. Compromises must be made on the rise to power and during its exercise. Moreover, they will be driven by a desire for fame and a historical legacy whose psychological energy is indispensable for the arduous tasks they face, the long years of honing one's views and winning adherents. The great leaders we examine in this book—Pericles, Lincoln, Churchill, FDR—embody this pattern, and the others who aimed high (without quite achieving greatness) illustrate it in their own various ways. The ambition for public honor is, to stress again, every bit as true of the decent man or woman who genuinely wants high office in order to do good for others as it is of the unscrupulous adventurer, opportunist, or callow timeserver interested only in enriching himself and his cronies. The puzzle has always been, and still is: How do we tell one from the other? And how shall our potential leaders themselves sift out their highest motivations from the lesser angels of their natures?

Let us turn to history—recent and ancient—for our answers.

PART I

A Generation Bids Farewell

The Saga of the Modern American Presidency

On January 2, 2007, official Washington ground to a halt for the state funeral of Gerald R. Ford, the thirty-eighth president of the United States. The capital had been through a particularly tumultuous period. The voters had recently delivered a resoundingly negative judgment on the presidency of George W. Bush, stripping the Republican Party of control of both houses of Congress in midterm elections that amounted to a referendum on the Bush administration's conduct of the war in Iraq. Bush himself, initially the hero of 9/11 who had vowed to bring justice to the terrorists—and made good on this promise by toppling two hostile regimes in the space of two years—had enjoyed unprecedented favorable ratings. Yet now he seemed the lamest of lame ducks, with approval ratings sinking to Trumanesque levels. As the White House scrambled to reexamine its strategy in Iraq, the triumphant Democrats paused on the brink, temporarily stunned by their own unexpected success, and wondering just how much latitude the public had actually given them to reverse the president's war-making strategy.

Yet the death of an American president, whatever the surrounding circumstances, compels attention and respect. For a prolonged moment, partisan differences were set aside. All the country's living

presidents gathered for the service, joined by much of the capital's political and cultural elite. Old faces, historical legends—such as Henry
Kissinger—from what now seemed like another age, reappeared
briefly on the stage of their former triumphs and reverses. As contenders began to emerge for what was to be the first presidential race
in fifty-six years in which no incumbent would be running, a feeling
was already in the air that the next presidential race would not just
be a change but a *generational* change. A new generation would take
over from the current one, which was coming to an end with the
second President Bush. The administration's principal foreign policy
architects, including the vice president and secretary of defense, were
veterans of five Republican presidencies stretching all the way back
to Richard Nixon. The state funeral for Nixon's successor seemed to
symbolize the historic transition that many were feeling was already
upon us.

At the core of that generation's perspective on the world was the
trauma of the war in Vietnam. A war that had begun with the shining
intentions of John F. Kennedy to defend freedom wherever required
around the world, it had ended in a debacle costing more than fifty
thousand American lives, American cities burning in riots, and the
downfall of two presidents. Nixon's presidency had been driven by
the need to bring the war to as honorable an end as possible through
a two-state solution, such as had prevailed in Korea. He pursued a
negotiated withdrawal by steady stages and the preservation of South
Vietnam. In the aftermath, with the final defeat of South Vietnam by
the communist North during the Ford presidency, aided by a venge-
ful Congress determined not to continue propping up America's
former ally, a bitter reaction set in among policy intellectuals who
believed that American power in the world must be reasserted in the
service of spreading the American ideal of democracy. These "neoconservatives," as they came to be known, reacted against both what
they saw as the hopeless pacifism of the Democratic Party, shattered
by Lyndon Johnson's conduct of the war, and the cynicism of the
Kissinger approach to international relations as an amoral balance of
powers regardless of whether the regimes included were democratic

or not. This new generation of "neocons," including Paul Wolfowitz and Jeane Kirkpatrick (many of them former Democrats), found in Ronald Reagan the vehicle for translating those policies into reality. In time, some of the older Nixon hands themselves, including Dick Cheney and Donald Rumsfeld, outgrew their roots in Kissingerian realpolitik to embrace the neoconservatives' professed revival of Wilsonian internationalism. Eventually, the Democrats themselves came around, at least in part, and through figures like Joshua Muravchik and Madeleine Albright found in Bill Clinton a Democratic president who was willing to use military force abroad, as in Kosovo, where it both served a moral purpose defending human rights and consolidated American influence in the region.

With al-Qaeda's unexpected assault on American shores on 9/11, George W. Bush, initially perceived in many quarters as a neo-isolationist, found that foreign policy would almost totally define his presidency. The neoconservatives of the preceding decades found their ideal cause at last: the defense of America from an ideological foreign foe whose defeat would proceed hand in hand with the extension of American ideals of liberty and self-government to oppressed peoples around the world, beginning in the Middle East. This time, the neo-cons resolved, there would be no detente with the enemy, the International Jihad. For Nixon's pursuit of detente with the Soviet Union, and especially the more toothless version carried on by Ford, they believed, had only encouraged the Soviets to think America lacked resolve. Moreover, there would be no stopping short of the final goal of deposing Saddam Hussein, correcting the error of the president's father, who had listened more to Kissingerian pragmatists like James Baker than to the neoconservative firebrands who had flourished under Reagan, but whom his successor distrusted.

The death of Gerald Ford, who had presided over the collapse of South Vietnam and the souring of detente, and who had pardoned Richard Nixon, summed up this whole remarkable saga. In truth, the solemn state obsequies drew together into a single narrative what had been a continuous process involving several generations and several layers of history in the twentieth century, reaching all the way back to John F. Kennedy. One trait they shared was the experience of war: A number of these men, and their electoral opponents, had been genuine war heroes—Kennedy, George McGovern, George H. W. Bush, Robert Dole, and Ford himself. Others, like Nixon and Reagan, had at least seen some form of service. Even the presidents who had not seen combat themselves employed top advisors (including Colin Powell and Donald Rumsfeld) who had done so. The experience of war formed a powerful moral spine in the outlook of these men, one that had already started to go into abeyance with the current President Bush (a number of the chief architects of his war strategy, including Vice President Cheney and his onetime deputy Paul Wolfowitz, had never served in the military) and which was, with the exception of John McCain, almost completely absent from the new generation of contenders.

Even more important than military service, however, were the historical lessons all these presidents had drawn from the cold war. For it was the cold war conflict between America and the Soviet Union that had fundamentally determined American involvement in Vietnam and shaped the moral horizon within which presidents of both parties acted, all the way down to the second invasion of Iraq and the overthrow of Saddam Hussein. Moreover, there was a powerful historical precedent for superpower conflict at the very dawn of the West, a precedent of which many of the twentieth-century leaders were aware. The ancient Greek historian Thucydides, in his masterful account of the Peloponnesian War (which we'll explore in Part Three of this book), told the story of the first superpower conflict, a decades-long struggle between Athens, the first democracy in Western history, and the grim collectivist oligarchy of Sparta. That conflict in turn stemmed from the earlier alliance between these two Greek states against Persian invaders from the East. After the common enemy had been vanquished, the two allies viewed each other with a distrust that at length broke into open conflict, sometimes through proxy wars between their allies, subsiding into long periods of cold war punctuated by violent armed clashes.

As we will see, Thucydides' history of that first democracy has never been forgotten in the West, and particularly in Athens's modern successor, the United States. It fed the atmosphere, and may even have provided a model, for Abraham Lincoln's Gettysburg Address. Theodore Roosevelt read Thucydides on at least two occasions (one of them during his presidency), contributing discerning comments of his own to the modern perspective on this ancient epic. Throughout the twentieth century, the ancient historian's lessons about the relationship between freedom and empire, and on the impact that combating tyranny abroad will have on democratic politics at home, seemed ever more relevant.

When John Kennedy, in tones reminiscent of Winston Churchill, spoke about the "long twilight struggle" against communist tyranny, the example of that earlier conflict between ancient Greek democracy and the despotism of Persia loomed large. JFK, along with Churchill and many other political leaders of the era, were intense devotees of history, including the history of the ancient Greek and Roman republics from which the modern West received so much of its heritage and inspiration—early in his presidential term, Kennedy cited Thucydides in urging the NATO alliance to speak with a common voice against continuing threats to freedom in the world.

It would be difficult not to be struck by the parallels between the Peloponnesian War and the cold war involving the United States and the U.S.S.R. After beginning with a survey of the reasons for the superpower conflict between Athens and Sparta, Thucydides warns that we cannot understand that conflict without going back further in time, to their original alliance against Persian despotism. Modern statesmen could make a similar deduction. Just as Athens had allied with Sparta to defeat the Great King of Persia, the United States had also allied itself with a grim collectivist oligarchy, the Soviet Union, to defeat the tyranny of Hitler. The eventual, inevitable falling-out between the two superpowers led to a prolonged conflict—one that ran sometimes hot, mostly cold, and was often fought through proxy wars, such as Korea and Vietnam. Most remarkably, just as Athens's potent blend of democracy and empire met its nadir in the invasion of Sicily—and the crushing defeat of the Athenian army and fleet that followed—so did the imperial idealism of the cold war meet its debacle in the jungles of Vietnam. In both cases, a great democratic empire had underestimated the size and difficulties of subduing "a piss-ant little country" (as LBJ called Vietnam).

JFK and his successors also believed it was important to look back to the origins of the cold war to see what was required of America today. It was crucial to recall the mistakes of Chamberlain's appeasement of Hitler if we wanted to avoid repeating them with the Soviet Union. It was equally important to recall the towering giants of the struggle against Hitler—Churchill, Roosevelt, and de Gaulle, our contemporary equivalents of the great Athenian wartime leader Pericles—if we were to live up to their example in the struggle with the new enemies of democratic civilization. In withdrawing from Vietnam, Richard Nixon believed he was imitating de Gaulle's statesmanship in leaving Algeria to save the French Fifth Republic from internal collapse. JFK and his advisors thought the torch had been passed to America from Churchill's Britain. The younger generation of neoconservatives believed that the Democratic Party—the party of Truman and JFK, of the wars of anticommunist containment in Korea and Vietnam—had been traumatized by Vietnam and sunk into a dewy-eyed one-worldism that dated back to Henry Wallace and Adlai Stevenson and their heirs George McGovern and Jimmy Carter. They saw themselves as JFK's true heirs, though by and large they left his Democratic Party to join Ronald Reagan's Republican surge in 1980.

This whole dizzying kaleidoscope of associations came to mind as President Ford's cortege rolled slowly through the streets of Washington. Truly a generation had passed. What would follow it?

The Titans: Winston Churchill and Franklin Delano Roosevelt

Two titanic figures dominated the American experience of World War II and the cold war that emerged from it—Winston Churchill and Franklin Delano Roosevelt. Time and again, from JFK to the present, their examples and their precepts have been invoked, and their legacies claimed. Let us examine some of their more striking features as leaders.

The complexity of Churchill's character was largely hidden from the public by the persona he had to assume as a wartime leader—John Bull, the British bulldog, the embodiment of the nation's stubborn pluck and grit. Like all great leaders, he was eventually reduced in the broader public's mind to a silhouette: Honest Abe, TR's flashing teeth and shouts of "Bully," FDR's head tossed back with a cigarette holder.

In truth, however, Winston Churchill was a man of many layers, both dark and light. As one of his close wartime aides, Field Marshal Sir Alan Brooke, summed up this larger-than-life personage, lovable even in his faults:

> I wonder whether any historian of the future will ever be able to paint Winston in his true colors. It is a wonderful character, the most marvelous qualities and superhuman genius mixed with an astonishing lack of vision at times, and an impetuosity which, if not guided, must inevitably bring him into trouble again and again. He is quite the most difficult man to work with that I have ever struck, but I would not have missed the chance of working with him for anything on earth.

In his moral certainty about the code of the gentleman, Churchill was every inch a Victorian. But he had more than a touch of Edwardian whimsy. His colleague during the war (and later his successor as prime minister) Harold Macmillan, a more straitlaced figure, marveled at Churchill's seemingly inexhaustible energy and ability to combine work with pleasure at a wartime conference in Casablanca:

> His curious routine of spending the great part of the day in bed and all night up made it a little trying for his staff. I have never seen him in better form. He ate and drank enormously all the time, settled huge problems, played bagatelle and bezique by the hour, and generally enjoyed himself.

The eminent British psychiatrist Anthony Storr believes that great leaders, artists, and thinkers often strive for achievement in order to fill an inner emptiness stemming from some early tragedy or rejection. In the overall emotional economy of life, the rest of us benefit from their unhappiness while neither enjoying their spectacular achievements nor suffering their inner hollowness. This is not to reduce great achievement by equating it with this sense of emptiness; depression is no guarantee of greatness. But greatness may require a degree of depression, melancholy, a sense of one's own frailty, and the vicissitudes of fate. It is precisely in overcoming one's inner demons to achieve something for the benefit of one's country or mankind that many men have risen to nobility and grandeur.

Storr entitled his book *Churchill's Black Dog*, after Churchill's private name for the crushing depression that would incapacitate him for days or weeks at a time, especially as a young man. It led to a periodic reliance on the opiate laudanum in his twenties to escape insomnia and, throughout the Second World War, to continuous self-medication by heavy drinking to deal with the extraordinary stress of his duties. We know from his biographers that as a boy Churchill felt ignored, virtually abandoned, by his mother, the beautiful American-born socialite Jennie Jerome, and his father, the brilliant but unstable Sir Randolph Churchill; he idolized both from afar, perhaps more fervently because he spent so little actual time with them. It is reasonable to surmise that he struggled all his life to deserve their love, to find in public fame the acceptance they had withheld.

This Freudian interpretation of the unconscious motive for achievement offers a way to grasp the traditional Aristotelian conception of "the great-souled man"—the exceptional leader who finds only the gravest challenges of statecraft arduous enough to demand his fullest talents. Such men are often bored by the ordinary domestic politics of budgets and taxes, and perform poorly when politics is confined to such issues. Yet the threat of war or civil war, stimulated by struggles worthy of their inner sense of greatness, allows them finally to show their full capacities. This is a hallmark of all the great leaders we discuss in this book, and it is preeminently true, for example, of Abraham Lincoln and Winston Churchill. Lincoln—who also suffered from a childhood sense of abandonment and lifelong depression—likewise appeared to find in the demands of his mission as a statesman the closet thing to a cure, converting the dark brooding into a source of energy to do good. Public service in the Aristotelian tradition, in other words, may be the most effective therapy for a leader in waiting who might otherwise drown in the vortex of his inner sense of alienation and loss.

Only Churchill's enormous hunger for honorable fame through statesmanship can explain his ceaseless drive to embody the spirit of Britain as a whole during the Nazi threat. The Welsh Labor Party politician Aneurin Bevan marveled at Churchill's performance:

> He cast himself in the role of the great advocate who put the case of Britain to the world and the destiny of Britain to the British. His name will stand . . . as a symbol of what inspired words can do when there is a strong, brave and devoted nation free and willing to back them up with deeds.

Charles de Gaulle, never excessive in praising others, nevertheless saw in Churchill a man whose greatness was summoned forth by the gravest national perils, and who played his role not only successfully but with a flair, gusto, and grandeur that were themselves sources of moral strength for the people he led:

> Churchill seemed to me equal to dealing with the most arduous tasks, so long as it was also grandiose. His character fitted him for action, for running risks, for playing his part wholeheartedly and without scruple. I judge him perfectly at ease in his post of guide and leader. From the beginning to the end of the drama, Winston Churchill appeared to me as the great champion of a great undertaking and the great actor in a great History.

As early as 1912, the Welsh prime minister David Lloyd George— no stranger to the value of a dramatic public presence and a love of the rhetorical flourish—saw Churchill's ability to play the part of a leader like a great stage role: "The applause of the house is the breath in his nostrils," he observed. "He is just like an actor. He likes the limelight and the approbation of the pit."

Sir William Milbourne James, a high-ranking naval intelligence officer during the Second World War, sensed a thirst for power in Churchill, but also the pure enjoyment he took from being the top dog, surely fed by his historical studies of great warriors and leaders like his ancestor the first Duke of Marlborough and the justified pleasure a man ambitious for public honor can feel in his leading role in the great affairs of state:

> He is virtually a dictator, as there is absolutely no one else to take his place and lead us to victory. He has a real sense of humor and I am sure has a silent chuckle when he reminds the house [of Commons] that he is entirely their servant.

As a student of the great historians Edward Gibbon and Thomas Macaulay, and an accomplished historian himself, Churchill knew all too well that historians would have the final say on his role in the twentieth century—and therefore determined to write that history himself. As one of Eisenhower's staffers, Captain H. C. Butcher, observed:

> The prime minister said it was foolish to keep a day to day diary, because it would simply reflect the change of opinion or decision of the writer, which, when and if published, makes one appear indecisive and foolish. . . . [H]e would much prefer to wait until the war is over and then write impressions, so that, if necessary, he could correct or bury his mistakes.

These morally ambiguous qualities—in addition to his overwhelming ambition, which amounted almost to a lust for public honor—might have made Churchill more repellent if not for his matchless charm. The British war correspondent G. W. Stevens remarked of Churchill as a young man of twenty-five:

He is ambitious and he is calculating, yet he is not cold—
and that saves him. His ambition is sanguine, runs in a torrent,
and the calculation is hardly more than the rocks or the stump
which the torrent strikes for a second, yet which suffices to
direct its course.

Even his detractors were disarmed by this openness, an almost
boyish ingenuousness and inability to conceal his ambition. Although
Churchill could play the role of populist, his aristocratic background
bred in him a contempt for artifice or concealment that is consistent
with the code of the gentleman stretching back to Aristotle and Cicero.
This code—which holds that a gentleman never stoops to dishonesty
because he stands in need of no one's good opinion so badly that he
would lie to achieve it—was part and parcel of Churchill's demeanor,
as the journalist A. G. Gardiner put it early in Churchill's career:

> To the insatiable curiosity and enthusiasm of the child he
> joins the frankness of the child. He has no reserves and no
> shams. You are welcome to anything he has, and may pry into
> any corner you like. He has that scorn of concealment that be-
> longs to a caste which never doubts itself.

During the war, Churchill's aristocratic candor even led him, on
occasion, openly to voice misgivings about his own policies. As his
close wartime aide R. G. Casey recalled, while watching a film of
British bombing raids against German towns, Churchill "suddenly
sat bolt upright and said to me, 'are we beasts? Are we taking this too
far?'" Casey assured him that he was simply being affected by the
graphic film footage, reminding him "that we hadn't started it, and it
was them or us."

Churchill did not attend university, and this failure to join the
other members of his caste at Oxford or Cambridge, settling instead
for the somewhat déclassé profession of cavalryman, always made him
feel a little insecure in the company of such learned figures as Prime
Minister Arthur Balfour. It also made him more of a throwback than

his contemporaries, a man whose Victorian moral code had not been undermined by an exposure to the hedonistic relativism and pacifism that had become increasingly characteristic of Oxbridge, culminating in the infamous Oxford Union resolution in 1933 in favor of refusing to fight for King and Country.

Churchill's lack of a formal education made him into a fierce autodidact who devoured books of history and philosophy in a ceaseless campaign of self-improvement. He craved respectability as a man of letters, but also because he desperately needed to make money: His parents' lavish scale of living, and their refusal to economize, left him almost no inheritance. He was determined to entertain on the same lavish scale as his parents, with daily enormous lunches for numerous guests and country-house weekends crammed with the cream of society, politics, and culture. As his biographer Martin Gilbert has established, Churchill commanded unprecedented fees for his books and journalism; most of this he sank into his country house, Chartwell.

Like de Gaulle and Lincoln, Churchill always felt like something of an outsider to the establishment he came to govern and embody. His lack of formal education and his ambition for fame and money could make him seem grasping and egotistical to his class. "It's a push-push world," he was fond of saying, "and we must shove with the best." Did his mother's American origins contribute to this can-do spirit? On a visit to New York when he was twenty, Churchill became very close to Bourke Cochran, an Irish-American lawyer prominent in Tammany Hall politics who was well known for his florid, rodomontade style of stump speech. One wonders if Churchill absorbed some of this style of rhetoric. His own style in the Commons was very different from that of other politicians of his time—from the arch whimsy of a Herbert Henry Asquith or from Arthur Balfour's smoothly honed syllogisms. In its flair, boldness, color, and drama, Churchill's rhetoric seemed more American than English. His wartime secretary has recorded how he would practice his speeches for dramatic effect in his office, dropping his voice to a rumbling growl on the key phrases.

Whatever its sources, Churchill's sense of being an outsider freed him from the establishment's limitations. What in peacetime could often seem bumptious, uncouth, and "American" to more refined members of his class also enabled him to soar above their conventions. Violet Bonham Carter, the daughter of the Liberal prime minister Asquith and a society fixture, saw in Churchill this remarkable freedom from his background along with the boldness of imagination and the alchemy that it effected on those around him and the public at large:

> Every time we met he exorcized in me any misgivings about his future; by the impetus of his mind, by his unerring instinct for the living thought and word, above all by his imagination; imagination, which, in truth, is but another name for absolute power. Although I knew he did not see the world we lived in as it was, I felt he had the latent power to make his world our own, to impose his shape and pattern on events.

All of these qualities coalesced in Churchill's capacity to inspire the British people through his speeches. Churchill's matchless rhetoric partook of an insight that has been shared by the greatest democratic leaders stretching back to Pericles and including Lincoln and FDR: The purpose of great political oratory is to describe the people *as they are* in such a way as to inspire them to be *what they should be*. Pericles' Funeral Oration, Lincoln's Gettysburg Address, Churchill's "We shall never surrender" speech—all purport simply to describe the qualities of the citizenry at their best in order to exhort them to persevere at this level. It is a way of encouraging people to be better without implying that they have failed to meet this high standard. They need not change what they are, merely to grow into it more fully by facing adversity. A leader must summon citizens to rise above themselves, but without appearing preachy or contemptuous of their present state of mind.

Churchill, in other words, saw it as part of his role to educate the public; his lack of a university degree only demonstrates that in the world of statesmanship character can trump formal education. Churchill never fully understood Nazism: He considered it a reemergence of traditional nineteenth-century Great Power ambition, of the militarism of Bismarck, the Kaiser, Helmuth von Moltke, and the German general staff. He failed to fathom the millenarian and apocalyptic side of Nazi totalitarianism, which (like its Bolshevik counterpart) required the creation of a "new man" through genocide to usher in a utopian epoch of peace and bliss. But Churchill knew as much as he needed to know. His view of Nazism was not wrong, merely partial. His depiction of "the Hun" was wildly out of date, fed by the experience of World War I, but it was sufficient to focus the energies of the British people, who needed only to recognize that Hitler was a menace to Britain and the world and had to be stopped. "Hitler," Churchill pronounced in his famous rumble, "is a monster of wickedness, insatiable in his lust for blood and plunder."

CHURCHILL'S GREAT ALLY Franklin Delano Roosevelt was as aristocratic an American as Churchill was a Briton. His pedigree stretched back to the first Dutch settlers of New York and forward from there to his magnificent cousin Theodore Roosevelt, whose patrician populism he emulated. He was highly conscious of his illustrious background, including his presidential forebear, and felt destined for public service. "Permeating everything Franklin Roosevelt said and did," the biographer Edgar Robinson observed, "was a mood of supreme self-confidence that was evident to everyone." Moreover, Roosevelt felt that his rank elevated him above petty self-interest and the need to enrich himself through cheap political deal making—and hoped that this sense of noblesse oblige would inspire confidence among the less fortunate. As the economist Rexford Tugwell, a member of FDR's brain trust of policy advisors, summed up the president's outlook:

> The people expect their president to be free from any interest or prejudice, to think singly of the national good, and to rally them to its support. He must force Congress, against its will, to do what has to be done, and he must often do it by raising the people—who want nothing so little as to be raised—against it.

FDR became the model for the president as the great national tribune, the upper-caste statesman who allies with the common people against petty officeholders, and who must, for their own good, inspire the people to rise toward his own high level of public service.

Roosevelt, however, was considerably more a twentieth-century man than Churchill, more willing to embrace the future, for ill or for good. Whereas Churchill ended the war with a hopeless wish to preserve the British Empire, FDR sympathized with the desire of colonialized peoples (including Britain's colonies) for independence. "To the President," recalled Churchill's physician and close friend Lord Moran, "China means four hundred million people who are going to count in the world of tomorrow, but Winston thinks only of the color of their skin; it is when he talks of India or China that you remember he is a Victorian." This anticolonialist streak rendered FDR somewhat more apt to credit Stalin's professed Marxist ideals of freedom and equality for all oppressed peoples than Churchill, who saw in Stalin a typical power-hungry militarist eager to exploit the vacuum left by Hitler's defeat to extend the Russian empire into Europe.

On a personal level, FDR was immensely charming, in the clubbable, breezy way of his class. Churchill found in him an antidote for his own periodic gloominess. "Meeting Franklin Roosevelt," he wrote, "was like opening your first bottle of champagne; knowing him was like drinking it." De Gaulle at first underestimated Roosevelt because of this charm, then realized how he used it to bring along his class: "Because of Roosevelt's sparkling personality, no one assumed more than a limited brilliance. . . . [I]t was with admiration that I saw the flow of this torrent of confidence that was carrying the American elite along with it." Others, including his longtime secretary of labor Frances Perkins, regarded FDR as sphinxlike, decrying his "youthful lack of humility," his "streak of self-righteousness," and even what Perkins saw as a "deafness to the hopes, fears and aspirations of the common lot." Yet in an impoverished nation saved by the policies of the New Deal, such voices were a distinct minority.

FDR's outer effervescence did serve as a buffer that helped him conceal a profound inner reserve. When off duty, according to the playwright and presidential speechwriter Robert E. Sherwood, he preferred the company of his own class: "When he could choose his own company, he preferred to be with old friends and relatives who had nothing to do with government and with whom he could talk about the old days in Hyde Park." He enjoyed the sport of politics as a game in which he excelled, occasionally reveling in his own deviousness. According to John T. Flynn, an early supporter of Roosevelt who later became an isolationist: "When he was bent upon some act which he was very eager to perform, yet which he believed would not stand exposure to discussion, he had a kind of childish habit of not only concealing his intention . . . but of even dissembling it like a small boy bent on mischief." Like all great statesmen, he was able to change tactics drastically and, his critics charged, shamelessly in order to pursue his main goals. "Those who wanted ideological consistency or even policy coherence were rightly exasperated with Roosevelt," writes the historian Garry Wills. "He switched economic plans as often as he changed treatments for polio." FDR might well have savored Ralph Waldo Emerson's motto "a foolish consistency is the hobgoblin of little minds."

Roosevelt was also capable of a cold-bloodedness that is, sadly and whether we wish to see it clearly or not, often the burden of leaders in dire national emergencies—a willingness to allow innocents to die to save a greater number or to realize an overarching national purpose. The history of statesmanship is replete with such awful choices. When France fell to Nazi Germany, Churchill ordered the Royal Navy to sink the French fleet rather than allow it to pass intact into German hands, which would have imperiled the sea-lanes on which Britain depended for survival. It was an act of political murder in which 1,297 French soldiers were killed in less than ten minutes. Yet even de Gaulle recognized the need to prevent German sea power from being so powerfully augmented and refrained from criticizing his ally for the attack. Lincoln endured the astonishing death toll of the Civil War in the cause of union, despite the personal agony it caused him, and allowed General Sherman to lay waste to Georgia to break the South's spirit of resistance. In FDR's case, historians have long wondered whether he knew about Japan's plan to attack in the South Pacific and did less than he might have to warn American commanders of the threat. His biographer Conrad Black concluded that Roosevelt was outraged by Japan's invasions of China and Indochina and that, by embargoing the oil on which Japan's economy depended, he could force the Japanese either to retreat or to attack the United States, thereby forcing America into the war. Great statesmanship may on occasion resemble villainy, and the reverse is also true.

At home, in creating the New Deal to address the misery caused by the Great Depression, FDR achieved an almost monarchical, Periclean sway in the reshaping of American life in the twentieth century—an accomplishment Churchill could never have matched and would never have desired. No American president had ever achieved this kind of power to do good, and Roosevelt's use of it set a new standard for the ambition of future leaders to serve the people. As the historian James C. Young wrote in 1936, FDR

> swept into office upon the crest of an emotional wave, demanding and obtaining powers that no other president had ever wielded, all but deified by a large part of his countrymen. . . . He yearns for the sanction of history as much or more than the approval of the present.

In an amazing feat of coalition building, Roosevelt rolled together the prairie populism of the old Progressives, which originated with William Jennings Bryan; the welfare statism pioneered by the Louisiana populist demagogue Huey Long; and an idealistic faith in world peace influenced by the beliefs of his wife, Eleanor, and his first vice president, Henry Wallace. To these disparate movements he forged a link with the old Democratic machine politics of the urban Northeast, with its dense concentration of ethnic working-class voters.

Roosevelt was in every way the great man, the omnipresent colossus of his times. His New Deal combined huge public works with a social welfare safety net that also redistributed income, enabling workers to afford to buy the goods they produced. Although the measures were slow to have a major impact, in the long run FDR saved capitalism from its own crisis of overproduction and underconsumption that had been forecast by Marx. He appealed to the patriotism of the capitalist classes by trying to enlist them in this cause, but some of those who joined him also profited enormously from the expansion of government as contractors for his huge public works. Because socialism was so utterly rejected in America, its defining ideas were largely unfamiliar—freeing FDR to borrow some of its redistributionist and central planning tenets without being identified as a socialist per se. Conrad Black credits Roosevelt with nothing less than "the re-invention of the American state." He continues:

> [FDR] involved the government in many areas where its presence had been limited or non-existent—industrial recovery, reflation, large-scale workfare programs, Social Security, reform of financial institutions, rural electrification, flood and drought control, stabilization of farm production and prices, conservation, refinancing of home mortgages and farm loans, public sector development and distribution of hydro-electric power, generous treatment of veterans, as well as the repeal of Prohibition.

As he presided over these vast transformations of society, Roosevelt himself took on an almost godlike aura in the American imagination. Deference toward him was remarkable. He spoke to the press seated in his open car like royalty, glasses flashing, cigarette holder dangling, head thrown back with a raffish smile. The public did not know he was seated because of polio—he looked like an estate owner addressing the field hands from his roadster.

But there were many who hated Roosevelt as well. Many of the wealthy regarded him as a class traitor. Many believed that his reforms had undermined the old-fashioned American principles of individualism and self-reliance with government handouts, while miring America in foreign wars—a sentiment that survived in some quarters for more than half a century, as evidenced by vice presidential candidate Bob Dole's awkward 1976 reference to the "Democrat wars" the opposing party had started. After Roosevelt's death, the tensions that had long been masked by the force of his personality, charm, and unique authority resurfaced. He had promised progress on civil rights, but delivered only mixed results. That unfinished agenda, along with the idealistic strand of anticolonialism and world peace, migrated to the liberal wing of the party, as embodied by Eleanor, Henry Wallace, and Adlai Stevenson, always uncomfortable with the more pragmatic mainstream and its Dixiecrat base in the segregationist South—a group FDR had believed essential to the Democratic Party's hold on power.

On the other hand, FDR's successor, Harry Truman, and some of the advisors Truman inherited—the so-called Wise Men, epitomized by the suave and steely Dean Acheson—reacted against what they saw as America's too benign, even naïve wartime reading of the Soviet Union's intentions. They thought America had woken up too late to the menace of Soviet imperialism, and were determined to combat it abroad if it could not be reversed in central Europe. This new desire to stop the "dominoes" from falling to the U.S.S.R.'s proxy liberation movements in the developing world sat somewhat uneasily with the idealist strain of Eleanor and Adlai. Before long, however, an implicit middle-ground credo emerged: We may have to fight Soviet proxies in the third world, but in their wake we will build true democracy. This uneasy combination of values has marked American foreign policy all the way from John F. Kennedy to President George W. Bush.

President Eisenhower, a managerial chief executive, maintained an even keel for the United States through most of the 1950s. On his watch, however, a resurgent nativism continued to grow on the far right, a movement that combined a resentment of "eastern" elites and big government with a long-simmering outrage that FDR and Truman had been "soft on communism" and "lost" Christian China. Personified by the Wisconsin demagogue Joe McCarthy, this new movement was an odd blend of contempt for Truman and Acheson for failing to conquer communism altogether, rolling it back from Europe and the rest of the world, and an older isolationism that eschewed *any* lesser, real-world intervention abroad. At its core, McCarthyism was more about the taint of communism at home than about a coherent foreign policy (it is no accident that Pat Buchanan, the most consistent isolationist of recent years, claims to be McCarthy's heir). While professing a wish to roll back communism everywhere, the extremism of which in fact safely guaranteed that it would never be attempted, McCarthyism was essentially an isolationist, moralistic protest. Though it died as a coherent force with McCarthy himself, the emotions behind it quietly endured in the coming decades, reemerging periodically through figures like the Republican senators Robert Dole and Jesse Helms. The tenets of American anticommunism were not effectively reconciled until Ronald Reagan, who combined a passion for decrying communism as anathema to the American soul, the pragmatic cold warriorism of Acheson and Truman, *and* the neo-Wilsonian idealism of FDR and JFK. Bringing these strains together, while championing entrepreneurialism over big government at home, Reagan became a kind of reverse FDR. In doing so, he achieved a magisterial sway in American politics that no one since FDR had possessed.

Passing the Torch: John Fitzgerald Kennedy and Lyndon Baines Johnson

The generational saga of the American presidency that is ending today properly begins with John F. Kennedy. It was he who had inherited the unresolved fragments of FDR's coalition and tried to recapture its dynamism after the grandfatherly interlude of Eisenhower. A pronounced Anglophile—he had even titled his 1940 book (originally his Harvard senior thesis) the Churchillian-sounding *Why England Slept*—Kennedy deployed a keen sense of irony and self-deprecating wit at press conferences (introducing himself in Paris as Jackie Kennedy's husband), demonstrating both his heritage of deadpan Irish humor and a personal suavity that recalled Anthony Eden. Kennedy's father had been known for a strain of wartime isolationism, a position that eventually drove FDR to sack him as ambassador to Britain; JFK worked hard to expiate his father's sins.

The issue of class was a complex one for JFK, as for his entire family. The Kennedys had the nimbus of New England aristocracy, but had achieved their status only through a fierce struggle for upward advancement. The parallels to Mario Puzo's *Godfather* saga, in which a Mafia don grooms his war-hero, Ivy League–educated son for the presidency, have been widely noted. Rumored to have begun his rise as a bootlegger during Prohibition, Joseph Kennedy gradually acquired the accoutrements of the Boston Brahmin, including the summer house on Cape Cod. But he often felt rejected—nursing a grudge against his Protestant neighbors, who were never sufficiently welcoming for his comfort. Moreover, the Kennedy patriarch's aspirations to the symbols of WASP gentility were undermined by the attraction of brash new money to Hollywood and his taking screen vamp Gloria Swanson as a mistress. His sons John and Robert inherited their taste for the movie world and its stars from their father.

This mixture of background influences made President Kennedy a complex figure, but they gave rise to a personality that enthralled the American public. There was something simultaneously aristocratic and swinging about it; Kennedy amounted to the first hipster in the White House. As Thomas Brown observed in his study of the Kennedy image, "in an era that prided itself on sexual sophistication, many were actually pleased or titillated at having had a 'swinging' president. The Kennedy image had always appealed most to that kind of American who prided himself (or herself) on being liberated from bourgeois restraints." Their supporters among the blue bloods enjoyed the Kennedys' swinging style and democratic energy, including the whiff of sexual outlawry. Temperamentally, JFK himself was somewhere between the Irish political cronies who handled the dynasty's backroom dealings and the genuine Boston Brahmins, the Episcopalian Ivy Leaguers straight out of Cheever's novels, whom he gathered around himself as a brain trust. That striking voice was not a Boston Brahmin accent at all, but a melding of the slow, slightly halting and self-preening syntax of Harvard Yard with the broad vowels and rasp of East Boston. As his longtime chum Ben Bradlee put it, Kennedy's character "was half the 'mick' politician, tough, earthy, bawdy, sentimental, and half the bright, graceful, intellectual *Playboy of the Western*

World." Still, the Anglophile showed most clearly in JFK's innate distaste for displays of emotion or ideological extremes. As the biographer James MacGregor Burns summed him up:

> One word describes Kennedy more exactly than any other—self-possession. He has never been seen—even by his mother—in raging anger or uncontrollable tears. [His humor] is a light, needling, slightly ironic banter, such as one often meets in war or in other times of stress. . . . This fear of making too much of a commitment, of going off the intellectual deep end, is locked into Kennedy's character.

Reflecting the zeitgeist, and the opening up of the bounds of personal behavior after the bourgeois staidness of the Eisenhower years, JFK—even if unconsciously—was the first American president to use the language of existentialism. This philosophical and literary movement had become something of a pop phenomenon by the late 1950s, with its avatar, Jean-Paul Sartre, appearing in a *Life* magazine profile and the American dramatist Paddy Chayefsky including a beatnik girl labeled "the existentialist" in his play *The Bachelor Party*. JFK's speeches were laced with what the social theorist Theodor Adorno termed "the jargon of authenticity." They spoke of "resolve," "courage," "commitment," "vigor" (always pronounced *vigaah*), "purpose," "decision." It is impossible to imagine Eisenhower speaking in this way. Sartre and Heidegger had crafted a similar lexicon of existentialism, but theirs looked inward, canted toward introspection and an intensification of personal relationships. The tousled, manly, energetic young president refashioned this language to galvanize, inspire, and rejuvenate the body politic, creating a Periclean existentialism suitable to what his poet laureate, Robert Frost, called "the glory of a next Augustan age." (Of course, the foxy old poet may have been slightly ironic in comparing JFK to the young *caudillo* Caesar Augustus with his manipulation of Vergil and other poets to fashion a propaganda cult for himself.)

Further fueling JFK's charisma—another European term that took on a new life with JFK's emergence—was the fact that he had been a genuine war hero, among the best and the brightest of the generation risen to young manhood during FDR's epic struggle against fascist tyranny. In his early forties, he was a physically beautiful man—sleek, hirsute, immaculately tailored, with that large handsome face and flashing smile, the youngest president in American history. Even the grainy Technicolor newsreel footage of that time radiates a strong sense of his style, compactness, energy, and presence. He had been a bookish boy, less athletic than his older brother, Joe Jr., who had been earmarked in the family's hopes for the presidency until his premature death during World War II. He remained a lover of history, reading Barbara Tuchman's masterful account of the First World War, *The Guns of August*, during the Cuban Missile Crisis to remind himself of how such hostilities can spin out of control. This was the flip side, less widely observed, of the White House hipster. Burns writes: "Many people think of Kennedy as a sunny gregarious type. . . . Actually, he is a serious, driven man, about as casual as a cash register. . . . He is happiest not in social gatherings, but sitting in bed, bespectacled, going through a recent biography."

In foreign policy, he inherited the outlook of the Wise Men of the cold war brain trust and their newer progeny, epitomized by the silken and iron-willed patrician Dean Acheson, the father-in-law of William Bundy. What had been lost in Europe—whether because of FDR's distraction by illness, or his naiveté about Soviet imperialism—would be fought by proxy in Vietnam, as it had been in Korea. Communism could not be rolled back in Europe, but it could be contained from spreading elsewhere. The remaining titan, Churchill, also distracted by exhaustion at the end of the war, reemerged in 1946 to take a more hard anti-Soviet stance with his Iron Curtain speech in Fulton, Missouri, arguably his most memorable remaining act as a world leader before retiring from the stage of events and another illustration of the power of vivid and well-crafted rhetoric in the affairs of democracies.

Kennedy's successes were decidedly mixed. The failed Bay of Pigs invasion of Cuba was a fiasco of irresolution, a project that should have been either abandoned altogether or executed on a far greater scale. The Soviet strongman Nikita Khrushchev rolled over Kennedy by building the Berlin Wall in flagrant violation of the city's treaty status. These mishaps earned Kennedy the contempt of de Gaulle for being a boyish amateur who approached governing with "the style of a hairdresser's assistant . . . he combed his way through problems." But Kennedy's deft resolution of the Cuban Missile Crisis was a triumph of grace under pressure (a Hemingway phrase that would henceforth be inextricably associated with the Kennedys). His adoring press secretary Pierre Salinger wrote: "[Those] six days were the most anxious of my life and, certainly, the grimmest of the Thousand Days of John F. Kennedy's presidency. But I never knew him to be more in command of himself or of events." The resolution of the missile crisis nipped the bud of further Soviet encroachment in Latin America so thoroughly that it would not return until the Sandinistas, and Khrushchev's loss of face probably contributed to his downfall. There has been endless speculation about how JFK would have handled Vietnam had he not been assassinated in 1963, when the mission was still confined to economic assistance, military advice, and counterinsurgency tactics. It seems clear that he did not oppose it continuing on this limited scale and may even have contemplated adding more personnel. But, based on his ability to face down the hawks in the Pentagon—who urged a full-scale invasion or even a preemptive nuclear strike during the missile crisis—it is safe to conclude that he would probably have opposed the massive expansion of the war, including the introduction of American combat forces, foisted on Lyndon Johnson.

Kennedy's death caused a generation gap in presidential leadership, a return—in the choice insult of my generation for its elders—to "baggy-pants" LBJ, a throwback to a duller era. In cultural terms, the gap was filled by the rock-and-roll revolution of the 1960s, with the Beatles inheriting JFK's dry press conference irony and putting their own twist on his hirsute good looks. The slain president's younger brother and dynastic heir apparent, Robert Kennedy, promised to reintroduce youthful vigor into the politics of the times; RFK alone could perhaps have been a bridge between his older brother's World

War II generation and the new generation, which forsook mainstream party politics for the counterculture—until he too was snuffed out by assassination.

Having begun as an anticommunist attack dog for Joe McCarthy, Robert Kennedy had evolved steadily into an attorney general who took on organized crime so thoroughly that some believe it may have contributed to his brother's death. He also became an energetic proponent of desegregation, the great moral crusade of the 1960s. As the son of Joseph Kennedy and brother of JFK, he never renounced his anticommunism in principle; the same considerations might well have kept him from simply withdrawing unilaterally from Vietnam if he had survived to win election in 1968. The Kennedys were never pacifists or one-worlders—the peacenik devotees of Adlai and Eleanor had always evoked their private scorn. But Bobby Kennedy might well have found his way toward the Nixonian solution of gradual withdrawal combined with negotiations to preserve South Vietnam.

Less charismatic at first than his brother, RFK seemed to grow deeper, more thoughtful, before the public's eyes, as he contemplated his own and the nation's mounting sorrow and bewilderment. He became more complex and ruminating as his death approached. Upon hearing the news of Martin Luther King Jr.'s assassination, he summoned up a graceful quote from Aeschylus—a spontaneous reaction that captured the Kennedys at their best. In that moment, Kennedy was drawing upon high culture to express a profound and widely mourned national loss in a way that has never recurred to this day: Whatever we may think of RFK's successors, one cannot imagine Nixon, Ford, Carter, Reagan, Clinton, or either President Bush quoting an ancient Greek poet to crystallize a tragic episode in American life.

The myth of Camelot has been done to death and much derided. But it did capture something real: a youthful energy; an idealistic belief that the best in high culture could reach people of all levels; an optimism brought low by the body blows of the war and the street and campus riots it provoked at home. As David Halberstam sagely observed in *The Best and the Brightest*, the war effort in Vietnam was doomed when Robert Kennedy's death severed the last link between the generation of World War II veterans and the baby boomers, the sons of the Wise Men, who, by rioting at Columbia and Yale, sent an unmistakable signal that the ruling classes would no longer play that role.

IN CONSENTING TO increase American ground forces in Vietnam to more than half a million men, Lyndon Baines Johnson was overwhelmed by JFK's brain trust. No longer restrained by the caution and slow study JFK had demonstrated during the Cuban Missile Crisis and the early stages of involvement in Vietnam, the offspring of the Wise Men (epitomized by the Bundys and systems management whiz kid Robert McNamara) combined a sophisticated disdain for moral crusades with a belief that America's edge in technology could overcome a backward guerrilla movement. The Johnson administration set about attempting to manage the war off center stage, without resorting to what it considered unseemly appeals to Red-baiting jingoism for public support.

For his part, LBJ shared with the older generation of the 1940s and 1950s a fear of appearing weak on communism, convinced that this would turn the country against him, a specter more and more from a former time. Moreover, behind his vulgarity and uncouthness he was deeply insecure about his lack of higher education and his humble origins in comparison to the pedigreed Ivy League advisors he inherited from his predecessor. As their social equal, classmate, and the original source of their government careers, JFK had never been under their spell; he could take their advice or leave it. LBJ, whose passion was for domestic politics, felt compelled to defer to their evidently superior expertise on international relations. The war with its spiraling death toll ground Johnson down, but he struggled not to show it in public for fear of appearing weak. His daughter Luci recalled many years later: "One of the most painful memories I have from my White House days was watching Daddy hear of servicemen who had been injured or killed. . . . None of these men were statistics to Daddy. They were all sons and daughters, husbands and wives, mothers and fathers."

As a public figure, LBJ represented a return to the old politics of smoky backroom logrolling, an ungainly figure whose effectiveness came not from charisma but from long years in the political trenches of Texas and on Capitol Hill. In contrast with the Kennedys' love of high culture, LBJ, according to his White House counsel Harry McPherson, "had no apparent interests outside of government and politics—not the theater, nor books, music, sports . . . [or] the study of history." A masterly congressional wheeler-dealer, he had been a remarkably effective Senate majority leader, before being picked to become JFK's running mate, a choice neither he nor the nominee was enthusiastic about. He was big, vulgar, and colorful, and went out of his way to revel in his hick side, as if to show he couldn't care less about not belonging to Camelot. The biographer Frank Cormier observed the he would "indulge in a very bad habit of belching loudly, without covering his mouth, after each healthy swallow. I saw him do this often and never could understand why he did it. Perhaps he wished to demonstrate that he was President and could be as uncouth as he pleased." He famously conducted foreign policy discussions while sitting on the Oval Office toilet, delighting in forcing his buttoned-down young Ivy League advisors and aides to draw closer to the open door from which they shrank in disgust. On occasion he even referred to African-Americans as "niggrahs," an embarrassingly crackerlike term. He held a dog up by its ears for a disgusted press corps at his ranch in Texas.

People of my generation found Johnson's presence on the public stage a dismaying reversal—so much so that we may have been blinded to his true elements of greatness. Had he not inherited the war, he might well have been a superlative president. As Cormier wrote:

> LBJ held to the simple, even stubborn patriotism of an age when Americans, bursting with confidence after taming a continent and subjugating its native inhabitants, believed that all things were possible in their best of all possible lands; when they had unquestioning faith that their country would always find itself on the side of God and righteousness.

Johnson, who had swept into politics on FDR's coattails, worshipped that idol from afar, and shared his yearning to do good things for the people. He used every technique he had acquired from his long congressional career—flattery, threats, cajolery, budgetary pork—to steer the Civil Rights Act to passage in 1964. The Kennedy brothers had made important strides toward such reforms, but their early deaths—and also, it must be said, their reluctance to embrace the Democratic Party's progressivist wing entirely, which would have risked alienating the Dixiecrats—stayed their hand. Sometimes it takes the leader who superficially most closely resembles what he wants to vanquish to succeed in doing so. The fact that LBJ looked and sounded like a cracker helped disarm those who might otherwise have opposed the "eastern," pampered Kennedys. With the passage of this legislation, LBJ offered the greatest leap forward for civil rights since Lincoln's Emancipation Proclamation, a long-delayed attempt to deliver on the equality of opportunity Lincoln's victory in the Civil War had promised.

Unfortunately for LBJ's reputation, this great achievement was long overshadowed by the mounting disaster of the war, which reached an American death toll of over five hundred a week during his last year in office. It was a bitter irony: At the very moment when his party's liberal wing was achieving so many of its aims, the civil rights movement at home was so radicalized by the war (which claimed a vastly disproportionate number of young black Americans) as to make the legislation seem almost irrelevant. The murder of Martin Luther King Jr. fueled the growth of the more revolutionary mood represented by the Black Panthers, who saw themselves as a national liberation movement parallel to the Vietcong whom the United States was fighting overseas.

King, arguably the greatest American moral figure of his age, was, like RFK, or at least what RFK may have promised, another link between the sixties generation and the old progressivism. Like Johnson, he had vowed to continue and complete Lincoln's work. His "I have a dream" speech, the most stirring piece of American civic rhetoric since the Gettysburg Address, was appropriately delivered in front of the shrine to the Great Emancipator on the National Mall in

Washington. The core of Lincoln's political mission had been—as he put it—that if slavery isn't wrong, *nothing* is wrong. If we can enslave another human being, we can commit any evil, and our ability to enslave another human being undermines any and all other claims we might make to decency as good family men, citizens, neighbors, and Christians. Furthermore, as Lincoln perceived, if people of one ethnic ancestry can be enslaved, then people of *any* ethnic background can be enslaved or otherwise brutalized: if slavery continued, it could extend to poor white people or to new immigrants. In this exact spirit, King argued that if civil rights are denied to any race, they can be denied to everyone. The extension of civil rights to black people is therefore the spearhead of their full realization for all of the poor, the disadvantaged, those without hope. King severely criticized the war, but he had no truck with revolutionary violence—staying within the tradition of peaceful civil disobedience represented by Mohandas Gandhi—or with the separatist strain of black nationalism. His loss for a time undermined these links between the contemporary civil rights movement and the larger American political tradition.

With American troops dying by the thousands abroad and the ghettos and campuses in flames at home, LBJ was driven from office. He voluntarily declined to run for a second term, aware that a second Johnson administration would have made it impossible for his party to seek a fresh way out of the conflict. With the perspective of time, his positive achievements have been increasingly appreciated. But at that juncture he was like a great statue that had been pulled to the ground, his Promethean energy and king-sized appetites reduced to a source of contempt. Two years later, in defending his own conduct of the war, President Richard Nixon remarked that he did not intend to stand by while America became "a pitiful, helpless giant"; one wonders if he was thinking of the fall of his towering but humbled predecessor. Johnson's party, having begun the war in the Achesonian spirit of containment and preventing more dominoes from falling, was shattered by the debacle and entered a period of prolonged guilt about what was more and more openly referred to, and not just on the margins, but in mainstream culture, as "the imperial presidency."

The immediate effect of Johnson's ostracism was the revival, in a new form, of a deep liberal stratum of the Democratic Party, the strain that traced it roots back through Adlai Stevenson and Henry Wallace, and even back to Thomas Jefferson, who, as we observed in the introduction, believed that America must be the friend of all nations in the world. This movement inherited aspects of the Progressive populism of William Jennings Bryan, the mildly socialistic "Wobbly" unionism of the 1920s, and a general reluctance to launch any military intervention abroad. American influence in the world, they believed, should be confined to giving succor to other progressive movements, in the interest of promoting world peace.

The Vietnam War shattered the long-uneasy alliance of cold war containment with Wilsonian internationalism. In its place, this more pacifistic movement filled the vacuum with a succession of leaders— starting with the 1968 insurgent candidacy of Eugene McCarthy, assuming dominance of the party by 1972 with George McGovern, and finally attaining the White House in 1976 in the person of Jimmy Carter. These new Democratic leaders were less concerned with the dangers of communism than with America's always seeming to be on "the wrong side" as the ally of reactionary, repressive oligarchies and juntas. The excitement and idealism of the party, especially among the young, went to McCarthy and later to McGovern and Carter, who very much summed up and refurbished this worldview.

Yet the Democratic Party was not so easily united under their umbrella. These new Democrats were viewed with suspicion by elements of the old FDR coalition, especially urban ethnic voters, who—as nicely captured in the 1978 film *The Deer Hunter*—were loyal to the old political machines of the industrial Northeast and fiercely patriotic as only those conscious of their immigrant roots can be. It was also true of white working-class men in the South. FDR and his successors had made peace with their Dixiecrat wing, usually proponents of Jim Crow and fierce opponents of civil rights, as the price necessary to retain national power for the greater cause. (Among these were figures like Senator Sam Ervin, later a brief national folk hero for his part in the Watergate hearings; Ervin had voted against every piece of civil rights legislation that came his way.) Both groups thought their party had given too much to minorities, and that it had become unpatriotic toward the war and the men in uniform They had always disliked what they saw as upper-class, effete egghead types like Adlai Stevenson and they viewed "Clean Gene" McCarthy in the same way.

The Alabama governor George Wallace, sensing the chance to break these groups off in a third-party bid for the presidency, imitated the conservative populism of Huey Long, whose original alliance of the dispossessed in Louisiana had been swept by FDR into his great national coalition for the New Deal. Implying that the party's "pointy-headed innerleckshuls" were soft on communism and contemptuous of middle-class majority values, Wallace won over both white working-class southerners and culturally conservative urban ethnics—and in so doing helped the Democrats lose the White House to Richard Nixon. In his landslide victory of four years later, Nixon swept these people entirely into the Republican fold, and the Silent Majority emerged full-grown. It was a watershed that has dominated electoral politics from that day until the present.

The President as Enigma: Richard M. Nixon

"If one hates Richard Nixon enough," wrote the journalist and historian Theodore H. White, "it is easy to describe the implacable vindictiveness and tenacity of the man as more important than the courage; the recurrent gusts of panic or fury as more important than the long thoughtfulness; his coarseness of discourse and lying as more important than his exceptional sensitivity to others' emotional needs; the cheapness and nastiness of his tactics as more important than the long-range planning of his exceptional mind."

It is hard to imagine another American president whose assessment would begin with the issue of the degree to which he was hated. Not whether or not to hate him, but how *much* to hate him. And White was no committed Nixon hater. He was a balanced observer who, before the "breach of faith" of Watergate, had been friendlier in his appraisal of Nixon than many observers in the journalistic mainstream.

Nixon saw himself as the American de Gaulle, a man whose conservative credentials were so impeccable that he could end the war in Vietnam without appearing to be a dewy-eyed idealist about world peace, without in any way conceding the moral superiority of the Vietcong's cause (widely assumed in the antiwar movement), or being mistaken for a leader who, by withdrawing, would make America appear weak in the eyes of the world. As he later put it about another striking departure from his own political pedigree, "Only Nixon can go to China" (also symptomatic of his odd tendency to speak of himself in the third person, as if his political persona were a separate entity from his real self). Temperamentally, Nixon was drawn to such challenges: While many presidents have squared up to crises they inherited, Nixon seemed to *love* crisis, to relish its stresses and opportunities for boldness and surprise. This was the man who titled his 1962 memoir *Six Crises*. The somewhat Mephistophelian air that for this reason surrounded him, mirrored in his genuine attachment for Henry Kissinger as the academically reputable partner in his labors who shared his worldview, helped explain the hatred he attracted. But he was hated even before the Watergate scandal.

First, there was the "Old Nixon." He had ridden the wave of anticommunism Joe McCarthy had made popular in the 1950s, labeling Truman's foreign policy as "Dean Acheson's Cowardly College of Communist Containment." He never went as far as McCarthy, who destroyed himself by attacking the loyalty of the military and thereby finally arousing the wrath of President Eisenhower. But Nixon's prosecution of Alger Hiss earned him a deep hatred that never went away. Elegant and well-bred, Hiss was the very embodiment of the "eastern" foreign policy establishment so much resented in the McCarthyite heartland. He had risen rapidly in the State Department during World War II; his supporters saw him as a high-minded moderate who wanted only to help foster good relations with the Soviet Union after their wartime alliance, in the interest of world peace. Nixon's pursuit of him implied that Hiss's stance—which might have struck many in his social class as a prudent middle ground—was tantamount to being pro-Communist, even a Soviet agent of influence in the government. The northeastern establishment from which Hiss sprang, and the world of fashionable well-heeled New York liberalism that regarded him as a martyr to the passions of the Red Scare mob, never forgave Nixon for bringing him to ruin.

That was why the old Nixon was hated. The New Nixon was hated mainly because he ended the war in Vietnam after the Democrats had tried and failed. It was no rout, but a phased, orderly drawdown in which the North was unable to achieve any decisive battlefield victories against the United States, and which left the government of South Vietnam intact, if embattled, as long as Nixon remained in office. As Henry Kissinger summed it up: "There is no question generosity of spirit was not one of Nixon's virtues; he could never transcend his resentments and his complexes. But neither did he ever receive from his critics compassion for the task his predecessors had bequeathed him." Today, even many of Nixon's detractors would concede that it was an impressive piece of statesmanship. By dangling the prospect of improved relations through detente, Nixon got the Soviet Union to stand aside from the conflict, even as his historic overture to China was cooling that regime's ardor for North Vietnam. Together, Nixon and Kissinger played a marvelous chess game of Great Power politics they called "triangulation"—detente for the Soviets as the carrot, the opening to China as the stick, luring both China and the U.S.S.R. into cutting Ho Chi Minh loose while making each want America's support against the other. As a result of Nixon's policy of Vietnamization, the phased replacement of U.S. combat forces with South Vietnamese, the last American troops left Vietnam in 1973. The antiwar movement fell momentarily silent. And when the North Vietnamese began to balk over negotiations, Nixon revealed that same capacity for calculated destruction we have witnessed in Lincoln, Churchill, and FDR: He bombed Hanoi and Haiphong without mercy, just as several years earlier he interdicted their supply lines in Cambodia. The antiwar movement returned to life and screamed its protest at what it considered a terror bombing campaign and the unauthorized invasion of a sovereign state, but a year into Nixon's second term, North Vietnam signed a peace agreement.

Partly because he was not a genuine conservative ideologue, partly because he did not want domestic political strife to distract him from the really important tasks of world leadership, Nixon preserved—indeed greatly increased—funding for Johnson's Great Society programs, including affirmative action. The Watergate scandal was many things, but at one level it was the revenge of the maturing sixties anti-war generation—now moving into responsible positions in the public and private sectors—against Nixon for seizing the political center and achieving so much at the Democrats' expense. In the 1972 presidential election, Nixon won every state but the liberal bastion of Massachusetts; it was the most impressive American history had yet seen. What could not be denied to him at the ballot box would have to be taken from him through the legal system.

Another source of the hatred Nixon attracted was undoubtedly his much-chronicled personal strangeness. His hardscrabble origins made him the archetypal American success story: a brutal failure of a father, a saintly but emotionally ungiving mother, a beloved older brother who died young of tuberculosis, Nixon chauffeuring his future wife, Pat, on her dates with other boys just so he could be near her—it was all a Freudian gold mine for speculation about Nixon's psyche. In his origins and his complexes, Nixon embodied the restlessness and anxieties lingering beneath the surface of American optimism—and he may well have realized as much himself. As a psychiatric profile by Eli S. Chesen put it, "Eisenhower knew that he was only part of the country; Nixon sees the country *as part of him*, an extension of himself." He drew upon his childhood vulnerability and channeled its negative energy into his outer will and determination to succeed: "While all of us experience anxiety in a multitude of forms, few people have been able to harness this energy as effectively and efficiently as Richard Nixon. This accounts for much of this man's greatness as well as weakness. . . ."

Still, while modern psychiatric insights are useful, we should take their reductionism with a grain of salt. As observed earlier, childhood deprival or abandonment of the kind Nixon experienced (along with Lincoln, Churchill, Reagan, Clinton, and many others, regardless of how one ranks them comparatively) are common to the experience of millions of ordinary people; they rarely produce a successful leader like Nixon, and therefore do not, on their own, explain the emergence of such personalities except as a minimal precondition at most, necessary but not sufficient. What distinguishes important leaders from the legion of people who experience such childhoods is an innate drive for achievement that may draw upon dark origins and anxieties, but cannot be fully explained by them. Richard Nixon, in other words, did not end the war in Vietnam because his father was abusive or his brother died a lingering death. But the toughness he gained from that background may well have added to his strength of will as a statesman.

Undoubtedly, Nixon was the object of some snobbery from liberals who came from privileged backgrounds, especially because of the Hiss trial. In private, JFK dismissed him as having "no class," and when Nixon learned of the remark it rankled deeply. But Nixon's own reaction to his remarkable success was much stranger—he seemed to court the disdain of the comparatively better born, "the Georgetown set" as he labeled them, to lacerate himself with it and search it out where it barely existed. It is by no means impossible to join the American elite if you have the credentials and achievements; Nixon possessed more than enough of both. He had attended a very decent liberal arts college, then Duke Law School; had served his country at war, and won election to the House and Senate on his first tries. The war hero General Eisenhower selected Nixon as his vice president, and dispatched him on the kinds of international troubleshooting roles he adored, becoming a national figure in his famous "kitchen debate" with the pugnacious Soviet leader Khrushchev, easily deflecting his claims for Soviet economic superiority. Finally, Nixon achieved his dream. Though defeated by Kennedy in 1960—and then defeated again in a run for California governor two years later—he returned from political purgatory to become a great foreign policy president, sealing his dominance with his smashing second-term mandate.

Yet none of it seemed to satisfy him inwardly. Even an ardent admirer like the speechwriter Raymond Price could write of his boss: "One part of Richard Nixon is exceptionally considerate, exceptionally caring and sentimental, generous of spirit, kind. Another part is coldly calculating, devious, craftily manipulative. A third part is angry, vindictive, ill-tempered, mean-spirited. . . ." Perhaps his most serious personal failing was that, when he finally rose to the level of the elite, Nixon then deliberately chose not to join it; instead he reveled in his alienation and solitude. By most accounts a loving father and family man, Nixon was also intensely shy, introspective, and private, a man who hated campaigning yet forced himself to press the flesh and appear likable to strangers. By keeping his warmer side so entirely under wraps, however, he was left to present only "Nixon Agonistes" (as Garry Wills dubbed him) to the public, the darkly brooding political opportunist. The public sensed this about him, and it made them uneasy: After all, the American rags-to-riches story is supposed to have a happy ending. Merit is what counts in a democracy based on the equality of opportunity for the earned inequality of result, and just about everyone is willing to pay it respect. Nixon was entirely free to bask in his countrymen's approbation. He could have won over his detractors, even the pedigreed Georgetown set, had he really tried. Yet, after his triumphant reelection in 1972, he seemed morose, uncomfortable, more driven than ever.

Nixon did display an occasional parvenu streak that betrayed his origins. He served cheap wine at White House dinners for congressmen, convinced that these rubes from the heartland would never know the difference, and reserved the finest vintages from the White House cellar for himself. But in his obsession with the Kennedys—who embodied the Georgetown set he hated—Nixon never grasped that what Georgetown liked about the Kennedys was precisely how rough-edged and untraditional they actually were. Through their family's rise from East Boston to Hyannis Port, they had shown that the democratic energy of the common man could reinvigorate the old patrician order while conforming to its style and manners. Nixon could have done the same, but instead he chose his isolation, perhaps because at bottom his scarred boyhood made him desperately afraid that his overtures would be rebuffed and laughed at. He told himself that the Kennedys were mere playboys and dilettantes while he was a man of "serious" mien. In this sense, his partnership with Henry Kissinger was a precious tendril of the acceptance he could never admit he craved: As a Harvard professor and former advisor to the blue-blooded Nelson Rockefeller, Kissinger was as close to "Georgetown" as Nixon would ever get, though he simultaneously resented and suspected Kissinger's ease in mingling with the Harrimans, Katharine Graham, and other denizens of the dreaded "set." For his part, Kissinger was surprised on first getting to know Nixon how sharp his mind was, a common experience among those who had known him previously only from his public persona. As the biographer James Humes observed: "Nixon enjoyed exchanges with curious minds who were young enough not to be biased by events of the past and who might shape policy in the future. He also relished an intellectual challenge."

In the end, of course, it was not hatred alone but the scandal of Watergate that brought Richard Nixon down. But what exactly *was* Watergate? The office building where the burglary took place became a footnote to history, lending its name to the crime, the investigation, and the Senate hearings that led to his downfall. But its name also carried the subliminal hint of a watershed, of gates finally giving way after holding back a torrent. The torrent that threatened Nixon was the 1960s counterculture—the combined forces of the rock revolution, the New Left, and the Age of Aquarius, many of its members upper middle class or loftier in their origins, and now grown older. Returning from their self-imposed exile from politics due to the sins of the fathers in Vietnam, they united to strike at *the* symbol of 1950s McCarthyism and the cold war hawks. There is no question that genuine crimes were at the heart of the Watergate scandal, and that the FBI's investigation was obstructed with the president's knowledge. Yet Nixon's predecessors had done as much or worse—RFK and LBJ had both authorized illegal wiretaps—and it should not go unremarked that he was held to a standard his predecessors averted. Although Nixon had ended the war, he was to be punished not for ending it sooner or on the counterculture's terms.

Ultimately, it could be said that Watergate was all about Vietnam: it flowed directly from it, and seemed to sum up its every implication. The powers Nixon abused, or that were abused on his behalf—bugging and burglary—had been assumed by the presidency to deal with domestic dissenters and to plug intelligence leaks. Indeed, the "plumbers" unit was originally formed by one of Kissinger's deputies to deal with such leaks, only later drifting into domestic political surveillance and dirty tricks. The criminal investigation and the Senate hearings took Nixon as their sacrificial victim, but in a sense their greater purpose was to exorcize the "imperial presidency" altogether—including the specters of LBJ and even JFK. Eventually the talk of scandal extended to the threat of impeachment for the American "incursion" into Cambodia—a military action that had nothing to do with the Watergate crimes themselves, but which afforded the Senate an opportunity to punish Nixon for his foreign policy altogether. Henry Kissinger narrowly escaped criminal investigation in several countries over his alleged role in war crimes and human rights abuses. The CIA was not so lucky, its powers of covert operation gutted in the Church Committee hearings of 1975. Soon the new Democratic presidential candidate, Jimmy Carter, was coupling the words "Vietnam" and "Watergate" into a single hyphenated entity that captured, for many, the immorality of government in the late 1960s and early '70s.

Above all, the Democrats were able to exorcize the illegal excesses of their own unnamed presidents and cabinet secretaries; only the Nixon administration would be openly punished. A powerful mythology began to rewrite the history of the times retroactively: in a well-known *Doonesbury* cartoon, the hippie Zonker Harris listened in bemused silence as a kindergarten student explained that Nixon had begun the war in Vietnam and JFK had ended it. The surviving dynast and heir apparent to "the dream," Edward Kennedy, consciously excised the hawkish, firmly anticommunist leanings of his two martyred brothers, until the Kennedy legacy appeared to be entirely harmonious with that of Eugene McCarthy or McGovern.

During his first presidential campaign and term, Nixon had positioned himself as a defender of "law and order" (a term given currency by his 1968 presidential rival George Wallace). During the Watergate investigations, the Democrats attempted to reclaim that turf, harping on the idea that they were defending "the rule of law"—a timely attempt to smooth over the radical character the party had assumed through its absorption of the antiwar movement. It was a delicious revenge: the radicals Nixon had dismissed as "the bums on campus" had grown into hip young professionals, and especially for those who became D.C. staffers, Watergate marked their own rise and return from exile with their parents' social status preserved or enhanced. The term "psychic emigration" became popular at this time among the baby boomers. It meant: Outwardly we may inhabit professions and wear suits, but inwardly we remain Aquarians committed to the values of the sixties revolution.

NIXON'S FATE WAS sealed with the discovery of the White House taping system. As his journalistic nemeses Bob Woodward and Carl Bernstein aptly put it: "The tapes provided a dark, almost Dostoyevskian journey into Nixon's fears [and] obsessions." Ironically, the taping system had been installed to give Nixon an accurate record of his administration's actions when he came to write his memoirs. In addition to revealing that he knew of his subordinates' attempts to throw the FBI off the scent of the Watergate burglary, the tapes also revealed Nixon at his most foulmouthed and conniving. Some of the crusty old pols who professed shock and schoolmarmish dismay at Nixon's language were obviously hypocritical: they knew well that JFK and LBJ trafficked in the same hardball locker room language most practical and powerful men of Nixon's era employed. The public at large, however, found it disillusioning that a president could talk this way.

But the real fascination was whether the taping system had been rooted in Nixon's own psyche. For its existence disclosed, in addition to a desire to preserve an accurate record for history, a perhaps subconscious desire to reveal his darker side. At an unconscious level, was Nixon longing to break out of his carefully crafted political shell—that mask of insincere laughter and salesman's smile flashed at the wrong moments—and bare his soul to the world? By the same token, not everything on the tapes was vicious and mean. There were many flashes of Nixon's boldness as a strategic thinker, of his generosity toward friends and family members, of his shrewdness as a political analyst. Maybe he unknowingly longed for others to see these sides of his character as well.

Or did he wish to be exposed, to be punished? Had his decades-long devotion to the achievement of presidential power become a prison he unconsciously wished to escape—and the tapes a way of provoking his own downfall? Even before the Watergate scandal, it seems astonishingly naïve to have supposed that Nixon could have edited his tapes before they were revealed to the public. Or did Nixon so relish the struggle against adversity, the narrative of crisis and redemption, having come back so many times from the wilderness—the cycle that had revived him after his razor-thin defeat by JFK, after his even more humiliating defeat in the 1962 California gubernatorial race—that, having achieved the zenith of possible public ambition, he prompted his own downfall so as to once again relish the challenge of an enemy?

Whatever the answer, Richard Nixon remains the most enigmatic of twentieth-century presidents and mirrors some central enigmas of America itself. In time, partial rehabilitation would come—not over Watergate but for his vision as an architect of international relations, where he rivaled if not equaled the master, Franklin Roosevelt. After resigning the presidency, the old lion returned to his native California, to the red-tiled Xanadu overlooking the Pacific that his extraordinary rise in life had brought him, left to contemplate the vicissitudes of fate. Like Shakespeare's Richard II, he might have mused, "For God's sake let us sit on the ground and tell sad stories of the deaths of kings." Even better: "I wasted time, and now doth time waste me."

The President as Penitent: Jimmy Carter

It was Jimmy Carter who returned the White House to the Democratic Party by winning the confidence of the sixties generation growing into careers and affluence—a segment of American society described at the time as the New Class or the Third Force. While they remained "psychic emigres" loyal to the sixties values of peace, love, and openness, they were able to combine a continuing pacifistic approach to America's role in the world with a comfortable acceptance of the traditional American desire to make money and get ahead. As a liberal southerner, Carter embodied the rising power of the Sunbelt and the ability of the New Class to be both economic go-getters and politically correct. The caricature of the South widespread during the Great Society days as a violent backwater of inbred hillbillies (as captured in the film *Deliverance*) was supplanted during Carter's presidency by a brief outbreak of "rural chic"—a time of plaid shirts, "urban cowboy" posturing among young professionals, and a fleeting media fascination with Carter's humble hometown of Plains, Georgia.

Carter's election was summed up in his promise to return government to being "as good and decent" as the American people after the twin evils of Vietnam and Watergate. He tried to reanimate an enduring American archetype, the Jimmy Stewart figure of the decent man who has no desire for political power—who, in fact, rather disapproves of its wheeling and dealing, but who must follow his conscience in a time of national need and step forward to serve the people. In this respect Carter was the polar opposite of FDR, who reveled in his skills in the sport of politics, and of Nixon, who was exhilarated by being the most powerful leader in the world. But Carter's approach was sincere, rooted in his Christian Baptist faith, with its distrust of worldly pomp and glory. His masterstroke was to try to reconcile the generations by making the political values of the sixties generation seem to flow directly out of an older American tradition of Jeffersonian agrarian populism and a distaste for the amoral Great Power realpolitik of the Old World—a cynicism engendered by the would-be Gaullist Nixon and his devious Metternich, Kissinger. Carter's stint as a peanut farmer only embellished this Jeffersonian conviction that the soul of American goodness remained embedded in the land and the "yeoman farmer" and not in the sophistication of the city.

Above all, the Carter presidency presided over a prolonged mood of penitence for the sins of the Vietnam War. The eastern foreign

policy establishment of Dulles, Acheson, and the Bundys, its confidence shattered by the debacle, had retreated into a kind of self-
laceration that took on the hues of New England puritan guilt. (Some,
like McGeorge Bundy, moved increasingly into the realm of chari-
table good works.) The establishment fathers—such as Cyrus Vance,
Carter's first secretary of state—assumed the burden of atoning for
the sins of the Vietnam era, allowing sons like Richard Holbrooke
to move back into the shell and style of the old ruling elite, but with
a reversal of values: the arrogant managerial pragmatism of the best
and the brightest was replaced by a new, sixties-inspired concern with
sensitivity, self-doubt, openness, and "change."

Carter was the perfect embodiment of this penitential interval.
After Ted Kennedy sanitized the Kennedy family legacy of its hawkish anticommunist streak, the pacifistic Carter was in many ways able
to perfect and patent for future use the Kennedy political nimbus—
the longish hair, the hand in the suit jacket pocket, the constant media
circus. Carter diluted and democratized the "Kennedyesque" style,
detached from the dynasty's personal ownership and drained of its
original punch, sex, and vinegar. Carter's attempt to dominate the televised ceremony for the opening of the JFK Library at Harvard was an
obvious bid for the succession—capped by an awkward moment when
he attempted to plant a peck on the cheek of Jackie Kennedy, who was
visibly repelled by this familiarity from a lower-caste stranger.

Carter had been a relatively unfamiliar figure before his run for the
presidency in 1976. This lack of background enabled him to mount a
candidacy based on the image he created: Carter distilled himself into
a cloud of soft vocal cadences, pastel shirts, a silver mane of hair, and
media frenzy and "momentum" did the rest. His rise was eerily predicted by the unseen candidate in Robert Altman's 1975 film *Nashville*,
whose reassuring voice lulls the voters like a southern lullaby. Carter
tried to make his lack of background itself a symbol of unity, walking
to his inauguration on foot and transforming the attendant celebra-
tions into a "blue jeans" affair. Like the chameleonic central character
in Woody Allen's *Zelig*, he was everything to everybody—navy lieu-
tenant and farmer, governor and nuclear engineer. Some found this an

appealing promise of competence; to others, it made Carter seem like a man searching for himself.

Carter was the first in a string of candidates about whom we know virtually nothing, figures with little or no long-term experience who come from nowhere to claim the role of commander in chief. Puff pastries of "big mo"—Gary Hart, Bill Bradley, Howard Dean—they have typically crumbled under the first serious pressure, a verbal gaffe, a skeleton in the closet revealed. As I write these lines, the jury is still out on the latest installment in this trend, the young Illinois senator Barack Obama. His 2008 campaign for the Democratic nomination showed extraordinary resilience, but suffered a series of wounds when his association with a controversial pastor was exposed, and when he was caught on tape characterizing small-town Americans as "bitter" because they turned to guns and religious fundamentalism to compensate for years of failed policies.

As president, Carter capitalized on the penitential mood of post-Vietnam, post-Watergate America—extending it to what became known as "the era of limits," a moral agenda disguised as an economic forecast. America's economic hubris, Carter implied, must be chastened to help us overcome the American taste for imperialism—our lust for riches from abroad—just as what he termed the American people's "inordinate fear of communism" must be chastened to curb the potential for jingoism. Real wars on trumped-up pretexts on behalf of immoral foreign allies, he argued, must give way to a purely spiritual war to curb our excessive consumption of fossil fuels. Carter called this "the moral equivalent" of war—as if to imply that no real war, no matter what cause it was fought on behalf of, could in itself ever be moral.

Carter manifested a similar contempt for Congress (he once referred to its members as "ravenous wolves"), reflecting his distaste for the dirty business of bargaining or making deals with the legislators. This was no mere personal tic, but summed up the contempt of the New Class for old-fashioned pork barrel and logrolling of the kind LBJ had epitomized. Carter's attempt to distance himself from this kind of horse trading began a strain of antipolitical politics that has included Gary Hart, Bill Bradley, and, most recently again, Barack Obama. Reluctant to outline hard policy options—perhaps out of a fear that they will be dragged down by the grubby compromising and trade-offs of Congress—they offer themselves as the princely personal embodiment of a higher vision. Their stock in trade is a string of abstract nouns—"change," "hope," "the future." The presidency they propose is as imperial as ever, but confined to the inner territory of noble intentions.

Carter's exercise of presidential power abroad was, in its impact on other countries, every bit as imperialistic in its scope as that of LBJ or Nixon, but it was an imperialism of withdrawal. Other countries were massively unsettled and transformed, not by the exercise of American power but by its rapid extraction. Human rights, in Carter's interpretation, was no longer a standard of conduct that America embodied, albeit imperfectly, for the rest of the world, but a standard of universal perfection that America herself must work to live up to along with the rest of the world, which had frequently done better. Though Carter revived the Wilsonian emphasis on the right of "peoples" to self-determination, his vision of human rights was not so much Wilsonian as a kind of penance for past American crimes and follies. Human rights under Carter became a free-floating, disembodied standard of universal perfection that no nation could live up to—certainly not the United States.

The utopianism of Carter's human rights ideal, which had no specific mooring in the American regime, pointed up the impossible contradiction of maintaining America's great power status while struggling to preserve a transcendentalist vision and the purity of an unsullied conscience. Although Carter preached noninterventionism, by castigating and peremptorily withdrawing support from such allies as the Philippines, the Somoza regime in Nicaragua, and the Shah's Iran, he in fact interfered directly in their internal affairs. This was not because communism or any other revolutionary ideology held any attraction for Carter, but because he harbored an evangelical zeal to purge and reform those who had chosen America as their ally—the same impulse that drove him to chasten America's own materialistic middle-class gas guzzlers. The Shah of Iran fell short of moral perfection; he was a fitful and halfhearted modernizer. But Carter would treat such recalcitrant allies like redneck sheriffs at home: If they failed to mend their ways immediately, America would pull their props out from under them—and do nothing to affect the results that would follow. Thus Carter stood by while Iran was overrun by one of the most bloodthirsty totalitarian dictatorships in the twentieth century. His administration's refusal to tolerate the lesser evil consigned a great country to decades of woe.

Carter's attempt to unify the sixties generation with the populism of an earlier era began to unravel as his failures mounted. His many personal idiosyncrasies began to intrude more and more on the daily operation of government. At length he became an object of ridicule, fatal for a president's authority; the once-charismatic southern agrarian was replaced by the eccentric who claimed to have been attacked on a hunting trip by what the press gleefully dubbed a "killer rabbit" that the president had subdued with a canoe paddle.

Ultimately, Carter's humble background would prove a liability. His brother, Billy—at first celebrated as a genial southern character—soon became an embarrassment even among the league of the damned of presidents' siblings, once it was discovered that he had befriended the Libyan dictator Muammar Qaddafi, partnering with him in various shady business dealings. By the end of Carter's presidency, his grassroots image was seen by many as a mock-humble denial of the symbols of national grandeur that had characterized the "imperial presidency," inviting the opposite extreme of the high-fashion glitz and patriotic pageantry of the Reagan era.

Carter's image was so distended and compromised by the end of his single term that Reagan's movie persona seemed like a valid promissory note for a return to real statesmanship. Miraculously, Reagan actually managed to grow into that role. But what was left behind, seemingly for good, was the expectation that our presidents should serve long political apprenticeships, the way Truman, LBJ, and Nixon had—should make a slow climb over decades from local to regional to congressional and finally to national office. Although only four years had passed since Nixon's resignation, we seemed to be an age away from his long slog from congressman to senator to prosecutor of Hiss, the vice presidency, the kitchen debate, the storming of his motorcade in Caracas, his first run for president, his failed gubernatorial bid, his stint as New York lawyer as he made serious money and gathered his kitchen cabinet for another run. It now appeared as if one could do an end run around this long slog by promising "new" (if unspecified) ideas and "a new vision."

Carter was a highly intelligent man, and the Camp David Accords was a landmark achievement for which he deserves all praise. Yet his temperament seemed ultimately unsuited for the office he held. Carter bared his soul compulsively to the public in a way that undercut his authority as a leader, using the public as a psychiatrist's couch. He confessed that he'd harbored "lust in his heart," and repeatedly declared his helplessness to the American people—as if they would somehow be reassured by a president who told them, *I'm just like you. I need your help. I feel your pain.* As Carter proclaimed his "love" for the entire population in a breathy, Marlene Dietrich–like delivery, the American people grew weary of his attempts at emotional intimacy. He claimed that he would "never lie" to the American people, a standard even less attainable in public life than private, and which would make statesmanlike rhetoric, with its inevitable exaggeration, an impossible task. And, as the world came crashing in on him—through the Soviet invasion of Afghanistan, the fall of Iran to violent revolutionaries, the ensuing hostage crisis, and the fall of Nicaragua to a Marxist-Leninist proxy of Cuba—Carter's passivity became a kind of existentialist ontology: *We can't do anything, such events are beyond our control.*

As "change" pressed in on America with one disaster after another, Carter's inner fragmentation and rootlessness became more and more obvious. His remark after the Soviet entry into Afghanistan—that he had learned more about the Soviet Union in the past two weeks than in his previous three years in office—was a sickening collision between his confessional style and the frightening prospect of a totalitarian regime that stood outside the American view of life. To give him credit, once his eyes were opened about the Soviet Union, he became a hawk during his last year, rather like Chamberlain when he finally saw Hitler for what he was. The penitential Cyrus Vance at the State Department gave way to the more hawkish Harold Brown at Defense, Zbigniew Brzezinski began organizing American help for the anti-Soviet mujahideen in Afghanistan, and defense spending was ramped up in a way that smoothed the transition to the Reagan buildup. Carter's collapse burst the sixties bubble and drove it from the real world, back out of the political center, to reemerge under Reagan as the "peace movement," a full-blown millenarian crusade to end all violence forever.

As these crises loomed on the horizon of his last year in office, Carter fled to Camp David as if to a religious retreat, desperate to find his way back to the political center. His only solution was to restate the inner core of the vision that had brought him to the White House, and it became the swan song of his dying presidency. In a televised address, he said that we were all in the grip of a "national malaise" caused by—of course—Vietnam and Watergate, the source of all our ills. In effect, the speech blamed the American people. *The problem, Carter implied, is not the actual disasters caused by my policies, but your spiritual shortcomings; rather than change these policies, I can only urge you to strive harder to share, care, love, and be open to change.* But Carter had himself *caused* the "national malaise," which was likely rooted in his own restless, driven, obscure personality. In challenging the country to overcome faults that were essentially his own, he had violated the golden rule of civic rhetoric exemplified by the words of Pericles, Lincoln, and Churchill: Don't blame your fellow citizens; rather, encourage them to follow their own noblest instincts.

New Day in America: Ronald Reagan and the Evolution of a Statesman

To understand Ronald Reagan, one must recognize not only his own personal appeal but his virtual monopoly of the political center during his presidency. This was not widely acknowledged at the time, but it became apparent in retrospect through his state funeral in 2004, which took on the proportions of a Wagnerian national myth of generational reconciliation: the moving formal obsequies of the ceremonies in Washington were capped by an almost Valhalla-like translation to eternity in the Simi Valley in California, against a background of glowing torches and a magnificent mountainscape. Rarely has an American chief executive attained such mythic proportions in both life and death: Among twentieth-century presidents, only Franklin Roosevelt brooks comparison.

The secret of Reagan's ability to bestride the political landscape like a colossus (to paraphrase Shakespeare's line about Julius Caesar) lay in the simple power of American patriotism—a force that was conceded to him by the Democrats, an act of folly that would take years to undo. Reagan's mystique had less to do with his powers of "communication," as was often alleged, than with the Democratic Party's willingness to allow the Republicans to monopolize the politics of hope for the future, economic growth, individual initiative, and love of country. This enabled Reagan, golden-tongued by nature, to spread himself across the entire rhetorical spectrum—so much so that eventually he seemed to embody the nation itself.

Rarely has there been such a disproportion between the prestige of a president and his own fairly modest intellectual acumen and uncomplicated personality. As even his admirers would concede, Reagan was far less complicated or intellectual than either Nixon or Carter. He was also less ruthless than Truman, and possessed none of the patrician air of command that allowed FDR to preside sphinxlike over the country. Reagan seemed to glide through life easily, untroubled by the burning passion for public approbation that drove a figure like Churchill. Reagan's followers appeared to come to him entirely of their own volition, drawn by his warmth—a welcome change from the hectoring many had disliked in Carter.

Yet Reagan's apparent simplicity masks the very complex evolution of political values that marked his political career—a journey that may seem difficult to reconcile with the genial sunshine of the man himself. It proves, as we have seen before with great leaders who begin their rise being generally underestimated and patronized—Lincoln and Churchill come to mind—that character can sometimes trump a sparkling intellect or a formal education.

This disjunction between Reagan's seemingly uncomplicated psyche—he slept well at night, there were no midnight Nixonian wanderings, no interrogations of presidential portraits—and his overwhelming public presence makes it hard to know where to begin in assessing a figure who even now looms so large over the landscape. Every presidential contender today openly or secretly longs to imitate the scale and longevity of his success. The Democrats ceded to Reagan so much of the American political center that he did not have to define himself with sharp edges, as had Nixon, for example, in selling himself as the man who would end the war and visit communist China precisely *because* he was a hawk and anti-Red—strenuous exertions against political typecasting Nixon had to carefully prepare over many years. Reagan's genial generalities about America's bright future had once been the staple of *all* presidencies; they had come to seem cheapened by overuse, but Reagan was able to make them fresh again, indeed to make them into political dynamite, because his opponents had abandoned them altogether. Carter's sackcloth-and-ashes mentality had left behind such a strong thirst for national self-affirmation that the ordinary platitudes of presidential rhetoric became an incredible gift, a blank canvas for Reagan's considerable oratorical dexterity and stagecraft.

The standard excuse the Democrats made for their historic electoral thumping by Reagan—that he was the "great communicator" who disguised bad policies with rhetorical gossamer—showed their inability for many years to think through the real basis of his success, and their unwillingness to reexamine themselves. It also betrayed a cynical willingness on their part to treat the presidential race *as* a game, a technique to gull the public. In attributing this manipulativeness to Reagan, they unwittingly let the public in on the fact that this was how they viewed politics themselves. For a long period, the Democrats could only alternate between whining about Reagan's rhetorical skills and trying to superficially imitate his mastery of public symbolism, summed up in their frequent pout that Republicans did not have "a monopoly on patriotism." Another variation of the attempt to imitate Reagan was to imitate the superficial *language* of toughness. Michael Dukakis, who ran against George Bush for the presidency in 1988, ludicrously styled himself "the Duke" like John Wayne, while remaining unchanged in his loyalty to the penitential Carter view of foreign policy. Driving around grinning foolishly in an Abrams tank for a photo op to prove that he favored a strong military did not fool anyone, and the electorate sensed they were being gulled. Political images are not and cannot be literally accurate—they inevitably simplify a candidate's personality. But they cannot simply be fabricated either, if they are to have any chance of success. They must tap into something authentic about the person and paint it in broad strokes that the widest spectrum of voters can relate to.

Reagan's critics loved to deride him for being "simplistic." Tip O'Neill, the charming and decent House Speaker, got on famously with his fellow Irishman Reagan in private (the two often enjoyed a few drinks at the end of the day—something the starchy Carter would never have abided). But even O'Neill couldn't resist calling him "simplistic," over and over again—as if it were a word the Speaker had just learned and loved to pronounce, in publicly lambasting Reagan's anticommunist and pro-market stances. At bottom, however, Reagan and Tip were both simple men, and doubtless in some ways simplistic. That was the source of their strength and integrity. As Reagan knew, often the truth *is* simple. Under FDR, Truman, and JFK, the Democrats had known as much. But in the 1960s and 1970s they had come to be seen as the party of the fastidious and overly refined, of those who flinch at a bald reality and prefer the kind of nuance and ambivalence that, while perfectly appropriate to savoring a work of art, can be disastrous when extended to the jungle of foreign affairs in a world where the majority of governments are oligarchies, dictatorships, and military juntas.

The truth about Reagan's success was also very simple. The electorate sensed that too many Democrats, for all their professions of populism, disliked capitalism, looked down on the middle class as gas-guzzling polyester-clad vulgarians, sneered at middle-class bourgeois morality, were soft on foreign policy, ashamed to express their patriotism, and contemptuous of religious faith. This is why the Democratic presidential candidates of the 1970s and 1980s wandered in the wilderness for so long—leaving aside only Jimmy Carter, the exception who proved the rule. To win the nomination, their presidential candidates had to respond not to the middle class itself but to the aging cadres of the counterculture who dominated the base of the party. In doing so, they alienated the country at large. During the Reagan years, it produced constant irresolution, petulance, and a cynical attempt to manipulate imagery to substitute for a lack of genuinely popular policies that the electorate somehow smelled as insincere—an effort that reached its nadir in that unintentionally comical photo op of Dukakis riding a tank. Only Bill Clinton, in some ways the reverse of Reagan, but also his mirror image opposite, was able to lead them out of this wilderness back to the White House.

Why Was Reagan So Successful?

As the Carter presidency was winding down, pop culture was already brimming with signs of longing for a Reagan-like figure. The 1978 nighttime TV drama *Dallas* already celebrated the return of capitalism and offered a reminder that the wellsprings of American success were found not in Washington but in the heartland. Texas embodied both traditional, full-blooded patriotism and the growth of the economic power of the Sunbelt over the old and declining industrial zones of primary industry in the Midwest and Northeast. But the tongue-in-cheek tone of the show pointed to a wider appeal, not only to Republicans but to emerging yuppies as well. The spell of Carter-induced guilt over the failure to live up to the dream of the sixties counterculture, and over Vietnam and Watergate, was shattered by the reemergence of old-fashioned bare-knuckled entrepreneurialism, brains, savvy, and ruthlessness.

While the liberal establishment bemoaned the return of the "ice age" (the slogan derived from the title of Margaret Drabble's novel about post-sixties disillusionment and the alleged loss of momentum in further social progress for minorities and the poor), people of all social levels found a guilty pleasure in the fun of J. R. Ewing's boyish, openly grasping villainy, his love of the chase, his delight in evil, but also his loyalty to family and soil. This zest for winning once openly manifested by presidential leaders, but driven underground by the prolonged guilt trip over the imperial presidency, was openly reemerging in the contest for entrepreneurial success, and it allowed Americans to begin reconnecting with a suppressed side of their national character. J.R.'s sharky little smile as he contemplated the numerous moving parts of his latest plan to grind oil patch rival Cliff Barnes into the dust invited a spirit of rebellion against the teary sadness of the Carter presidency, its smiling through tears and spankings of the middle class for its greed. The treacly bucolic atavism of John Denver or *The Waltons*, emblematic of the Carter era's attempt to tap into the Jeffersonian preference for simple agrarianism over urban sophistication, burst its polite bounds and surged back to the Republicans, merging their traditional clientele of Main Street small-business and country-club old money with the new, brash, thrusting ambition for megabucks embodied by J.R. The Ewings used their oil wealth to maintain their *Junker* status as landed Texas aristocrats. As cattlemen ranchers, they were frontier blue bloods. But the family fiefdom, Southfork, could only be maintained in its magnificent sprawl and splendor because of J.R.'s ceaseless maneuvers in the glass tower downtown. Symbolically, it summoned up the approaching Reagan era.

Dallas also recalled a deep-grooved theme in American success stories—the grafting of new wealth onto old blood, often against the backdrop of the open frontier, the limitless canvas for the ambition of new talent. Figures like the Sterling Mortons come to mind—moving west to Nebraska as homesteaders in the 1850s, over successive generations they became tycoons, philanthropists, and served in the cabinets of Grover Cleveland and Theodore Roosevelt, all the while moving steadily back eastward. The Bush family had in fact embarked on a similar odyssey during the Carter and Reagan years; they would eventually embody its apotheosis when the grandson of a gentlemanly Connecticut senator, enriched by Texas and in many ways a genuine Texan himself, succeeded his patrician father as president. In the 1970s, however, it was the rise of Ronald Reagan that embodied this exciting new zeitgeist, an antidote and answer to the long dreary years of American failure, setback, and withdrawal. The "era of limits," of penance, was over. There is an uncanny magic to great leaders, or leaders who aspire to greatness, whereby history itself can sometimes seem to take their side, seems to walk with them, guiding their steps. Reagan was not on a level with Lincoln, Churchill, or FDR, but he had something of this magic that defined a country anew and enabled a country to see itself in him.

Yet the gauziness of Reagan's renewal of American confidence should not blind us to the fact that this was *not* the free market ethos of the 1950s, much less of the Horatio Alger era, that was frequently invoked by both friends and foes of the Reagan administration. The capitalism of the 1950s had still been fueled by a Victorian legacy of self-restraint, piety, probity, personal abstemiousness, and a certain shame about excessive wealth; conspicuous consumption was to be avoided as vulgar and the mark of a parvenu. This Protestant work ethic went together with expiatory good works—the building of libraries, art galleries, and universities by the Carnegies and other robber barons, to avoid the scathing label Theodore Roosevelt gave them as "malefactors of great wealth." The new entrepreneurs of the Reagan era, by contrast, rarely demonstrated a 1950s-style Christian probity or a devotion to anticommunism. Oddly enough, the sixties disdain for capitalism as a value system had been embraced by the new entrepreneurs themselves—in many cases, after all, they were the same people—who happily accepted the morally disparaging argument that capitalism is about nothing more than getting the better of others to make limitless money.

The sixties generation, in other words, abandoned its objections to capitalism, even as it retained its low opinion of its moral value. It was in fact not morally admirable, except insofar as it demonstrated your brains and if you had a taste for the hunt. Morality properly speaking was reserved for politically correct projects such as the peace movement. Combat manuals like Sun Tzu's *The Art of War* became popular

with management gurus. Now you made money *for* the sake of pleasure, consumption, fame. The "natural life" of the counterculture was
steadily upgraded to include fine wines and furniture typified by the
artists' colony of newly enriched rock and movie stars in posh Mill
Valley, California. In the past, a staunch moral character and background were said to be essential to success in business. That emphasis
on moral character now gave way to a pure meritocracy of test scores
and a mania for "good schools"—even preschools that were said to
"track to the Ivy League."

Ironically, the new money class of the Reagan era shared the withering view of capitalism fomented by Karl Marx and Herbert Marcuse.
Contrary to the Marxist caricature, the United States of America had
not been founded for the sake of capitalism alone. Commercial success
was merely one among many of the individual liberties it fostered.
Freedom of speech, association, and worship were at least as important. Now, oddly enough, the Reagan-era capitalists agreed with the
New Left that "Amerika" had been created for no other reason than
to liberate greed. As Oliver Stone's creation Gordon Gekko says in his
pep talk to shareholders in the film *Wall Street*, "greed is good." Life
as a successful capitalist, in other words, was unconnected with any
traditional conception of moral behavior—it was entirely compatible
with drugs, sex, and gargantuan consumer pleasures. The emerging
class of young, newly super-wealthy Wall Street traders was a crazy
quilt of once-contradictory patterns—a group who wore Chinos and
built lavish wine cellars, while indulging in bodybuilding, cocaine,
and free love.

It was also discovered during the Reagan years that capitalism
could also be combined with the "internal emigration" of the baby
boomers after the Age of Love was over. The thirtysomething software millionaire might resist unionization of his employees and deny
them a pension plan and other benefits. But on the weekends he would
take his young children to a peace rally. It was a pretense of Reagan's
critics that only the Republicans promoted excessive materialism. In
truth, the pattern fit neither party exclusively. But the Democrats in
general left this renewed capitalist vigor to the Republicans to exploit

politically. The Democrats were unable to part with their missionary conception of government and the liberal grandee conception of vast state spending to help the underclass. At the same time, however, while the software tycoon could take his kids to a peace rally while hiring people on contract so as to avoid paying them pensions, he could never embrace Reagan's foreign policy if he voted for the Democrats. That kind of patriotism was still regarded by many baby boomers as jingoistic and fearmongering. Moreover, as the economist Kevin Phillips correctly opined, although the American economy as a whole may have expanded, the gap between classes had widened. There were issues brewing that the Democrats could eventually exploit.

Faced with his country's pent-up longing to make money without limit or guilt, Reagan did something very simple: He let people do it. With the Democrats trapped in their Carter-era wailing about compassion and limits, Reagan had a clear field to put across a scheme so "simplistic" and circular that it became all things to all people: supply-side economics. The operating principle of supply-side economics could be expressed as follows: *Liberate greed to pay for government.* It was a recipe for self-perpetuating nongovernance, with the president as inexhaustible cheerleader on the sidelines. The business of government was reduced to following the mantra "no new taxes"—but after the Carter era, simply leaving people alone to make and spend money looked like vigorous leadership on a grand scale.

With supply-side economics, Reagan co-opted, more effectively and convincingly than Carter, the mantle of Jeffersonian populism and little-man entrepreneurialism. He even freed himself to absorb the nimbus of the grand national activism of FDR, offering hope and movement across the whole country—not through state action, as FDR had, but through abstention from it. He got the state out of the people's way. In a sense, Reagan was the inevitable answer to FDR: He reenergized FDR's grand coalition by letting it fly apart for good. That answered to a deeply held American belief first expressed by Montesquieu, the Enlightenment thinker most often cited by the Founding Fathers in *The Federalist* and repeated by Paine and Jefferson: "That government is best which governs least." Reagan also reanimated the long-standing American conviction that individualism and the pursuit of economic self-interest is natural, and that America, having been founded uniquely among nations to promote it, is a world unto itself, where nature makes the taint of government largely unnecessary.

Far from being a throwback to the age of the robber barons, Reagan was in many ways a man of his age—more so than, say, Nixon, with his nostalgia for Gaullist and Churchillian "seriousness." The old Horatio Alger myth about free enterprise had stressed probity, pain, sacrifice, piety, and deferred gratification. True success meant joining Victorian Christian civilization, standing for public virtue, and setting an example for the masses. As soon as you made your fortune, you or at least your children must aspire to a higher gentlemanly purpose, such as public office, one of the learned professions, or becoming a patron of culture. By contrast, Reagan's recipe for expanding the economy was painless, morally contentless, and value neutral—compatible with hedonism, and thus surprisingly consistent with the values of the sixties generation. Reaganomics and the Reagan boom gave the New Class the financial means to actualize the back-to-nature fantasy of *The Greening of America*—dotting the enclaves of the wealthy with eco-friendly teak and glass mansions in the mountains, adobe complexes with Persian carpets, solar-powered air-conditioning, a lap pool, and a dance rail. *Making money itself is public-spirited*, the supply-side ethos whispered. *You don't have to do anything else.* Buying luxuries created new service economy jobs, and that was just as civic-minded as founding a library or running for Congress. This was the most potent appeal to the New Class: You don't need to cut your hair or clean up your sex life to join the Reagan revolution. No wonder rock stars like Sammy Hagar were among Reagan's supporters.

Reagan's vulgar yet doubtlessly sincere view of capitalism was probably aided by the fact that he had no experience of the business world himself, only experience in promoting its worth as a spokesman for General Electric. He had always been a cheerleader for the idea of the little-man entrepreneur and the hometown values of Main Street. He had portrayed these kinds of men in his movies, then sought out their counterparts in the real world and extolled their value to America at a time when the smart set looked down on them. But being confined to the role of a rhetorical cheerleader probably enabled him to think that capitalism really was just about moneymaking, and that this was truly its claim to merit. He seemed to hero-worship the titans of business.

By contrast, an actual self-made tycoon like Joseph Kennedy had wanted to rise above business and remove its taint as quickly as possible—even the legitimate investment business that succeeded his shadier origins. He made money so that he, or his sons, could rise to the level of statesmanship and national service, and so prove that they deserved acceptance by their old-moneyed social betters. Men who had held high appointed office during the 1950s, like John Foster Dulles, Dean Acheson, and Averil Harriman, were on good terms with the corporate elite, but they were never reducible to its chief concerns. Their money was out of sight, its origins delicately confined to the past. Their houses were discreetly shrouded, their summer retreats safely out of view. Public service alone could vindicate the robber baron antecedent, the "one who made the money," and wash away its grubbiness. The Reagan era, by contrast, began the arguably loathsome practice of saying that people invited to assume high government positions like a cabinet post are doing the rest of us a favor because they will make less money—as if no public honor, including the highest magistracies of the republic, could quite trump a temporary loss in income. It was a vulgarization of the business ethic that escaped many conservatives because it seemed so successful and American and escaped liberals because of their own low moral view of capitalism left over from their protest days. The cheesiness and mock-humble hayseed air of Carter's inaugural gave way to the splashy excess of Reagan's—a Gilded Age mélange of Versace-draped trophy wives, the legendary saloon singer with the rumored mob connections, and the department store heir whose million-dollar affair with his beautiful young mistress erupted in a notorious palimony suit with allegations of S&M, ending in her violent murder by another lover.

. . . .

REAGAN'S PERSONALITY AND skills and how they contributed to
his success are easier to understand in the context of the era. On the
broadest level, Reagan represented the reconciliation of the generations by appealing to a universal desire to advance in life and pros-
per—"democratic capitalism." It was a great national volunteer project that reunited the country. Nixon had been the last president who
achieved national unity—albeit briefly—through his policies alone,
staking his claim on ideas like Vietnamization and superpower detente that had taken years of nurturing. The resulting tensions with
his opponents, too great to be contained, burst the bounds of the political center during Watergate and could not be sorted out into a new
consensus. The centrist foreign policy of the Wise Men, embraced by
Truman and JFK and revitalized by Nixon, had itself become divisive.
In attempting to heal the wounds, Carter and Reagan shared the techniques of the new politics—the politics of gesture and media symbols
to paper over divisions that hard policy could no longer reach. Both
leaders furnished a simulacrum of an older America to mask those
divisions and give a new consensus time to solidify. The presidency
came to absorb more and more of the role of a symbolic national
unifier, leading to an emphasis on image and gesture (including the
debate over flag burning that preoccupied Reagan's successor, the first
President Bush) over substance. The decline of New York as America's
cultural and intellectual hub, and the rise of the Washington policy
intellectual, was another symptom of how everything was being absorbed into the presidential aura.

In answer to Carter's vision of the nation as a community of
penitence, Reagan offered the simple release of populism divorced
from any historical content except self-interest. Reagan himself was
an ahistorical figure: He shared none of Nixon's admiration for past
statesmen, JFK's passion for history, or RFK's taste for Aeschylus. His
administration contained at the highest level no intellectual heavy-
weights comparable to Kissinger, although it was full of able managers
and pragmatists like George Shultz, as well as young Turks like Paul

Wolfowitz and his brain trust at Policy Planning awaiting their chance for larger actions. But Reagan's lack of historical grounding reflected a genuine, if not entirely admirable, strand of the American experience, recalling the Gilded Age boom years of President McKinley.

In the absence of a credible alternative from the Democrats, Reagan's presidency smoothly absorbed all national symbols by default. There was a seemingly endless succession of beautifully choreographed patriotic pageants: for the fallen troops in Grenada, for the Bicentennial of the Constitution and "Lady Liberty," for the space shuttle victims, the skies spangled with fireworks as the president rolled out mellifluous yet oddly generic phrases, often going overboard for the gravity of the occasion ("let slip the surly bonds of earth to touch the face of God"), the leader always upright, perfectly groomed, a catch in the throat and a tear in the eye. It was as if destiny had granted Americans a reprieve in which to learn how to feel the love of country again by slow baby steps, before the Iron Age descended on 9/11 and the troops began to die, not by the handful in America's backyard in Grenada but by the thousands in Iraq.

Reagan's past as a B-movie star was often sarcastically noted as the source of his rhetorical smoothness, artificiality, and "simplistic" belief in good guys and bad guys. This easily purchased contempt blinded many to what was really novel in Reagan's link with show business. It was not the mere fact of a Hollywood pedigree: The Kennedys had been Hollywood people like their father, numbering movie and music stars among their intimates. Carter had already converted the presidency into a victory for media technique and was chummy with Willie Nelson and Mary Tyler Moore. In later years, Jonathan Demme directed a film biography about him. Stars fascinated by politics and Hollywood-loving politicians were nothing new. Indeed, the rise of the socially concerned celebrity during the civil rights era of the 1960s and later during the peace movement of the 1980s (with Paul Newman lecturing Johnny Carson on *The Tonight Show* about the urgent need for arms control) helped make Reagan's Hollywood pedigree seem less unusual.

The real significance of Reagan's Hollywood past was how well it equipped him to offer the electorate a simulacrum of the American tradition. Reagan was often called a throwback to the nineteenth century. But he was really a throwback to that version of nineteenth-century Christian entrepreneurial individualism as simplified and sentimentalized *by* Hollywood films of the 1940s. Neither Reagan nor his voters knew or cared much about the past itself. Besides his broad articulation of New Right social issues, Reagan evidenced no coherent view of the American tradition—apart from the pluck, cheerfulness, and grit of the characters he had played on film like "the Gipper." The economist and sometimes Republican strategist Kevin Phillips, who admired some of Reagan's achievements, nonetheless took an unsparing view of his shallowness. Writing about his diaries, Phillips observes: "Nowhere does this popular president speak of the challenges of the coming millennium, of history and its turning points, of the squeeze on the same middle class that provided him with enormous support, or the transformation of the American economy as manufacturing gave way to speculations and finance. These, apparently, were not his concerns."

Though he brought fundamentalist Christians back into politics as a major force for the first time since the Populists, it is debatable to what extent he was a devout or at least a conventional Christian himself. His own church attendance was limited to the traditional presidential minimum of important holidays and state funerals. He never persuasively defended the Victorian view of moral uplift through hard work, the deferral of gratification, and piety, and did little to forward the New Right take on social issues like abortion except to talk in general terms about preserving the family. As the biographer Lou Cannon observed: "While I do not doubt Reagan's sincerity in advocating an anti-abortion amendment, he invested few political resources toward obtaining this goal." Ultimately, it was the vacuum of public virtue he inherited from the Democrats that made Reagan's unobjectionable platitudes about patriotism and loyalty to the American way of life sound like rhetorical dynamite, an affront to sophisticated opinion. They were, in fact, minimal gestures devoid of controversy, meant to appeal to just about everyone.

Since his days as governor of California, Reagan had an ingenious knack of running for office to the right and then governing from the center. He in effect detached his conservative self from his governing self, running with the first one and holding office with the second. In a strange kind of political coquetry, he even let his followers believe that his true conservative self was imprisoned by bureaucrats and handlers he was too good-natured to override, like a damsel in distress inviting his most loyal supporters to rescue him from his prison tower and "let Reagan be Reagan." But this *was* Reagan. Just as Nixon preempted the New Left by ending the Vietnam War, it was Reagan, of all people, who began drawing down America's nuclear arsenal and edging up to the discussion of total nuclear disarmament with Gorbachev, thereby coming closer to meeting the practical agenda of the peace movement than any Democratic officeholder could.

On the domestic side, Reagan's defense of "free enterprise" was in many ways a nostalgic balm to help ease America through the disappearance of its primary industries and its conversion to a service economy. For most people, "democratic capitalism" meant white-collar and service-sector jobs with lower pay, fewer benefits, and diminished job security. The Reagan presidency was in many ways a form of tribal politics, presenting large, bright, and reassuring cartoons of tradition in a society where economic globalization was rapidly eroding previous social bonds. As hard-core movement conservatives later conceded, federal programs continued to grow exponentially under Reagan. As his short-lived budget director David Stockman learned to his cost, Reagan had no intention of souring his honeymoon with America by actually cutting the entitlement programs of the Great Society.

Altogether, the Reagan era represented the boiling down of the centuries-old ethos of Christian capitalism and Protestant uplift to a series of mass-marketable, homogenized gestures meant to elicit a certain mood of patriotism and decency at the least possible cost in depth of feeling or psychological and historical complexity. If this was what he drew from his movie roles, Reagan was only emulating what the great movie moguls like Louis B. Mayer, and before him entertainers like George M. Cohan and Irving Berlin, had furnished—a broader, gauzier version of the American founding creed in which newcomers, whether Catholic, Jew, immigrant, or nonbeliever, could join. The moguls disarmed the Know-Nothing nativist strain in American culture by perfecting a sentimental, picture-perfect version of their own American world in which Christian decency dictated that no man of merit or ambition should be excluded from a chance to rise, regardless of faith, color, or creed. Reagan reenergized this ever-expanding American ethic of inclusion by acting it out as president—down to the catch in the throat, the dewy eyes, the Jimmy Stewart stance of a good and unassuming man pushed too far by bullies.

Reagan far exceeded Jimmy Carter's prowess in acting out the role of the unpolitical man who has a deep distaste for the cheap opportunism and greed of political life, but who is driven to take it up because no one will speak for the people—a character perfected in films like *Mr. Smith Goes to Washington* and *State of the Union*. Even when answering a sharply critical questioner, Reagan would cock his head, grin, and begin with that characteristically drawn-out "Well," as in, *Well, now, settle down, young feller, and try to see the other man's view*, as if indulging a hotheaded nephew. When he issued his heroic and inspiring call in front of the Brandenburg Gate in Berlin, he sounded less like the American commander in chief with thousands of ICBMs at his back than a small-town mayor who has finally had enough: "Mr. Gorbachev, tear down this wall!" Reagan's few truly intransigent remarks—like his description of the Soviet empire as an "evil empire"—were the exception that proved the rule, and the hysterical reaction it prompted from some liberals only showed how far from the center their party had strayed. The Soviet Union, after all, had deliberately killed at least thirty million of its own people through collectivization and slave labor on behalf of a utopian economic experiment that had accomplished next to nothing in a half century. What morally grounded person could object to calling that empire evil?

One of Reagan's key assets was his air of kindly-old-man sweetness. Even as late as the 1950s and early 1960s, Reagan had seemed a bit precious, like the teacher's pet who harangues his class about doing their homework and leaves an apple on her desk. With his child-actor pompadour, cheeky grin, and often-petulant voice, he seemed the smart aleck who wants his hair tousled—it all grated. Age and incumbency transformed Reagan into a wise and patient father figure who admonished the rebellious to calm down and think twice. At the same time, his air of ingratiation, which once seemed cloying, now seemed touching, like a grandfather shyly seeking to win over his grandchildren. As Lou Cannon observed, Reagan's past was not entirely in keeping with the sunniness of his personality; his personality was almost certainly shaped by his boyhood need to cope with his father's alcoholism. "Relatively few studies," Cannon observes, "have focused on the experiences of successful children of alcoholics, of whom Reagan is an outstanding example." Reagan's terminal boyishness might originally have been a coping strategy for dealing with his father. Children of abusive parents sometimes try to seem harmless, young for their age, in order not to seem threatening to a parent's volatile temper.

But the striking thing is that Reagan set about making himself over to fill the emptiness of his dark childhood. He wanted love, and he was successful in finding it—first through movies, and later in public service. Cannon writes: "In his early days, Reagan's extraordinary optimism had enabled him to cope with the dark spells caused by Jack Reagan's drinking. Later, it permitted him to forge ahead relentlessly, changing courses, careers, and ideology in his climb to the presidency." Reagan came to embody American optimism itself. America's hopes for the future became his own best therapy. In contrast with Nixon, some of whose childhood troubles he shared, Reagan never allowed his dark origins to drag him down. He made himself into what he wanted to be, and it was genuine. His speechwriter Peggy Noonan has described Reagan's "trust in the future, his sunny belief that change, big change, was possible." For therapy he drew on the balm of the American experience itself, and especially its unending search for a better future for everyone. "This belief," according to his first press secretary, Marlin Fitzwater, "was at the core of his political principles—that conservatism was good for America, and America was a good, hardworking, ethical nation that should be a model to the world." By embracing America as his cure, Reagan was able to act on his need for the love of others by radiating to them the confidence in the future that they themselves most needed. As Noonan put it, "it is the oddest thing, and true, even if everyone says it: It is not possible to be nervous in his presence. He acts as if he's lucky to be with you." The presidential historian Thomas Cronin compared him to JFK. Although their views on policy were not identical, both had "a way of talking about issues in simple terms that made them interesting and got people to listen." And both had a "contagious optimism" that others basked in like the sun.

Past and present, reality and acting, came together for him when he was shot in front of the Hilton Hotel in downtown Washington, D.C., in 1981. His remark while being wheeled to the operating room to Nancy—"Honey, I forgot to duck"—summed up everything most appealing about the 1940s leading man, ready with a wisecrack to put others at ease and deflect any praise for his bravery. That moment immediately ended the snickering about his having been a Hollywood soldier during World War II who saw action only before a camera making morale-building films for the troops. Reagan, in a sense, had taken a bullet for the country.

There was a genuinely monarchical aspect to Reagan's presidency that returned to a magisterial role once inhabited by George Washington, Theodore Roosevelt, and Franklin Roosevelt. John Kennedy reached for it as well, although he died too young for it to flower. The monarchical side of the presidency was lost almost entirely in the conflagration of the 1960s and 1970s, when we became accustomed to seeing presidents brought low in public, watched Lyndon Johnson slowly self-immolate under his burdens, followed by Nixon's self-induced downfall and Carter's jangly, fitful anxiety and professions of helplessness, cries for a massive joint therapy session with himself as the chief analysand. Reagan's tenure restored a sense of noblesse oblige to the office: He loved time off, putting in eight-hour days and going to bed early, and somehow these habits were reassuring. They showed that the modern presidency needn't overwhelm a man, that he could remain a real person. Reagan's natural grace and stagecraft greatly enhanced this role: Striding across the White House lawn toward the helicopter in riding boots, pointing genially to his ears to signal that he couldn't hear the reporters' questions because of the noise of the propellers, giving a crooked grin in response to the crisp marine guard salute—all of this had an aristocratic air of breezy, sporting affability that was not Reagan's birthright, but which he grew into naturally and brought off with remarkable believability.

Reagan's favorite vacation pastime, cutting away the brush at his ranch, linked him to his white-hat cowboy movie roles, while at the same time imparting the air of the country gentleman who likes nothing more than to put on his wellies and get out in the fresh air with his dogs and horses. There is an interesting cultural theme here: Americans have never quite understood how middlebrow the English landed gentry is. The English aristocracy has always loved country life and always rather distrusted people who make too much of a show of their intelligence. They are impressed not by brilliance and deep learning, but by bluff simplicity and the ability to get along without getting too intense or familiar. It was no coincidence that Queen Elizabeth, the best pedigreed and most convincing example of royalty left in the world, got on famously with Reagan. His countrified qualities—the ranch was a genuinely American equivalent of the great estates of Europe—together with his personal modesty and amiability, must have very much suited her own temperament. It confirmed the British sense that manners and affability are much more important than mere IQ—which, after all, anyone at all might possess.

When Reagan visited Britain in 1982, there was a widely reproduced photo that showed the president and Queen Elizabeth riding horses on the grounds of Windsor Castle. Like the queen herself, Reagan was easily mounted, erect, and completely confident in the saddle, chatting with the queen in a casual way that clearly delighted her. The symbolism was rich. The queen, a product of centuries of horsemanship and country living, was enchanted with the American president, a former B-movie star and son of an alcoholic grocer. Meanwhile, it was as if Vice President Bush, the closest thing in the

Reagan administration to a genuine American aristocrat, had faded away like Casper the Ghost.

An early incident in Reagan's presidency's summed up many of its qualities. When American fighter jets got into a dogfight with Libyan jets and downed them, the president's aides decided not to wake the president but let him sleep until 4:24 a.m. On hearing of the skirmish, Reagan approved and then immediately went back to sleep. An explosion of criticism resulted about Reagan's lack of qualifications for the job, that he was asleep at the switch. These criticisms completely missed the mark. The fact that Reagan could be allowed to sleep through this event showed both that it was not terribly important in the order of things and that the people around him were sufficiently competent that he did not have to personally manage every mini-crisis. In the eyes of many, the incident contrasted favorably with Carter's constant stress on "competence," which amounted to round-the-clock micromanaging, anxiety, and a meddlesome immersion in details, culminating in the fiasco of the abortive hostage rescue mission. The Libyan dogfight incident supported the impression that the presidency had not grown too big for human control, that a normal, relaxed, and well-adjusted man could handle the presidency, that the government was much of the time able to run itself. Reagan had always been a brilliant delegator, the very opposite of Carter. He did not mind letting go of the reins, taking care of the big picture while the experts handled the implementation. It was a tendency that didn't always serve him well—as he discovered later, during the Iran-Contra scandal, where the president's distraction left a vacuum that allowed junior and unbalanced figures to engage in some disturbing and illegal adventurism. On that occasion, the president really was asleep at the switch, and showed his sometimes excessive deference to letting "the fellas" take care of the details.

Reagan's Foreign Policy

In Lord Charnwood's great biography of Abraham Lincoln, he remarks that a statesman's likely reward for his labors is ingratitude and the bland assumption of lesser men that "anyone" could have done the same thing. Ronald Reagan, whose greatest achievements were in the realm of foreign policy, was frequently the victim of this syndrome. Despite the fact that his policies had a great deal to do with encouraging the rise of Mikhail Gorbachev and discouraging the last of the Soviet old guard, many journalists of the era insisted blandly that Reagan deserved no credit for the collapse of the Soviet Union—that it was "inevitable," a completely internal process that would have happened no matter what, and that, if anything, Reagan slowed its unfolding through needless saber rattling.

Later, after Reagan left office, the American contribution to the end of the Soviet empire was claimed as an entirely bipartisan achievement, which to a great extent it was—the Reagan administration could not have encouraged its breakup through Gorbachev's reforms without the support of centrist Democrats like Daniel Patrick Moynihan, Henry "Scoop" Jackson, Sam Nunn, and Al Gore. By the same token, however, the celebration of the "end of the evil empire"—alluding to Reagan's famous denunciation of the Soviet Union before Gorbachev assumed power—encouraged the impression that *everyone* had easily and contentedly accepted the president's moral judgment on the Soviet adversary in the first place. In truth, the comment had unleashed a firestorm of invective from figures on the left like Ted Kennedy and George McGovern, who regarded Reagan as a warmonger leading us straight to nuclear Armageddon. That Reagan's apt formulation should at length have become a part of the American political consensus—when at first it had provoked such hysteria—is the soundest tribute to Reagan's achievements in foreign policy. The genuinely bipartisan mourning that accompanied Reagan's funeral was a tribute to both his success and the convenient amnesia about the historical record that is the price inevitably paid for becoming a national icon. As his great comrade and close friend Margaret Thatcher put it in her eulogy:

> He will be missed not only by those who knew him and not
> only by the nation that he served so proudly and loved so deeply,
> but also by millions of men and women who live in freedom

today because of the policies he pursued. Ronald Reagan has a higher claim than any other leader to have won the Cold War for liberty and he did it without a shot being fired.

Although Reagan's rhetoric about the Soviet Union sounded very tough after detente and its sputtering out under Ford—with talk of the "convergence" of the two systems in the notorious memo of Helmut Sonnenfeldt, a top Kissinger aide—his anti-Soviet agenda was not precise and, as usual, he actually governed as a centrist. Despite an initial and fumbling attempt to have a genuine movement conservative, Richard Allen, as national security advisor (with his retrograde use of the term "Bolshevik" to label his critics), Reagan relied heavily on the old Nixon-Kissinger brain trust, including Alexander Haig and George Shultz, while his vice president, George H. W. Bush, had headed the CIA under Ford. In some ways, though not all, Reagan continued Nixon's policies, which is to say the centrist foreign policy that had once resided with the Democrats of containing further Soviet expansion while pursuing arms negotiations and other attempts at improving bilateral relations. Recalling the Eisenhower years, and in marked contrast with President Reagan's occasionally very tough anti-Soviet rhetoric, the Reagan administration showed an aversion to the use of large-scale military force. Its main military action was to reverse a radical Marxist coup on the tiny island of Grenada. American military aid to the Nicaraguan Contras was largely spearheaded by civilians like the neoconservative policy intellectual Elliott Abrams, part of a younger generation whose careers had originated with the attempt of Democrats like Daniel Patrick Moynihan and Scoop Jackson to return to the centrist foreign policy their party had largely abandoned.

Although Reagan's arms buildup was often portrayed by the peace movement and the press as unilateral and provocative, many congressional Democrats considered it necessary, and the buildup projected by Carter's defense secretary, Harold Brown, and by Gary Hart during his bid for the nomination did not fall far short of the increases Reagan actually implemented. Reagan's first major success was in thwarting the Soviet Union's "peace offensive" to prevent NATO from carrying out the ordinary and necessary upgrading of its medium-range missiles in West Germany. Blown up to ludicrous and apocalyptic proportions by the peace movement in both Europe and the United States, the upgrade—requested by West Germany in the first place— vanished as an issue once the weapons were in place. To have caved in to Soviet objections would have amounted to giving the Soviets a veto over internal NATO military policy. Reagan and his advisors recognized this as setting an intolerable precedent.

Whatever the student protestors might have thought, the Soviet "peace offensive" was a calculated last gasp by the Stalinist old guard, headed by Andrei Gromyko. They knew from long experience—going back to the days of Joseph Stalin—how much foreign policy headway could be achieved by bluster and playing upon naïve Western longings for peace. By standing up against this hypocrisy and supporting the NATO alliance's military needs, Reagan helped convince the old guard that their day was done. In doing so, he helped Mikhail Gorbachev move people of his own generation up and sweep the Brezhnev veterans off the stage. This spelled the death knell of the regime. Increasingly bogged down in their own Vietnam in Afghanistan—itself a disastrous move by Brezhnev to breathe some ideological vigor back into the decaying Soviet regime at home—the Soviets failed in their desperate bid to change the subject and reassert some Soviet muscle in Europe. By checking it vigorously, Reagan helped send the U.S.S.R. in a new direction.

The Uncertain Successor: George H. W. Bush

Ronald Reagan cannot be ranked on the same level as Franklin Roosevelt. The challenges he faced were not as many or as difficult as those of FDR's time, and he did not display the same brilliance, ingenuity— or, indeed, ruthlessness—in dealing with them. Yet there are resemblances: The sweep of Reagan's coalition had a breadth comparable to FDR's, bringing together a comparable number of diverse constituencies—business conservatives, movement conservatives, neoconservatives, evangelical Christians. While adored by the white working

class, Reagan cheerfully promoted the global free trade policies that
doomed their unionized jobs in primary industry and enriched the
class of arbitrager. His sunny personality, mildness, decency, and mastery of the politics of gesture and the symbols of intergenerational
reconciliation—plus the nation's eagerness to recover from the tur-
bulence of the LBJ-Nixon-Carter whirlwind beneath the umbrella
of his regal amiability—welded these disparate, often hostile forces
together.

And there was another likeness: Like Roosevelt's, Reagan's coalition fragmented after he passed from the scene. His successor, George
H. W. Bush, was a return to a more managerial, middle-of-the-road
approach in the vein of Eisenhower and the caretaker Ford, whose
fate he involuntarily shared of filling a gap between more vivid and
compelling leaders. Bush continued Reagan's lazy attitude toward the
deficit, and was savaged for this by loyal Reaganites, who felt free to
challenge him on the point in a way they would never have dared
with the Old Man himself. On the foreign policy front, he distrusted
the neoconservatives. With his Kissinger-era veteran James Baker as
secretary of state, he returned to a balance-of-powers approach that
sometimes savored of moral neutrality—as in Baker's initial inclina-
tion to favor the "territorial integrity" of the surviving communist-
era Yugoslavian regime despite its oppression of ethnic and religious
minorities. "Stability" was the watchword.

On the other hand, Bush also undertook America's first major military operation since Vietnam—a full-scale land invasion of Iraq that
made the Reagan administration's operation in Grenada seem like a
Sunday-school picnic. He used the formidable instrument left to him
by Reagan, the world's strongest military force, on a scale from which
Reagan himself had always shrank. Yet, unlike the second invasion
of Iraq his son would conduct, Bush's Gulf War was a strenuously
nonideological exercise in maintaining the international status quo.
Bush justified it solely on the grounds that existing sovereign states
must not be invaded. Other Arab nations embraced Operation Desert
Storm in a way they could not embrace the son's toppling of Saddam
Hussein precisely because the invasion was morally indifferent to the

kinds of rule within state borders. Having liberated Kuwait and restored the status quo, Bush and his advisors deliberately chose not to
topple the Saddam Hussein regime, since his Arab neighbors much
preferred having Saddam Hussein's wings clipped to seeing America
establishing through force of arms that tyrannies deserve toppling—
their own records not bearing scrutiny in this regard. This supremely
Kissingerian exercise in realpolitik bitterly alienated the neoconservatives, who avenged themselves through the son's completion of the
job in 2003.

The senior President Bush marked a return to the northeastern
country-club conservatism of the Nelson Rockefeller wing of the
party. He was a throwback to the man in the gray flannel suit, his
slicked-back hair fins and reedy voice recalling the cartoon character
Dagwood, or the old-fashioned Wall Street gentleman banker who
had a couple of martinis before dinner and golfed on the weekend. As
blue-blooded Yankees with old money, the Bushes eschewed—and
presumably disdained—the vulgar consumerism of Reagan's *nouveau
riche* buddies. Their summer retreat at Kennebunkport was suitably
old-fashioned and screened from public view, all wooden shutters,
rowboats, and horseshoe pit. When Kevin Phillips describes Bush on
vacation, the president sounds uncannily like Dana Carvey's famous
imitation of him:

> George H. W. Bush had his own distinctive preppy streak.
> In addition to his famous narration while playing horseshoes—a
> triumphant "Mr. Smooth does it again" with each ringer—his
> recurrent bursts of enthusiastic schoolboy phraseology even as
> president were sometimes described as "Bush-speak."

A mild and genial man in person, known for his many long and
loyal friendships—which he tended in Victorian fashion, penning
a stream of letters over the decades—the senior Bush nevertheless
exuded a faint whiff of cynicism about politics, a patrician hint that
he was slumming a bit to be president. The biographer John Robert
Greene described him as "the least introspective of men, never com-

fortable with articulating any abstract idea, much less with talking to the nation about what he stood for." His famous inarticulateness—the fodder of late-night comedians, parodied by Tom Clancy in *A Clear and Present Danger*—cut a striking contrast with his predecessor's flowing wordcraft; to some, it seemed to stem not so much from shyness as from an aristocratic disdain for explaining oneself, for stooping to offer arguments to one's servitors. As the Reagan speechwriter Marlin Fitzwater observed, the difference between Reagan and Bush was that when they looked to the future, "one looks through the gauzy lens of his dreams, the other through the viewfinder of a telescope." When asked by a reporter about his larger aims for the country, Bush rather snidely replied: "Oh, the vision thing?" Like his son who succeeded him in the White House, he tended to wave off the details—weren't there people who took care of those things? A *Newsweek* photo of his cabinet on the eve of the 1992 election could later be seen clearly to spell his doom: a collection of elderly men in expensive but discreetly unstylish suits, red ties, silver-haired, monolithically Anglo-Saxon, and with the same air of slightly lazy, slightly smug complacency, smiling ironically at the need to be on display, unable to imagine the electorate would be so mad as to part with their sober guidance.

George Bush was not so much disliked as abandoned by the Reagan loyalists. In their minds he had never been one of them, and they didn't care enough about reelecting him to stave off the very real threat that a Democrat would take back the White House for the first time in twelve years. Nothing was more unconvincing than to hear the elder Bush, a man who was the living embodiment of Episcopalianism—what one wag termed the Church of the Correct Fork—claiming that he had been "born again" and had accepted Christ as his "personal savior." The evangelicals didn't buy it, and many of them sat out the election (his share of their vote fell by 20 percent between 1988 and 1992). The neoconservatives, social issue conservatives, and evangelicals preferred to nurture their views in radical purity, in their think tanks, political action committees, and journals, rather than have them diluted or ignored by a lukewarm interloper from the world of Rockefeller liberal Republicanism with its barely disguised contempt for the great booboisie of the Bible Belt. They could come back through Congress, and lie in wait for the White House down the road.

Return from the Wilderness: Bill Clinton

Bush's failure to galvanize the Reagan core constituency paved the way for Bill Clinton, who literally restored the Democrats at the presidential level as a great national party, bringing them in from the wilderness and reeducating them in how to use the instruments of state power without a guilty conscience. The first Democratic president to serve two full terms since Franklin Roosevelt, elected by solid majorities, Clinton was a historic success, a counter-Reagan. Like Reagan and FDR, he could have gone on running for president for multiple terms had he wished and had the law permitted it. He was also a bewitchingly clever, joyous, golden-tongued, and charismatic man, both scalawag and deadly serious policy wonk, a psychological Rubik's Cube right up there with Reagan, FDR, and Churchill, if not on their level in all regards. Like Reagan—and diametrically opposed to Nixon—he genuinely liked people and basked in their love of him. Like all the greats, his personality somehow meshed with the elements of his sprawling constituency and became the glue that held them together. As the biographer John Brummet put it, Clinton was "the best politician of his era and a man of dizzying brainpower and awesome policy command. There was his disarming charm; he was almost impossible to dislike in a personal meeting."

The key to Clinton's success was a bold readjustment of American politics, in a way that drew on elements of both old stalwart Democratic client groups and newer elements that might otherwise have leaned toward the Republicans. Like his opposite number in the United Kingdom, Tony Blair, he did not reverse the global free trade policies of his conservative predecessors, but embraced them with a vengeance and campaigned for them with tent revival fervor. For the first time in recent memory, a great Democratic politician was singing the Milton Friedman song of a rising tide raising all boats. No more sackcloth and ashes about being the world's leading economy. Clinton was entirely at ease in the company of newly made software billion-aires and Wall Street traders, but he could also legitimately remind people that it was his own party, the party of FDR, that had once res-cued capitalism and made it work for ordinary people. Clinton shared the missionary zeal for democratic capitalism that the Democrats had handed over to the Republicans starting in 1968, and which Reagan had raised to a pitch of rhetorical perfection. Indeed, Clinton was Reagan's match in reaching the broad public as a speaker; he was Democrats' own long-awaited "great communicator." As *Newsday* ob-served after his first year in office, "Clinton is a president very adept at selling. He believes, with good reason, that he can convince most people of almost anything."

Clinton buoyantly urged everyone to get their piece of the incred-ible economic boom with which his presidency coincided. Wall Street loved him at least as much as it had Reagan, and more than Bush, who was seen as more Main Street than Wall Street, more about business than trading. Roger Altman, Clinton's deputy treasury secretary, em-bodied this connection, having come to the administration from the world of high-stakes investment banking in New York. If J. R. Ewing had prophesied the coming of Reagan, Clinton could have been best buddies with Michael Douglas's barracuda trader in *Wall Street*—rich, savvy, sophisticated, stylish, testosterone-driven. Without a trace of hesitation, he followed Reagan in abandoning workers in the old in-dustrial and textile sectors, cheerfully consigning their jobs to obliv-ion on the promise that they or their children would end up with better jobs in hipper white-collar conditions, trading the assembly line for the keyboard. As for deficit reduction, after years of Repub-lican rhetorical tub-thumping about "big government" accompanied by steadily burgeoning entitlement programs, Clinton actually did it—including making cuts to the welfare state that would have caused a firestorm of outrage had they been undertaken by a Republican.

Even so, the outrage was pretty vociferous. But Clinton had nerves of steel in this regard. Where else in the political landscape could the visible minorities and the disadvantaged turn? They knew they would still be better off under him than under a Republican, and he knew they knew it. Moreover, as a liberal on all hot-button social issues that did not require new entitlement programs, he balanced his abandonment of the old Democratic fixation on a managed economy with a rhetorically unimpeachable record in supporting extended rights for women, gays, and minorities. However unhappy they might be with his cutting back of social welfare programs, and with his cautious go-slow approach on their issues apart from symbolic gestures, he knew that they had nowhere else to go.

In a brilliant piece of political theater during his first presidential campaign, his famous public putdown of the African-American hip-hop activist Sister Souljah, Clinton did what no Republican would have dared to do and none of his Democratic successors has since attempted: Clinton signaled that he and the party establishment would no longer be intimidated by professional black radicals. It was another nail in the coffin of the Carter-era mantle of perpetual guilt over American racism and imperialism: Clinton was saying yes to progress, but no to self-laceration. America has its share of shortcomings to overcome, he was saying—but if you are antiwhite or believe that America is irredeemably evil, you should vote for someone else. In one fell swoop, Clinton rescued the Democratic Party from years of self-imposed marginalization, brought it roaring back to the political center—and, in order to do this, took the heat for all the broken promises and perceived betrayals.

As is so often the case with exceptionally successful leaders, their striving is in part aimed at healing an emotional wound from childhood—with Clinton, as with Reagan, an alcoholic father. Like many children of alcoholics, Clinton had early assumed an adult role in his family, turning his obligatory responsibility to manage his family into an ambition to govern for good purposes in the larger world, thereby redeeming the family's fallen reputation. As the biographer David Maranis writes:

> In the literature on children of alcoholics, there is a type sometimes referred to as the Family Hero, who plays one of two well-defined roles, either as caretaker and protector of the

family or as its redeemer to the outside world. [Clinton] was the prototype of the Family Hero in both definitions.

Abandoned by his alcoholic father, Clinton seems to have felt an early loneliness that made him reach out almost obsessively to others—both for friendship and, with women, for sexual contact. The Arkansas journalist Meredith Oakley observed: "Clinton is almost compulsive about seeking people out; many of those midnight calls for which he is famous have no bearing on politics or business of any kind. Sometimes he has no more on his mind than contact with another human being." His neediness led others to find him lovable, and this powerful erotic bond with a legion of supporters on his rise from the governorship of Arkansas to the White House provided a cadre of passionate loyalists to staff his campaigns. Not for the first time, a need for love in private life fueled an ambition to serve the common good and created a bond between leader and supporters that was akin to a private love affair. Of course, neither Clinton nor the voters were always well served by this blurring of the lines between public duty and personal erotic craving.

MANY AMERICAN PRESIDENTS end up devoting a large proportion of their time to international relations whether they intend to or not. The very power and position of the United States makes this inevitable: whatever events transpire overseas, America will inevitably be involved in some fashion—praised or blamed, called upon for help, told to butt out, or condemned for standing aside. This is true in spite of a long-standing aversion to what George Washington in his farewell address called "foreign attachments," based on the conviction that America was not an oppressor like Old World powers, and that intruding in the affairs of other peoples would somehow infect American life with corruption and Caesarean ambition. From the Founding Fathers forward, American leaders have often shown a profound ambivalence about seeking honor and power on the world stage, especially through military might. It seems to violate the spirit of democracy and equality.

Some presidents have had international crises thrust upon them; others anticipated them and relished the prospect. Still others have discovered that, whereas domestic politics could remain stubbornly resistant to even minor change, the president's almost limitless power of command over the military, and wide latitude for waging war and making peace, were irresistible, a way of achieving something important and final in a way that seldom happened when Congress had to be satisfied. FDR came to power focusing on the crisis in internal American affairs caused by the Great Depression. But he was also looking ahead to the dangers posed by imperial Japan and Nazi Germany, and worked long and hard to build the consensus needed to go to war. JFK famously announced in his inaugural address that the United States would bear any burden and pay any price to defend and extend liberty around the world. Lyndon Johnson, by contrast, loathed war making; his real interest in the presidency was in using it to achieve civil rights and better the lives of real Americans, in the tradition of his idol Roosevelt. Vietnam consumed him entirely against his will. Nixon relished the chess game of foreign policy above all else; he came to office chiefly concerned with ending the war and negotiating detente with Russia, at the same time checking their ambitions and keeping them uneasy by opening up to their enemy, China. Domestic politics bored Nixon; he left it mainly to others, and did not rock the boat by eroding the civil rights and affirmative action initiatives inherited from the Democrats. Jimmy Carter's election was in part a reaction to the feeling of being drenched in foreign entanglements and cynical realpolitik from the Nixon-Kissinger era. But Carter, too, came to be enthralled by the wide leeway a president has in foreign affairs, and he brokered the first peace accord between Israel and an Arab state.

Clinton blended all of the above. He, too, campaigned chiefly on the issue of improving the lot of Americans at home; his campaign manager, James Carville, famously rallied his staff with the cry, "It's the economy, stupid!" Yet during his formative years as governor of Arkansas and a major participant in the center-right Democratic Leadership Council, in thinking out his future presidential strategy, Clinton was interested in restoring the Democratic Party as one that was not inherently pacifistic and would wield military force abroad if necessary, both to protect the United States and to promote democracy, as had his predecessors FDR, Truman, and JFK. Although he had avoided the draft during Vietnam, he apparently had no objection in principle to the use of military force. His shrewd and tough-minded secretary of state, Madeleine Albright, presumably spoke for him during her famous sparring match with the ever-cautious Colin Powell when he headed the Pentagon: "What's the use of having this superb military you're always talking about if we can't *use* it?" Ridding the Democratic Party of the reputation for one-worldism and appeasement with which Republicans had been able to brand it since the days of McGovern and Carter was key to moving it back to the center, just as it was essential at home to make it clear that Democrats were not against prosperity and moneymaking. From the outset, Clinton listened to hawkish Democrats like Joshua Muravchik on foreign policy matters, just as he listened to centrists on domestic affairs like William Galston and Amitai Etzioni. If *Commentary* was the journal that embodied Reagan, the *New Republic* embodied Clinton and shared his vision for the party. The choice of Al Gore—closely associated with Sam Nunn and virtually a neoconservative in the Senate—as his running mate, of Albright as secretary of state, and of Republican William Cohen for Defense were immediate indications of this shift.

The results were largely impressive and in some ways put the Republicans to shame, when measured against their own principles, in the sphere of international relations for the first time in living memory. While Bush had been perceived as willing to invade Iraq in order to protect oil-rich reactionary Arab states—but unwilling to topple Saddam Hussein and thereby consigning hundreds of thousands to death and oppression under his grim rule after encouraging them to rise up—he took no action when presented with a clear-cut opportunity to use military force to prevent genocide in the Balkans.

More fearful of "instability" than of the oppression of Muslims in Kosovo, Secretary of State Baker and his British counterpart, Lord Hurd, accomplished little, while Sarajevo was soon in ruins and starving wraiths behind barbed wire appeared in central Europe for the first time since the Holocaust.

Though the provisional peace brokered by Clinton and the new British prime minister Tony Blair in Kosovo was not flawless, it brought an immediate, drastic reduction in the carnage. The ensuing air campaign over Kosovo sent a clear signal that the West, led by the U.S. militarily, would not allow death camps to reappear in Europe. This was not why we had fought the cold war to a successful conclusion.

Among Republican opinion outlets, Bill Kristol and the *Weekly Standard* were among the few who had the moral courage to admit that this was the right policy, whatever its limitations, and that Republicans would have applauded had it been one of them. Others argued that Clinton's plan was so ineffective that it would have been better to do nothing at all—a position that was tantamount to condemning the Kosovars to continuous repression. More strangely still, some congressional Republicans, including the Oklahoma senator Don Nickles, revived the almost vanished isolationist strain represented by Jesse Helms and Bob Dole's faux pas about "Democrat wars," dusting off the New Left slogan to proclaim that America should not try to become "the world's policeman."

Clinton also performed with great skill in attempting to broker a land-for-peace deal between PLO chief Yasser Arafat and Israeli prime minister Ehud Barak. The accord failed only because, at the last minute, Arafat refused to accept the resulting agreement—which would have granted 90 percent of his demands—because it would mean giving up the dream of destroying Israel entirely. This was in no way Clinton's fault, and may well have saved Israel from a disastrous gamble originating with Barak. Finally, Clinton's renewal and extension of the Bush administration's no-fly zones in Iraq helped create a de facto autonomous Kurdish statelet, bringing that people the first respite from Saddam Hussein in years, and at least curtailing his power to menace the Shiites. These efforts paved the way for George W. Bush's subsequent invasion of Iraq and rapid overthrow of the regime, which had been weakened by the Clinton administration's measures more than was realized at the time. Clinton, moreover, argued tirelessly about the threat Saddam Hussein posed, citing his continuing attempt to develop weapons of mass destruction, his menacing of Iraq's neighbors in the region, his genocide against his own people, and his involvement in a plan to assassinate the senior President Bush. On these grounds, Clinton encouraged Congress to pass a declaration that it was American state policy to bring about Saddam Hussein's "removal"—which certainly provided his successor with some legislative precedent for the invasion.

One cannot judge Clinton for these efforts by the same lights as we would have after the attacks of September 11, 2001. He was not confronted by the same threat to American soil as his successor, and so of course he did not undertake actions as major or decisive as the deployments in Afghanistan or Iraq. "Lobbing cruise missiles into the desert" to try to pick off Osama bin Laden may have looked ineffectual with twenty-twenty hindsight after 9/11. At the time, however, Clinton was way ahead of the game in understanding the threat he posed. No Republican president would likely have done more without the paradigm shift of 9/11. After all, even President Reagan had taken no action against those responsible for bombing the marine barracks in Beirut in 1982. By any fair standard, Clinton was at least a moderate success as a foreign policy president.

This is not to suggest that Clinton did it all on his own, or that he never made tactical compromises. The presence of Republican majorities in both houses of Congress after 1994 was a powerful extra nudge to fiscal balance and to downsizing entitlement programs. The health-care plan championed by his wife was unworkable, portending a vast new government bureaucracy. And of course there were other problems: His conduct in the Lewinsky scandal dishonored him as a president, a husband, and a father. A onetime fervent loyalist, George Stephanopoulos, witheringly summed up his disillusionment:

How could a president so intelligent, so compassionate, so public-spirited, and so conscious of his place in history act in such a stupid, selfish and self-destructive manner? . . . I came to see how Clinton's shamelessness is a key to his political success, how his capacity for denial is tied to the optimism that is his greatest political strength. He exploits the weaknesses of himself and those around him masterfully, but he taps his and their talents as well.

Clinton's dalliance with Lewinsky was not the only ethical lapse of his presidency: His last-minute pardon of the shady businessman Mark Rich stank of a payoff for murky services. Still and all, Clinton did spearhead the drive to balance the budget and the first actual shrinking of entitlement programs, which had expanded exponentially since the days of LBJ's Great Society. When he made his farewell appearance at the Democratic Convention that nominated Al Gore (who imitated none of his successes), he was fairly able to claim that he had begun his two terms as president with the clear aim of moving the Democrats back to the center in both domestic and foreign policy. Who could seriously challenge him?

Fortunate Son? George W. Bush and the End of a Saga

The presidency of George W. Bush, which is coming to an end as this book goes to print, remains so close to us that less can be said about him with certainty than about his predecessors. We are still in the throes of the events sparked by 9/11 and a more judicious perspective will come only with time.

Before 9/11, like Carter and Clinton before him, George W. Bush came to office appearing eager to curtail America's international role and concentrate on domestic issues. His catchphrase "compassionate conservatism" suggested a feeling that the Republicans had become Scrooge-like in the voters' minds, too apt to blame the poor and suffering for their own afflictions. He appeared ready to entertain a view gaining ground among conservatives, notably Irving Kristol, that the U.S. military role in Europe had ended with the demise of the Soviet empire and its forces should therefore be withdrawn. Concern was expressed that he was a neo-isolationist. Yet foreign policy necessarily became his defining mission after the worst attack on American shores since Pearl Harbor. As James Carney wrote in *Time* during those awful early days:

> The President is growing before our eyes. . . . He's trying to become the leader that America needs right now, just as America is trying to become the nation it needs to be. . . . Bush had told a number of friends and advisors that he has never known such clarity of purpose, such certainty that he is the right person for the moment. He is buoyed by his faith that God has chosen him to lead the country during this perilous time.

Bush acted with remarkable speed to unseat the Taliban regime in Afghanistan—and to topple Saddam Hussein, a job left unfinished by his father and called for by Clinton. In both projects, the neoconservative cadre that had evolved through five Republican presidencies played a leading role, especially through Dick Cheney, Donald Rumsfeld, and Paul Wolfowitz. Bush himself, by all accounts, acted decisively and enthusiastically to carry out both actions. He continually galvanized the bureaucracy and the military planners with what often seemed like impossible demands for rapid deployment. In a way that compelled admiration among his closest aides—but which his critics would later say was supremely irresponsible—he spent little time delving into the details of military planning and occupation. Some have connected this neglect of detail to his strong religious faith. As the Bush speechwriter Michael Gerson observed: "He does have a strong belief in providence, and in the necessity of gathering information, making good choices, doing your best, and trusting the result to God." Bush appeared to see his main role as both coach and cheerleader, providing blunt, unambiguous directives that carried the powerful aura of the commander in chief, while trusting the experts to make it all come together. For the neoconservatives, Bush's assertiveness was initially exhilarating. At last, they had a chance to use American military power to overthrow a tyranny that threatened both America and its own neighbors and supported terrorism. Its overthrow would spark democratic reform throughout the Middle East. Yet the results were mixed at best; many have called them disastrous.

The second President Bush is difficult to read psychologically, and not only because we do not yet possess the perspective of time. He is unusually laconic and self-contained, and has left little evidence about his innermost feelings. In this regard, he provides the sharpest possible contrast with Clinton, who could not get enough of sharing his feelings with the people. In this, perhaps Bush has inherited the reserve of his Yankee forebears. As the journalist and pundit Jeffrey Toobin wrote of Bush early in his first term, "elite opinion mattered little to him; Bush was steeled by a sense of entitlement that protected him from criticism." But that sense of entitlement coming from his privileged background was very likely a source of strength in acting against the Taliban and Saddam Hussein so decisively. His patrician origins arguably made him not care if people, especially media pundits, didn't think he was an intellectual or a sophisticate. The French president François Mitterrand, like other European critics, never grasped, owing to their inadequate knowledge of the United States, that Bush's pedigree in American terms was usually far superior to their own in their respective countries—certainly superior to that of Mitterrand, whose father had been a vinegar maker. Bush didn't crave their approval.

Some things about him can be observed fairly close to the surface. While his father moved to Texas to expand the family fortune, no one quite bought into him as a Texan—the senior Bush was "all hat and no saddle," as the saying goes. The son, however, really does appear to have become a Texan. Although he has the usual Bush Ivy League pedigree, he enmeshed himself with Texas through marriage and children. His wife, the gracious, demure, and ever watchful Laura, always seeming to be on the verge of a caring and gentle reproof like the former schoolteacher she is, recalls Lady Bird Johnson in her warmth and fortitude, with none of the leathery Kate Hepburn salt-water and mackinaw briskness of the president's mother, a true New England matriarch. If Barbara Bush is about morning coffee on the dock as the leaves turn in Maine, Laura Bush is about doing her own grocery shopping and taking the kids to piano lessons. Bush's Lone Star accent sounds genuine, and his Latino connections (by marriage) suggest an attractive leavening of the purebred WASP bloodlines of his background. One believes he really does enjoy pork rinds and that dusty-looking ranch.

Bush also shares his father's inarticulateness. Although he delivered a few good speeches, he often seemed bizarrely and dismayingly tongue-tied about the enormity and high stakes of the war on terror. One could only wince at his joint press conferences with Tony Blair when, after Blair rolled on effortlessly about the meaning of the struggle in long, rounded sentences with clauses and subclauses dancing in the air, the president would blink and mumble something about "bringin' good democracy to those folks." Even the conservative columnist and supporter Mark Steyn described Bush's rhetorical style as "stagger[ing] like a groggy prize-fighter, stumbling through the same lines over and over ('Saddam Hussein is a dictator. He gassed his own people. He's a dangerous man. He gassed his own people. He's a dictator')." Bush's greatest moment, unscripted and spontaneous, came during his first visit to Ground Zero, three days after the cataclysm, when he escaped his security detail and jumped on top of the wreckage to embrace the firefighters and speak to the shattered New Yorkers gathered there. When someone shouted that they couldn't hear him, he turned it into a symbolic moment, shouting back through his megaphone like an old-fashioned stump politician of yore: "I can hear you. And whoever knocked these buildings down are going to hear from every one of us!" It was a moment of greatness, Bush at his best. The crowd's roar of approval was cathartic and therapeutic for both the bereaved and stunned New Yorkers and the president himself, reconnecting with his people. It struck exactly the right combination of consolation and defiance: *We are licking our wounds, but don't ever imagine that those who did this to us won't be hearing back from us soon.* That sentiment was polished in what were probably the best two lines of his address to a joint session of Congress in 2001: "Whether we bring our enemies to justice, or bring justice to our enemies, justice will be done. Our grief has turned to anger, and anger to resolution." Solemn, quietly menacing, it was suitably Roman in its firm clarity: This is what we are going to do. Prepare yourselves. Whereas the elder Bush had a somewhat whimsical air of cynicism about politics, the son was blunt and straightforward, speaking in short, unadorned declarative sentences, never vulgar, though often reverting to slang drawn from football games.

Above all, Bush's evangelical Christianity was obviously sincere, and it has wedded him to the Bible Belt in a way that was never possible for his father. Loyal adherents among evangelical Christians who knew him personally view his decisive moves against the Taliban and Saddam Hussein as rooted in his bedrock faith. He has repeatedly credited his experience as a born-again Christian to his transformation from a heavy-boozing, ex–frat boy who was once arrested for drunk driving into a solid family man. It rings true with his coreligionists. Several million of these people, lured to the ballot box by Bush's campaign strategist Karl Rove, probably secured Bush's 2004 reelection against John Kerry, and it is unlikely that foreign policy was as important to them as the faith Bush shared with them. Indeed, the most remarkable feature of Bush's presidency was that he conducted an entirely neoconservative foreign policy from the thin base of an evangelical constituency that, while it was certainly patriotic, was not otherwise preoccupied with world affairs or eager to see American forces sent abroad. It was Bush's support from heartland Americans that enabled the heavily pedigreed policy intellectuals of his administration (Wolfowitz had been both a distinguished academic and a former ambassador) to overthrow two hostile regimes.

Before the 2000 election, George and Laura Bush seemed to embody the zeitgeist in that mysterious way that promises success. They meshed with their era as had Clinton and Reagan before them. They seemed like ordinary, real middle-class people, Sunbelt rather than Northeast, barbecue rather than sushi, the kind of people who take the kids to school in the van then do the grocery shopping. The image was not precisely true, of course—Bush was Yale, Harvard, Skull and Bones. But it was fashioned out of elements that were genuine about Bush and his family. Bush came to the White House with an easygoing unpretentiousness that was not merely a dividend of his untroubled sense of caste, but in some ways repudiated those privileged origins in favor of the open manners of the heartland, cemented by his marriage. As the White House aide Vance McMahan put it, "it's often said that he's a man comfortable in his own skin—and I think that's exactly right. . . . He was somebody who has as little degree of pretension as anyone I've ever met. You'd think that someone exposed to the life experiences he has would be full of himself—but that was the furthest thing from the truth."

Who would presume to speculate about the personal side of all this? Was the son trying to be a more real and convincing version of what the father had achieved only in part? Was the determination to overthrow Saddam Hussein an implicit moral criticism of his father for leaving the Kurds and Shiites in the lurch after encouraging them to rise up? It will be a long time, if ever, before we know for certain. The Bushes do not like to talk about themselves or bare their souls. In this, whether in Texas or Florida, they remain New Englanders. What is clear is that the whole of our saga stretching back to JFK has played itself out. The neoconservatives will never return to the prominence they achieved under the second President Bush. Their worldview, conditioned by the cold war, the fear of appeasement, the passing of the torch from Britain to America, had its final and clearest testing ground in Iraq—a morally detestable and strategically dangerous foe, a clear agenda for exporting democracy to Iraq and beyond, and overwhelming military superiority to accomplish these aims.

Debate will continue for many years about the effectiveness of the Bush administration's war on terror. One fact is undeniable. Seven years after 9/11, America has not suffered another such attack, while cities in other countries have. In my view, the fact that Bush toppled two hostile regimes within two years of 9/11 cannot be unconnected to that fact. While Homeland Security doubtless foiled other intended attacks, a committed terrorist cell like al-Qaeda would have to be sobered by the observation that the cost of a single attack was the rapid crushing of the Taliban regime, their earthly outpost for the pure Islamic society to come, and Saddam Hussein, who shared their hatred of the West and succored terrorists nearby. State sponsors of terrorism, including Syria and Iran, will also have been given pause by the lightning rapidity with which the tyrant next door was crumpled. Cause and effect may be difficult to determine in the cauldron of international relations, but to my mind, Bush's vigorous military action contributed to the ensuing respite from another 9/11 with about as much certainty as we can ever possess. On the other hand, having liberated Iraq from its brutal dictator, America's confused occupation strategy in the aftermath did not prevent murderous civil strife and may have intensified it through blunders of omission or commission. Still and all, while the president's record is mixed, it contained a dimension of real greatness. Scorned by many opinion elites today, he will be missed in years to come as his achievements sink in.

The neoconservatives to whom Bush gave the implementation of his foreign policy succeeded in many ways, but not in others, and perhaps not enough in any of them. Elderly or discredited, they are leaving the scene, and we will not see their like again. Bush was not one of them—he was not an intellectual. But he did genuinely share with Paul Wolfowitz the Jeffersonian belief that the love of individual liberty is natural to all mankind, a gift that America must not selfishly keep for herself but must share with the world, because this freedom is not America's gift to the world but God's gift to America and mankind.

Will the new generation of leaders waiting in the wings to walk onto the stage of history pick up the torch, or leave it in the dust to sputter out? We will know soon enough.

The Presidential Algorithm

In the introduction to this book, I used the fictional TV president Josiah Bartlett as an example of an ideal leader combining character traits and experiences that would be difficult, if not impossible, to find combined in a single leader in real life. But the emphasis in the phrase "if not impossible" should be on the "if." The reason people remain inspired by politics—by the hope that they might do some real good—is that men and women still believe it possible to find someone who combines many or all of these desirable traits, and who therefore deserves our passionate and reasoned support. It's always a risky prospect, because precisely those strong qualities of mind and will that are the hallmarks of a good leader can also fuel the ambition of an unscrupulous leader for sheer power, and it can be difficult ahead of time to know which is which. Just as unpromising leaders can grow into their office, those who start out promisingly can be led astray by their own hidden demons.

What, then, might we say of the presidents we have considered in Part One? Do they add up to an ideal type if one sifts through their best qualities? When thinking about their careers, it's hard not to put together such a prototype—the algorithm, so to speak, of the ideal leader. He or she would have the charm and historical sensitivity of JFK; the earthy and strong-willed longing to help the disadvantaged of LBJ; the keen intellect and chess master's skill of a Nixon in foreign affairs; the well-intentioned Baptist decency of Jimmy Carter; George H. W. Bush's sterling personal character and ingrained sense of service; Ronald Reagan's sunny optimism about America's future and his comfort in his own skin; Bill Clinton's ebullience and love of connecting with the people while encouraging them to rise in life; and the simple strength of purpose and bedrock religious faith of George W. Bush.

But it is just as easy to compile a list of negative qualities that would codify the algorithm of a bad leader—and, unfortunately, such a list can be drawn from the very same men. That would give us the irresolution of JFK and his tendency to equate gesture with real policy; the paranoid vulgarity of Johnson and his inability to think past the failed strategy in Vietnam; Nixon's creepy solitude and crass view of politics; Carter's habitual moralizing and tendency to see his own country's role in the world as villainous; Reagan's laziness and distaste for tough decisions about the deficit; the jadedness of the senior Bush and his inability to see the big picture or inspire the country; Clinton's sexual adventurism and tendency to rhetorical overkill; and the junior Bush's crippling inarticulateness in defending his war aims and his tendency to leave too much of the hard planning to subordinates.

Is there any leader in American history who comes close to embodying the good traits sketched above, while partaking least of the bad ones—or at least sublimating his negative energies to fuel a higher mission on behalf of justice? There is, I think, one man who at least comes close, and who therefore remains a bellwether for honorable, brave, and thoughtful presidents. He was very great, but also very complicated and even dark in a way that rivals or surpasses any of the men whose personalities we have sketched above. To him we now turn.

PART II

Democracy and Empire

Lessons in Leadership, from Napoleon to Lincoln

No first-time visitor to Washington, D.C., can fail to be profoundly moved by the Lincoln Memorial, which immortalizes Abraham Lincoln's legacy in a temple of shimmering white marble. Larger than life, the figure of Lincoln himself is seated like a stern judge in a Roman magistrate's curial chair, a moral giant delivered to posterity as the ultimate consul of the New Rome. Yet this Lincoln is dressed in the stolid, slightly rumpled middle-class clothing of an ordinary American of the Victorian age, reminding us that the modern successor to the ancient republics is a democracy, under God, and that its power is wielded for the sake of equal rights and the good of all, not for aristocratic pride or imperial glory. The marble Lincoln is entirely human and recognizable, his face etched with distant concerns and sadness, the wide mouth creased with worry and compassion. He is with the ages, but also somehow still with us, pondering the elusiveness of justice, the frailty of mankind. He is our backwoods Cincinnatus, yet greater than the ancient heroes, for it was justice, more than honor, that moved him—justice for the slaves even at the risk of taking his country to the brink of annihilation to restore it, purified of this dreadful taint. Better a broken union than one based on the ultimate injustice and corruption, as poisonous to the master as it was wicked to the slave.

Lincoln could be loquacious, but he also had an unmatched genius for stating the truth briefly and irrefutably. Behind the somber beauty of the Gettysburg Address lies the more forthright purpose uttered shortly after issuing the Emancipation Proclamation in 1863: "If slavery is not wrong, nothing is wrong." This is why slavery was the poison root out of which all the branches of American life radiated, and why American life would be undermined and poisoned by it until that root was removed. If slavery isn't wrong, nothing is. If we are capable of enslaving another human being, then we are capable of any conceivable cruelty or injustice. If we are capable of enslaving another human being, no other act, however generous or loving, toward family, friends, and fellow citizens, can escape being poisoned by its rot. This Lincoln understood: Nothing in America would be sound, none of its good fortune deserved, until this wrong was righted.

The real Lincoln was, of course, a good deal more complicated, his character more shaded, than the marble monument. According to some who knew him, the famously stern and sad expression he assumes in all the photographs, his long curving mouth tugged down at either side by a nameless melancholy, was an accident of technology, reflecting the need to hold his expression immobile during the half minute or so that it took for the photographer to expose the plate. By most accounts, Lincoln smiled frequently and laughed loudly and often. Sometimes he was convulsed with laughter before he reached the punch lines of his own jokes. "None of his hearers enjoyed the wit—and wit was an unfailing ingredient—of his stories half as much as he did himself," recalled the battlefield correspondent and abolitionist Henry Villard. "It was a joy indeed to see the effect upon him." He loved hearing jokes and stories, and loved regaling others with them.

Yet the face in the photograph clearly reveals something real about the man when he was prevented from finding a momentary release from his burdens in humor. Lincoln's life was weighed down in many ways—by the superhuman responsibilities he bore during the Civil War, but also by his sorrow over the young lives lost on both sides of the conflict, which gnawed at him as if they had been his own sons.

Visiting the battlefields, he internalized the sorrow of the hundreds of thousands of bereaved parents and spouses, and that national grief etched deep furrows on his long face. "He is exceedingly thin, not so very tall," the French diplomat Marquis Adolphe de Chambrun wrote of Lincoln after a personal meeting at the White House. "His face denotes an immense force of resistance and extreme melancholy. It is plain that this man has suffered deeply."

The war exhausted him with its inexhaustible crises, the intransigence and vanity of pompous, shirking generals like McClellan who would not stain their bright gleaming columns with actual combat, allowing the outnumbered but more daring Confederates to carry the day. The men of his cabinet, like William Seward, though in time they came to admire and even venerate him, began by viewing him as an undereducated bumpkin who had chanced into a position that they, as men of background and breeding, were far better suited by nature and circumstance to inhabit than himself. (Seward once reproached the president for polishing his own boots.)

Then there was the long litany of bereavement in his personal life—the death of a newborn brother when Lincoln was three years old, of his mother, aunt, and uncle when he was nine, and of a newborn sister when he was eighteen. These deaths gave him an early and permanent sense of emptiness and abandonment—a sensitivity that was intensified by the death of an early love, Ann Rutledge, in 1835. Many believed that Lincoln never recovered from Rutledge's death, and indeed he seemed to fear that he would be abandoned by any woman he loved. His wife, Mary Todd, tormented him with her suspicions of his attachment to Rutledge, and dragged at him in bitterness at a time when he needed every ounce of energy and moral fiber to lead the nation. Of their four children, only two survived to adulthood; his son Willie died in 1862, while the war was raging. Although he wept convulsively in private, Lincoln never permitted himself to grieve openly for the boy before others when hundreds of thousands of young men were falling in battle—a relief he denied himself partly because of what he considered his own failure to find generals who would fight to win.

McClellan's evasion of combat, General Ambrose Burnside's timid half victories, and Meade's premature withdrawal (having defeated Lee at Gettysburg, he allowed his army to escape intact), all tormented Lincoln personally because he knew they were needlessly prolonging the conflict and would cost far more lives in the long run than a decisive blow delivered immediately. He fired six generals before finding the commander he needed, Ulysses S. Grant. Whether intensified by these events, or exacerbating their drain on him, Lincoln suffered all his life from what in those times was called "the hypo," for "hypochondria," and which today would likely be diagnosed as serious, possibly clinical depression. As his close friend Henry C. Whitney observed, "no element of his personality was so marked, so obvious and ingrained as his mysterious melancholy." Another close associate, his law partner and later biographer William Herndon, described him as "a sad man, a terribly gloomy one—a man of sorrow, if not of agony." As with Churchill during World War II, the burdens of leadership Lincoln assumed might ultimately have been the most effective therapy for his melancholy, for he simply could not allow himself to be sucked into the vortex of despair.

But the complexity of Lincoln's character, so instructive for our attempt to understand the soul of a leader, goes even further than this. Consider the words of an aspiring politician of twenty-eight, as he contemplated the meaning and place of political ambition and honor in American democratic life in an 1838 address to the Young Men's Lyceum of Springfield, Illinois—words far removed from the Periclean cadences of the Gettysburg Address or the ashen grandeur of the second inaugural. They begin simply enough:

> Many great and good men sufficiently qualified of any task they should undertake, may ever be found, whose ambition would aspire to nothing beyond a seat in congress or a presidential chair.

So far, this is the Lincoln we think we know. Surely his ambition was fully satisfied by achieving first a seat in Congress (he ran unsuccessfully for the Senate in 1858) and then the crowning honor, the presidency. But he continues:

> *But such belong not to the family of the lion, or the tribe of the eagle.* What! Think you these places would satisfy an Alexander, a Caesar, or a Napoleon? Never! Towering genius disdains a beaten path. It seeks regions hitherto unexplored.

Is this our sainted hero from the marble temple on the Mall, Honest Abe, the Great Emancipator? Or are these the words of a passionate extremist, recalling the hungry young men of nineteenth-century European novels—men like Julien Sorel in Stendhal's *The Red and the Black*, burning for distinction in a world where the departed glory of the fallen French emperor has left a vacuum for pride.

Lincoln's fervor intensifies as he contemplates towering genius:

> It sees *no distinction* in adding story to story, upon the monuments of fame, erected to the memory of others. It *denies* that it is glory enough to serve under any chief. It *scorns* to tread in the footsteps of *any* predecessor, however illustrious.

And, most shocking of all from the man who would one day free his enslaved fellow Americans:

> It thirsts and burns for distinction; and, if possible, it will have it, whether at the expense of emancipating slaves, or enslaving freemen.

Had Lincoln set his sights on becoming an American Alexander? A Caesar or Napoleon? A man so ambitious that he thought his craving could be as readily satisfied by enslaving other citizens as by freeing the slaves, as if the moral difference meant nothing to him? A man who is absolutely unsatisfied to merely continue the traditions of past American statesmanship, of the Founding Fathers? His eloquence in describing this "towering genius" makes it impossible not to suspect that Lincoln was to some extent describing how he saw himself—what he hoped, or perhaps feared, he might become. He is far too involved and convincing in the case he makes for us to consider his words merely cautionary. And yet this is the man who, in his crowning speeches as president, grafted his own work entirely onto the precedent of the Founding Fathers and represented it as bringing their promise to fruition in "a new birth of freedom." Far from disdaining a beaten path, he tended it reverently while furthering it, all the while denying that he was doing anything bold or novel—he was only doing what "our forefathers" would have wanted. This is why the word "I" never appears in the Gettysburg Address: All the honor, Lincoln insists, belongs to those who have fallen in battle for the Union.

How can the man of the Lyceum speech have become the man of the Gettysburg Address? Did he change? Did he compromise his own ambition? Or did he outgrow the desire for fame? Does a great leader *need* the added motivation of recognition and honor? Or do such desires drag him down and obstruct his nobler goals? If we can shed some light on these questions, we will have gone some way in understanding the magic of leadership and the soul of a leader. And to do that, we must look more closely at the young Lincoln's understanding of the role of honor in the America of his day.

The Tribe of the Eagle: Political Honor in a Democracy

The topic of Lincoln's speech at the Lyceum was "the perpetuation of our political institutions." It was within this respectable context that he introduced the rather jarring question of whether democracy can find room for "an Alexander, a Caesar, or a Napoleon." In turning to the problem of ambition and its outlets, Lincoln provides a sharp contrast with an earlier and very distinguished observer of American manners, Alexis de Tocqueville, whose great work *Democracy in America* became a mirror from abroad in which Americans have repeatedly sought themselves out, especially when it comes to the challenges of statesmanship. When Tocqueville visited the United States six years before Lincoln's Lyceum address, he worried that the egalitarianism of American life might not encourage the emergence of extraordinary leaders. Pondering why "there are so many men of ambition in the United States but so few lofty ambitions," the French visitor observes:

> Among democratic nations ambition is both eager and constant, but in general its aim is not lofty. Life is generally spent in eagerly coveting small prizes that are within reach. . . . The Americans are constantly driven to engage in commerce and industry. Their origin, their social condition, their political institutions, and even the land they inhabit, urge them irresistibly in this direction . . . in the midst of a new and boundless country whose exploitation for profit is their principal object. . . . They strain their faculties to the utmost to achieve paltry results, and this speedily and inevitably narrows their range of vision and circumscribes their powers.

Lincoln, however, has more in common in this regard with his contemporary Ralph Waldo Emerson, the distinguished Unitarian clergyman and transcendentalist. Emerson wrote that "it is natural to believe in great men. . . . Nature seems to exist for the excellent. The world is upheld by the veracity of good men: they make the earth wholesome." Emerson was also impressed (although not uncritically) by Napoleon, cited by Lincoln among "the tribe of the eagle"—Napoleon the great liberator and champion of the rights of man, as some believed, though many others considered him a criminal usurper and bloodthirsty conqueror. In whichever version, Napoleon loomed large over the nineteenth century, especially when it came to contemplating the permissible limits of political ambition.

In exploring his theme of "the family of the lion," Lincoln is also taking issue with some of the original Founding Fathers. Alexander Hamilton had argued that America's reliance on laws, institutions, and checks and balances might not include a role for great statesmen like the leaders of the ancient Greek and Roman republics, but would by the same token exclude the rise of demagogues disguising their ambitions under the cloak of public service and, in general, avoid the wild careening between tyranny and anarchy that characterized Athenian democracy. Because Athens was the *only* historical precedent for a full-scale democracy, the Founding Fathers took pains to distinguish the nascent American republic's respect for property, merit, and the rule of law from the "mobocracy" of the first egalitarian regime. Yet Lincoln returns to a much older rubric within the history of leadership, one broached by Plato, Aristotle, and Cicero and passed down to the European Renaissance through thinkers like Castiglione and Vergerius: how to strike the correct balance between honor seeking and the cultivation of the mind. These thinkers were concerned with how statesmen could sublimate longings for glory in the service of country, family, and piety, and elevate the cultivation of mind, soul, and moral strength above the not inconsiderable virtues of battlefield courage.

Lincoln began his Lyceum speech with a survey of America's success since the founding:

> We find ourselves in the peaceful possession of the fairest portion of the earth, as regards extent of territory, fertility of soil, and salubrity of climate. We find ourselves under the government of a system of political institutions, conducing more essentially to the ends of civil and religious liberty, than any of which the history of former times tells us.

These great achievements, however, have been accomplished *for* us, not accomplished *by* us:

> We, when mounting the stage of existence, found ourselves the legal inheritors of these fundamental blessings. We toiled not in the acquirement or establishment of them—they are a legacy bequeathed us, by a *once* hardy, brave, and patriotic, but *now* lamented and departed race of ancestors. Theirs was the task (and nobly they performed it) to possess themselves, and through themselves, us, of this goodly land; and to uprear upon its hills and its valleys, a political edifice of liberty and equal rights.

Lincoln's tone and language, as he speculates on whether his generation might make an equal contribution to the American legacy, is distinctly ambivalent. The honors to date, he contends, belong to the founding generation alone; we merely receive and pass along their achievement. A quarter century later, in his Gettysburg Address and second inaugural, Lincoln would claim a continuity with the founders, honoring the present generation for not only passing on, but *extending*, the founders' achievement—a "new birth of freedom," a second American Revolution. By that point, however, Lincoln's own desire for distinction through public service has been so thoroughly subsumed by the demands of his presidency that he was able to attribute all the honor to those who had given their lives.

How, then, might the current generation contribute? As Lincoln observed at the Lyceum, there was little risk of future danger from a foreign foe: America was effectively impregnable to a Napoleon.

> Shall we expect some transatlantic military giant, to step the Ocean, and crush us at a blow? Never! All the armies of Europe, Asia and Africa combined, with all the treasure of the earth (our own excepted) in their military chest; with a Buonaparte for a commander, could not by force, take a drink from the Ohio, or make a track on the Blue Ridge, in a trial of a thousand years.

Rather, the future danger facing America was inner rot:

> At what point then is the approach of danger to be expected? I answer, if it ever reach us, it must spring up amongst us. It cannot come from abroad. If destruction be our lot, we must ourselves be its author and finisher. As a nation of freemen, we must live through all time, or die by suicide.

The greatest danger Lincoln foresaw was a growing trend of lawlessness and mob rule—a by-product of the pioneer spirit, whose aggressive energy, once turned outward to tame the frontier, was now turning in on itself:

I hope I am over wary; but if I am not, there is, even now, something of ill-omen amongst us. I mean the increasing disregard for the law which pervades the country. . . . This disposition is awfully fearful in any community; and that it now exists in ours, though grating to our feelings to admit, it would be a violation of truth, and an insult to our intelligence, to deny.

Lincoln painted a picture of an America increasingly racked by violence:

Accounts of outrages committed by mobs, form the everyday news of the times. They have pervaded the country, from New England to Louisiana;—they are neither peculiar to the eternal snows of the former, nor the burning suns of the latter;—they are not the creature of climate—neither are they confined to the slaveholding, or the non-slaveholding States. Alike, they spring up among the pleasure hunting masters of Southern slaves, and the order loving citizens of the land of steady habits. Whatever, then, their cause may be, it is common to the whole country.

It's impossible to avoid measuring the Lincoln of these sentiments against the towering figure he would later become—and by that standard it's difficult not to find Lincoln's concerns here a tad overblown, as if he is trying to convince *himself* that the country was on the verge of a complete breakdown, that his nation faced a danger sufficiently grave that his generation could earn distinction by confronting it. He goes on to temporize:

I know the American People are *much* attached to their Government;—I know they would suffer *much* for its sake;—I know they would endure evils long and patiently, before they would ever think of exchanging it for another. Yet, notwithstanding all this, if the laws be continually despised and disregarded, if their rights to be secure in their persons and property, are held by no better tenure than the caprice of a mob, the alienation of their affections from the Government is the natural consequence; and to that, sooner or later, it must come. Here then, is one point at which danger may be expected.

How are we to combat this danger? The answer—perhaps less than uplifting—is redoubled loyalty to the law and vigilance on its behalf. Again, Lincoln's rhetoric, his call for a "political religion," feels slightly overblown, desperate in its quest for a great issue. It is also somewhat Jacobin in its zeal to impose such a civil religion on all:

> The question recurs "how shall we fortify against it?" The answer is simple. Let every American, every lover of liberty, every well wisher to his posterity, swear by the blood of the Revolution, never to violate in the least particular, the laws of the country; and never to tolerate their violation by others. As the patriots of seventy-six did to the support of the Constitution and Laws, let every American pledge his life, his property, and his sacred honor;—let every man remember that to violate the law, is to trample on the blood of his father, and to tear the charter of his own, and his children's liberty.

Lincoln seems to envision a project of universal indoctrination involving all regions, social levels, and institutions, rather like the civil religion famously called for by Jean-Jacques Rousseau in *The Social Contract*:

> Let reverence for the laws, be breathed by every American mother, to the lisping babe, that prattles on her lap—let it be taught in schools, in seminaries, and in colleges;—let it be written in Primers, spelling books, and in Almanacs;—let it be preached from the pulpit, proclaimed in legislative halls, and enforced in courts of justice. And, in short, let it become the *political religion* of the nation; and let the old and the young, the rich and the poor, the grave and the gay, of all sexes and tongues, and colors and conditions, sacrifice unceasingly upon its altars.

But now we come to the psychological core of the speech, the theme that was likely Lincoln's chief concern. Despite his efforts to whip himself into foreseeing a total breakdown of law and order, he now contends that America's gravest danger is actually its own great success. Why? Because the times no longer called for outstanding leaders of the caliber of Washington and Jefferson—and thus the ambitious young men of Lincoln's time, with no civic mission to satisfy their thirst for achievement, would be tempted to seek glory through usurpation.

> But, it may be asked, why suppose danger to our political institutions? Have we not preserved them for more than fifty years? And why may we not for fifty times as long?
>
> The experiment is successful; and thousands have won their deathless names in making it so. But the game is caught; and I believe it is true, that with the catching, end the pleasures of the chase. This field of glory is harvested, and the crop is already appropriated. But new reapers will arise, and *they*, too, will seek a field. It is to deny, what the history of the world tells us is true, to suppose that men of ambition and talents will not continue to spring up against us. And, when they do, they will as naturally seek the gratification of their ruling passion, as others have so done before them. The question then, is, can that gratification be found in supporting and maintaining an edifice that has been erected by others? Most certainly it cannot.

Lincoln followed this passage with his vivid evocation of the family of the lion and the tribe of the eagle, cited above. The words recall Hamilton's profession of "disgust" and "horror" in the ninth Federalist Paper at the unscrupulous demagogues of the ancient republics, but the import of Lincoln's words is very different. Hamilton believed that American institutions, the rule of law, and the channeling of personal ambition into success through commerce and the other peaceful arts would help the young nation forgo the need for a Pericles or a Cato, and therefore avoid the danger of a Catiline or Caesar.

The importance of commerce in taming and redirecting excessive ambition, echoed by James Madison, conveys an important theme of the Enlightenment as expressed by Locke, Montesquieu, and Voltaire. In the famous tenth Federalist, Madison makes his jarring observation that government cannot remove the causes of vice from men's souls, but it can control their outward bad effects. One way to do this is to channel political ambition into three branches of government, each of which represents the people in a different way, and therefore prevents any of those branches from ganging up on the rest and creating a tyranny. But the other way, equally important, is that the encouragement of agriculture and commercial enterprise through westward expansion will gradually dissipate the danger of glory seeking by channeling it into success in business. The Old World code of martial honor and aristocratic pride, often issuing in the longing for war as a way of proving one's courage and in dueling and other retrograde pursuits, will be absorbed into the gentler drive for material well-being, softening the manners of society as a whole and giving every individual an opportunity to rise above his origins. Madison's prescription rapidly became the American reality. As Tocqueville observed during his visit to America in the early 1830s, for better or worse, the old European aristocratic code of martial pride had been replaced by the heroism of westward expansion and free enterprise, princes by royal descent replaced by self-made princes of commerce.

But Lincoln is saying something rather different. According to him, men belonging by nature to the tribe of the eagle will emerge in America in *any* event. Tocqueville need not have worried that manly pride would vanish in a democracy. No change in civilization or manners effected by the New World, Lincoln is claiming, would eradicate this fundamental human type. It was a point that could be traced back to Periclean Athens, to Thucydides, the great narrator of the Peloponnesian War: Responsible leaders like Pericles will emerge in any era, but irresponsible demagogues like Alcibiades will reliably emerge as well, for human nature remains constant, and so do the attractions of honorable statesmanship and the temptations of tyranny. For Lincoln, the danger was that this new crop of would-be lions would not be able to find glory in serving an egalitarian republic of laws and institutions whose aim is to eliminate the need for men like themselves.

One is reminded of Rousseau's famous argument about the great founders of republics like the Spartan lawgiver Lycurgus. As Rousseau puts it, we can only hope that such towering figures will find their ambition for immortal fame satisfied by founding a regime of good laws that will discourage charismatic revolutionaries like themselves from emerging in the future to disrupt its communal harmony. Just as Lincoln calls for the creation of a "political religion," Rousseau contended that the founder of a well-ordered republic should "change human nature," and invent a "civil religion" to bind citizens together. Then, like Cincinnatus of the old Roman republic, he would voluntarily resign his dictatorial powers and retire to his farm, because the republic of equal citizens devoted to serving the common good could not proceed untroubled while a giant like himself remained in their midst.

But Lincoln is asking: What if such a titan emerges and *isn't* content with serving the republic, because the glory of the founding is already past?

> Is it unreasonable then to expect, that some man possessed of the loftiest genius, coupled with ambition sufficient to push it to its utmost stretch, will at some time, spring up among us? And when such a one does, it will require the people to be united with each other, attached to the government and laws, and generally intelligent, to successfully frustrate his designs.

Lincoln brings us face-to-face with the old problem of how such ambition might instead be channeled into honor seeking through public service. How might a potential tyrant be educated, his passions sublimated, into the eminence of what Aristotle calls "the great-souled man," a leading citizen who seeks the honor of other reputable men by serving the republic? Perhaps the fact that Lincoln was largely self-educated enabled him to vault over the general opinion of his times that burning ambition would be tamed by commerce and return to this ancient, hardheaded perspective on the recurring dilemmas of statesmanship and political ambition. We have already observed how character and common sense can trump formal education in great statesmen, such as Churchill. It is remarkable that Lincoln rejects one of the central premises of the Enlightenment and its American devotees Jefferson, Madison, and Hamilton—that the danger of excessive honor seeking could be largely erased by channeling the pursuit of power into self-preservation and economic enterprise. Not only does Lincoln find this impossible given the constants of human nature, he does not even think it altogether desirable—because even the best governed republics will *need* such men from time to time, and must hope that they will strive on behalf of the republic rather than seek glory, like Caesar, by crossing the Rubicon to overthrow it. To find a man who will free the slaves, in other words, you must entertain the risk that the liberator may be a tyrant-in-waiting who may choose to enslave his fellow citizens instead.

> Distinction will be his paramount object; and although he would as willingly, perhaps more so, acquire it by doing good as harm; yet, that opportunity being past, and nothing left to be done in the way of building up, he would set boldly to the task of pulling down. Here then, is a probable case, highly dangerous, and such a one as could not have well existed heretofore.

In this sentiment, Lincoln was following the spirit of ancient thinkers like Aristotle and Thucydides rather than the benign bourgeois materialism of Locke and Madison. Political ambition is natural to a certain kind of man, Lincoln is saying. It cannot be reduced to comfortable self-preservation and success in commerce. Once we recognize that it will never go away, the question is, how might its energies be redirected toward a decent patriotism?

To these dilemmas of excessive and unsatisfied ambition, Lincoln then adds another danger—the challenge to civil order posed by the commonplace passions of jealousy, envy, and greed:

Another reason which *once was*; but which, to the same extent, is *now no more*, has done much in maintaining our institutions thus far. I mean the powerful influence which the interesting scenes of the revolution had upon the *passions* of the people as distinguished from their judgment. By this influence, the jealousy, envy, and avarice, incident to our nature, and so common to a state of peace, prosperity, and conscious strength, were, for the time, in a great measure smothered and rendered inactive while the deep rooted principles of *hate*, and the powerful motive of *revenge*, instead of being turned against each other, were directed exclusively against the British nation. And thus, from the force of circumstances, the basest principles of our nature, were either made to lie dormant, or to become the active agents in the advancement of the noblest of causes—that of establishing and maintaining civil and religious liberty. But this state of feeling *must fade, is fading, has faded*, with the circumstances that produced it.

The American Revolution, Lincoln is arguing, submerged and channeled these passions of envy and revenge into hatred of the British occupier, turning them outward in a common cause. Now that the common peril has passed, those passions are running amok and generating the climate of lawlessness decried earlier. There is an echo here of Pericles' famous Funeral Oration as it was handed down by Thucydides—one of whose chief themes, as we will see in detail in Part Three, is the problem of envy in democratic societies and how it can undermine a spirit of cooperation for the common good. In a society where all are said to be equal, exceptional merit and success may invite jealous indignation and a base desire to level all distinction. Lincoln read voraciously to improve himself; Shakespeare and the Bible were among his mainstays. But he had a roving and fertile mind, and he may well have absorbed the temper of classical writers like Thucydides from the age of the Greek Revival in America. Yet it's also possible that his beliefs about the recurring capacities of human nature for virtue and vice, for public service and tyrannical ambition, were products of his own common sense and his observations about the society around him.

With the passion of revolutionary fervor now outmoded, Lincoln argues, the private vices are likely to rebound. The glory of the revolutionary struggle will not be forgotten, Lincoln admits, but its direct impact will fade with time. The passion that once ensured the nation's survival now fueled lawlessness, frontier justice, and mob rule. Therefore, cold reason and dedication to the rule of law must replace passion:

> I do not mean to say, that the scenes of the revolution *are now* or *ever will be* entirely forgotten; but that like everything else, they must fade upon the memory of the world, and grow more and more dim by the lapse of time. In history, we hope, they will be read of, and recounted, so long as the Bible shall be read;—but even granting that they will, their influence *cannot be* so universally known, nor so vividly felt, as they were by the generation just gone to rest. At the close of that struggle, nearly every adult male had been a participator in some of its scenes. The consequence was, that of those scenes, in the form of a husband, a father, a son or a brother, a *living history was* to be found in every family—a history bearing the indubitable testimonies of its own authenticity, in the limbs mangled, in the scars of wounds received, in the midst of the very scenes related—a history, too, that could be read and understood alike by all, the wise and the ignorant, the learned and the unlearned. But *those* histories are gone. They *can* be read no more forever.

To Lincoln and those of his generation, the Revolution was no longer a living memory, with its lessons in the proper employment of passion in the service of liberty. Yet Lincoln clearly regrets that the "giant oaks" of the founding era have been "levelled" by the malignant influence of envy and mob rule.

> They *were* a fortress of strength; but, what invading foemen could *never do*, the silent artillery of our time *has done*; the

levelling of its walls. They are gone. They *were* a forest of giant oaks; but the all-restless hurricane has swept over them, and left only, here and there, a lonely trunk, despoiled of its verdure, shorn of its foliage; unshading and unshaded, to murmur in a few more gentle breezes, and to combat with its mutilated limbs, a few more ruder storms, then to sink, and be no more. They *were* the pillars of the temple of liberty; and now, that they have crumbled away, that temple must fall, unless we, their descendants, supply their places with other pillars, hewn from the solid quarry of sober reason.

All that remains for statecraft today, in this lesser age, is a dedication to reason and reverence for the laws:

> Passion has helped us; but can do so no more. It will in future be our enemy. Reason, cold, calculating, unimpassioned reason, must furnish all the materials for our future support and defence. Let those materials be moulded into *general intelligence, sound morality* and, in particular, *a reverence for the constitution and laws*; and, that we improved to the last; that we remained free to the last; that we revered his name to the last; that, during his long sleep, we permitted no hostile foot to pass over or desecrate his resting place; shall be that which to learn the last trump shall awaken our Washington. Upon these let the proud fabric of freedom rest, as the rock of its basis; and as truly as has been said of the only greater institution, *"the gates of hell shall not prevail against it."*

Lincoln's well-crafted peroration endeavors to sound passionate in defense of the need to be dispassionate. Yet one senses the anticlimax as he reaches his conclusion, his turning away from the dark and sparkling ruminations on the tribe of the eagle, the troubling greatness of a Caesar or a Napoleon, to a rather halfhearted civics lesson. In a way he could not yet foresee, Lincoln would later be called upon to lead his country through perils that easily matched those of the revolutionary period, and that summoned from him spiritual and moral energies every bit the equal of those displayed by the Founding Fathers.

In the years that intervened, Lincoln showed caution and bided his time. The conformism of the Jacksonian era suited him, allowing him to pose as an unremarkable timeserver while nurturing an inner radicalism. Like Aristotle's great-souled man, like Pericles before him and Churchill afterward, he found that only the direst national peril could truly satisfy his ambition by drawing from him every ounce of his talents. For the Civil War itself would resolve the dilemma set forth in the Lyceum speech. Lincoln himself would prove to be that member of the tribe of the eagle who chooses to save the republic, not topple it, and to free the slaves rather than enslaving his countrymen. And in serving the common good at this extreme juncture in American history, he could uphold the highest principles of justice and morality while remaining true to the fiery creed of his youth: "Towering genius disdains a beaten path."

Leadership Ancient and Modern: The Dilemmas of the Founding Fathers

Lincoln's Lyceum speech suggests that Tocqueville need not have worried so much about the American democracy's capacity to generate men of heroic striving. For Lincoln, the danger was that when such men did emerge, they would not find challenges equal to their ambition. Lincoln's contemporary Emerson wrote that it was natural to believe in great men. His conclusion sounds almost Lincolnesque (the Lincoln of 1838) in its taste for the extreme case: "The stronger the nature, the more it is reactive. Let us have the quality pure. A little genius let us leave alone." This is precisely the kind of man Lincoln included in the tribe of the eagle.

There is no question that the American Founding Fathers were haunted by the problem of grand political ambition, and the question of whether and to what extent it could be harnessed to serve the republic without courting the risk of nurturing a tyrant who emerges as the seeming servant of the common good but then throws off his democratic sheep's clothing to reveal the tyrannical wolf beneath.

Several issues come together around this theme. Given that today we live in a world with dozens of relatively successful democracies, and where almost all regimes at a minimum profess democratic principles, it's hard to imagine how rare and risky a project the American founding was. In contemporary terms, it would be like settling another planet. After all, Thucydides' portrait of Athens had helped give democracy a bad name among the educated and propertied classes of Europe. Between the American Revolution and the final ratification of the Constitution in 1790, this conservative fear of democracy was thought by many to have been amply justified by the French Revolution of 1789, which seemed to confirm Thucydides' worst nightmares about mob rule, unscrupulous demagogues, the confiscation of property, and the wholesale slaughter of the privileged orders.

As noted, the Founding Fathers were keen to ensure that no one draw conclusions about their new American democracy based on these other, more troubled models. James Madison was likely trying to distinguish America from the revolutionary egalitarianism about to break out in France when he wrote in the tenth Federalist that the new Constitution would not lead to agitation for "an abolition of debts, for an equal division of property, or for any other improper or wicked project." This was not to be the collectivist and lawless "mobocracy" of the Jacobins. Even though America had fought Britain for her independence, the American experiment would more closely resemble the Glorious Revolution of 1688 in England—based on the principles of Locke, defender of property rights, rather than those of Rousseau and his vision of a classless society pursued by the Jacobins. British statesmen like Pitt and Burke had clearly understood this about America, which is why they decried Britain's making war on a brethren people who only wanted the same rights as the British themselves had achieved. Like the Glorious Revolution, the sole purpose of the American Revolution was to establish representative government, due process of law, religious tolerance, and the rights of the individual, especially the right to acquire property. It did, of course, proclaim as a matter of principle that all men are created equal, an assertion of outright egalitarianism that Britain's more class-bound politics and monarchical principle had always avoided.

Alexander Hamilton, writing in defense of the new Constitution, did everything in his power to separate the new American republic from those of ancient times:

> It is impossible to read the history of the petty republics of Greece and Italy without feeling sensations of horror and disgust at the distractions with which they were continually agitated, and at the rapid succession of revolutions by which they were kept in a state of perpetual vibration between the extremes of tyranny and anarchy. If they exhibit occasional calms, these only serve as short-lived contrasts to the furious storms that are to succeed. If now and then intervals of felicity open themselves to view, we behold them with a mixture of regret, arising from the reflection that the pleasing scenes before us are soon to be overwhelmed by the tempestuous waves of sedition and party rage.

Hamilton was describing precisely the world set forth by Thucydides in his *History of the Peloponnesian War*, and the course of the very first democracy in the West. Athens rose to predominance in Greek affairs by leading the struggle to save Greece from Persian invasion. That predominance in turn provoked a long and bloody war with Athens's chief rival, Sparta—a battle that gradually undermined the internal fabric of life among the allies of the two superpowers, leading to appalling civil wars as the oligarchical supporters of Sparta and the democratic supporters of Athens tried to install their own regimes at home. When men of substance heard of the horrors in revolutionary Paris, they were already primed by Thucydides' unforgettable descriptions of the mass reprisals based on class, the confiscation of property by the lower orders, and the downfall of all moral decency: The Jacobin Terror only proved that the ancients had been right to decry any form of popular sovereignty.

Hamilton is well aware of Thucydides' somber reflections on how sound and prudent leadership such as that provided by Pericles can rarely prevail in the long run against the passions of the mob. He and the other Founding Fathers must do everything they can to assure the educated and propertied classes of the New World, and the friends of responsible government in England and Europe, that this new American democracy will be a republic of laws in which institutional checks and balances will prevent any one faction or unscrupulous demagogue from seizing power and oppressing the rest. By contrast, in the ancient republics, everything depended on the occasional and fortuitous emergence of virtuous leaders like Pericles. But these leaders were frequently undermined by the vicious partisan strife by which one party wanted to use government power to tyrannize over its foes. Hamilton continues:

> If momentary rays of glory break forth from the gloom, while they dazzle us with a transient and fleeting brilliancy, they at the same time admonish us to lament that the vices of government should pervert the direction and tarnish the luster of those bright talents and exalted endowments for which the favored soils that produced them have been so justly celebrated.

Accordingly, the new American republic would primarily rely for its soundness not on the hope that brilliant and responsible leaders like Pericles will emerge, but on the endurance of its institutions:

> The science of politics, like most other sciences has received great improvement. The efficacy of various principles is now well understood which were either not known at all, or imperfectly known to the ancients. The regular distribution of power into distinct departments; the introduction of legislative balances and checks, the institution of courts composed of judges holding their office during good behavior . . . these are wholly new discoveries, or have made their principal progress toward perfection in modern times. These are means, and powerful means, by which the excellences of republican government may be retained and its imperfections lessened or avoided.

Still, however much the new American republic tried to lessen its dependence on the fortuitous emergence of great men willing to serve the interests of the common good rather than subvert it for tyrannical aims, the founders could not altogether dispense with the problem of ambition and honor. For, even given the crafting of more durable laws and institutions, men of character would still be needed to serve—and calling for such men would always run the risk of luring would-be tyrants and demagogues in the process.

Closely connected to the distrust of democracy was the question of whether a gentleman could find a place in the leadership of a democratic government, without betraying his own background, cultivation, and breeding. One of Tocqueville's chief motivations in writing *Democracy in America* was to try to convince the gentlemen of his own class back in Europe not to desert the emerging democratic movement there because they were repelled by its vulgarity, but instead to guide it toward a more moderate and responsible outcome such as the American experiment, following the British precedent, had begun to establish. Among the American founders, some were self-made men with fairly modest backgrounds as tradesmen or merchants. But others, like Jefferson, Madison, and Washington, came from the planter class of Virginia. A goodly number of their generation had been liberally educated at such colleges as William and Mary, Yale, Harvard, Princeton, and the future Columbia, and grew up in refined circumstances on a par with the landed gentry in England. They experienced from early on the quandary of how to adjust their genteel origins to the populist demeanor suitable to an egalitarian society. The nineteenth-century man of letters Julian Hawthorne, son of the famous novelist Nathaniel, describes the balance Thomas Jefferson tried to strike between an outwardly accessible, democratic, and informal manner for his political dealings and his private world of gentlemanly cultivation, centered on his ingeniously designed Palladian house Monticello with its collection of European art and antiquities:

Jefferson by birth belonged to the patrician class, and was therefore the readier to observe the forms of democracy. Accident having placed within his reach all that birth could give, he could slight it and carry out the theory of equality by his example as well as by his precept. . . . At all events he chose to be democratic in his manners as well as in his ideas.

The founders often entertained Greek and Roman precedents when cautioning themselves always to restrict their love of honor to what was best for the preservation of the republic and the good of the people. One of their models was Cicero's *Dream of Scipio*, the paragon of a statesman who serves the republic without personal gain both on the battlefield and in the counsels of government, but who places the life of the mind and a concern with the immortality of the soul even higher than civic honor. Educated in or at least exposed to the values of the classics, Jefferson, Hamilton, Washington, and Madison were also keenly aware of the tension between civic honor and personal ambition, of the dangerous precedents of Caesar, Catiline, and Alcibiades, who flattered and enflamed the passions of the mob and its resentment of the upper orders. Hamilton warned repeatedly that the new American republic must beware of the emergence of "Catilines and Caesars." Sallust's *Conspiracy of Catiline*, which recounted how Cicero saved the Roman republic from the tyrannical subversion of the debauched flatterer of the mob, was a staple in the founders' classical education.

George Washington is one of the most revealing cases in point. His modesty and bravery, his steady course in preserving the Continental Army through the severest hardships of hunger and poor equipment and then winning through to victory, earned him a cultlike stature even in life. The honors paid to him after his victory at Yorktown came close to making him an American monarch in all but name. As Julian Hawthorne wrote:

> The reason is that here, for once, we find a man sincerely resolved to give himself unreservedly to the work of helping others (namely his countrymen), and entirely forgetting all personal claims, ambitions, and sufferings in that single aim.

. . . On learning of the surrender, Congress went to church to thank God, and Philadelphia blazed with illuminations. Honors were showered upon Washington. . . . Franklin wrote to Washington that this success brightened "the glory that must accompany your name to the latest posterity."

Admirers from afar like the English Whig leader Charles James Fox praised Washington's nobility and compared him to the great generals and statesmen of classical antiquity, bemoaning the Old World's lack of men of such quality:

How infinitely superior must appear the spirit of principles of General Washington in his late address to Congress compared with the policy of modern European courts! Deriving honor less from the splendor of his situation than for the dignity of his mind. It must, indeed, create astonishment that, placed in circumstances so critical, and filling a station so conspicuous, the character of Washington should never once have been called in question.

Washington was particularly enamored of Joseph Addison's immensely popular drama *Cato*. Addison's story was based on the life of Marcus Porcius Cato, the most intransigent and relentless enemy of Julius Caesar, whom he regarded as a traitor to the senatorial class bent on fanning the resentment of the plebeians in order to overthrow the republic and proclaim himself king. In the play, Cato is waiting for the victorious dictator Caesar to arrive at the camp of the defeated republican army in north Africa. Although Caesar is willing to make peace and offer Cato pardon, Cato prefers suicide by falling on his own sword rather than accept the hated usurper's clemency. The play was a roaring success in both England and the American colonies. Clearly Washington saw in Cato and Caesar the two exemplary extremes of republican government; he even had the play performed for the Continental Army at their beleaguered camp in Valley Forge, doubtless viewing it as a valuable civics lesson for his officers and men. While determined to embrace the good model Cato, Washington must have been sensitive to the temptations of the Caesarean alternative—the renegade aristocrat who courts the mob to become the darling of the masses and for a time is loved by almost everyone.

Washington clearly intended for his men to see their own impending battles as imitating the virtuous struggle of Cato, although presumably with a different outcome. But he may also have meant to impart to them that, even if they should lose, they must preserve their honor intact and never submit to British tyranny even at the cost of their lives. It is a vivid example of how Washington and other chief actors in the American Revolution saw themselves as consciously re-enacting the origins of the most famous republic in history—while avoiding the pitfalls of the classical era. Some scholars believe that a number of the most famous speeches from the American Revolution were closely inspired by the play. For example, Patrick Henry's ringing ultimatum, "Give me liberty or give me death!" parallels a scene from Act II of *Cato*: "It is not now time to talk of aught / but chains or conquest, liberty or death." Even more strikingly, a line from Act IV, "what a pity it is / that we can die but once to serve our country," appears to anticipate Nathan Hale's immortal cry, "I only regret I have but one life to give for my country."

These dilemmas surrounding the permissible limits of ambition and honor seeking among leaders of a democracy were already complex enough. But the challenges were intensified by the unfolding of the French Revolution and the subsequent rise of Napoleon Bonaparte. In its early phase, the French Revolution took the Glorious and American revolutions as its models. The leaders of this first phase—men like Talleyrand, Lafayette, and Honoré Mirabeau—were great admirers of the American founders, including Ben Franklin and Jefferson, both of whom had lived among them in Paris. Lafayette had even served as an aide-de-camp to Washington and came to love and honor him like a father. But in its second, purely revolutionary phase, spearheaded by the Jacobins, the revolutionaries wanted much more: pure equality overnight, and the abolition of private property and religion. Their goal was to create a heaven on earth, a return to the primitive Arcadian collective of the Year One, and to bring about the transition by the literal extermination of the privileged classes.

It was against this backdrop of idealistic terror and bloodshed for the sake of the brotherhood of man that Napoleon Bonaparte arose. The greatest conqueror in the West since Julius Caesar and Alexander the Great, Napoleon for a time ruled an empire that rivaled either of theirs. Rousseau had already written ominously of "the legislator" who "changes human nature" and takes on a godlike quality in order to found a just regime. Napoleon seemed to spring straight from these pages of *The Social Contract*. As we observed in Part One, the most impressive leaders can sometimes emerge from outside the governing classes—as was true in different ways of Lincoln and Churchill. On the darker side of leadership, where tyranny and mass murder are employed to achieve utopian aims, the trend is striking. Hitler, as an Austrian, and Stalin, as a Georgian, both came from the hinterlands of their respective civilizations. In both cases, their origins were looked down upon as backward and uncouth in comparison with their civilizational center. Stalin was mocked by Russians for his heavily accented speech; Hitler's exaggerated courtliness to his female staff was snickered at behind his back as the mark of a Viennese rube. Bonaparte, as a native of Corsica, was never fully accepted by some as truly French, and it lent him a simmering resentment that never entirely left him. His detractors often sneeringly used the Corsican version of his name, Buonaparte, as if the spelling alone could refute his claims to empire.

Napoleon's sensitivity about being an ethnic outsider from a somewhat barbarous outback was compounded by his childhood experience of alienation. Obsessively devoted to his mother, becoming almost a substitute spouse for her in widowhood, he was aloof, withdrawn, and arrogant toward other boys his age. I remember as a child seeing in my parents' encyclopedia the reproduction of a painting of him as a cadet at Brienne. It showed the ten-year-old boy standing alone as the other boys played and frolicked, glowering in his military cape and tricorn hat like a miniature version of his future self. The painting conveys the feeling that his arrogance is a self-protective pose for his desire to join the other boys, his inability to do so, and his fear of being rejected. No matter how many medals, titles, and palaces he accumulated, this solitary mien never left him. Battlefield portraits often show him standing utterly by himself as he surveys the situation, his suite hanging back as if to avoid disturbing the isolation of his genius. He particularly detested his servitors among the old aristocracy like Talleyrand, whom he correctly suspected of looking down on him as an uncouth parvenu.

Talleyrand and other moderates had enlisted the young General Bonaparte to overthrow the government in a military coup to prevent the Jacobins from returning to power. From that ruthless beginning, his swath of astounding conquests in the Middle East and Europe unfolded, prompting comparisons with the military brilliance of Cyrus the Great, Hannibal, and Caesar. The animating vision of Napoleon's statecraft was that he used military conquest to spread the French Revolution's ideals of liberty, equality, and fraternity. Wherever he prevailed militarily, he liquidated what remained of the old feudal and aristocratic regimes of Europe and tried to leave in their place a modern state with representative institutions and the rule of law. The Napoleonic Code was adopted by much of Europe as its legal system and remained in force after his downfall.

At the same time, Napoleon made himself the emperor of this new liberal cosmopolitan order, liquidating the surviving Austrian rump of the Holy Roman Empire and effectively arrogating to himself the legitimate descent it had claimed from Augustus Caesar, Constantine, and Charlemagne. He was something new in history: a tyrant who liberates, a conqueror who spreads the rule of law and elected government. Like Alexander or Cyrus the Great before him, Napoleon offered the opportunity to young men for glory and to rise in life: many of his marshals were sons of the revolution, from humble origins, who ended up loaded with titles, wealth, and aristocratic marriages. Those who weren't suited for a warrior's life garnered the solid benefits of orderly government and individual rights.

The version of the revolution that Napoleon spread through his fifteen years of bloodshed was the original, more moderate version. His conquests employed violent Jacobin means to impose peaceable bourgeois ends. That was why a moderate like Talleyrand supported him—and why Talleyrand would be reviled by his class and the restored Bourbon monarchy as a traitor. This was the cardinal difference between Napoleon and his predecessors among the tribe of the eagle, as Lincoln characterized them. Alexander and Caesar had used their conquests to spread values that were essentially aristocratic; they invited the meritorious among their conquered peoples and allies to become Greek and Roman gentlemen. Napoleon, however, was spreading the modern democratic value of equality for all, and that had a deep resonance with the Christian assumption of the equality of man before God. His particular genius as a modern statesman was to understand that the solid material comforts extolled as the fruits of modernity by men of the Enlightenment, such as Voltaire or Alexander Hamilton, were not enough to satisfy precisely those fiery young men Lincoln was talking about in his Lyceum speech—the few who crave extraordinary distinction and honor. Napoleon wanted to supplement bourgeois self-interest with Caesarean glory by enlisting the honor seekers to spread by force of arms bourgeois rights to all the peoples of Europe.

This is why opinions about Napoleon differed so profoundly in the political and literary classes of the West; even individual observers veered from one extreme to another in their judgment of the emperor. Like Tolstoy's Pierre Bezukhov in *War and Peace*, many who identified themselves with the Enlightenment while living in reactionary regimes with feudal political authorities were excited by the young emperor's spread of the rights of man. But at the same time, as patriots, they could not stomach the idea that it would be up to a foreign conqueror to improve their lands, however much they needed improving. Pierre eventually sides with the old Russian patriotism embodied by General Kutuzov, convinced that Russia's much-needed reform must wait until the foreign peril to her survival has been repelled. Napoleon was often both oppressor and liberator at once. His creation of a confederation of German states, while aimed primarily at checking the power of Austria, led to the first stirring of German nationalism and the desire for a modern nation-state. Enlightened opinion in England was initially ambivalent toward the revolution, as it had been in America. The Whig leader Charles James Fox, who had extolled Washington's Roman virtues, was also attracted to the French Revolution as the destroyer of the ancien régime throughout Europe. But he finally came to view Napoleon as dangerous to Britain and the entire continent. As Napoleon's power grew, as his obsession with pomp and glory veered toward megalomania, Britain began to see itself as the defender of the republican spirit—of constitutional government and the rule of law—against this new universal tyrant "old Boney." The Duke of Wellington, Napoleon's eventual nemesis, could be seen as the modern equivalent of Lucius Junius Brutus defeating Tarquin the Proud, Scipio Africanus defeating Hannibal, or Marcus Junius Brutus the Younger taking on the dictator Caesar. Behind it all, as ever, observers of the time could see the example of the epoch-making struggle of Athens, the first free government in the West, against the Great King of Persia.

The French historian and statesman François Guizot gives us a sense of the ambivalence toward Napoleon throughout his spectacular rise and fall:

> For the first time since the death of King Louis XIV, her history finds once more a center, and henceforth revolves around a single man. For fifteen years, victorious or vanquished, at the summit of glory, or in the depths of abasement, France and Europe, overmastered by an indomitable will and unbridled passion for power, were compelled to squander their blood and their treasure upon that page of universal history which General Bonaparte claims for his own, and which he has succeeded in covering with glory and crime.

This fascinating mixture of "glory and crime" entranced, and repelled, young men of spirit and imagination everywhere in the West. Although Tocqueville worried that Americans might be too averse to glory seeking, he also worried about the emergence of a permanent syndrome of Napoleonic rulers—demagogues who would rise to power by cloaking themselves as the radical champions of democracy. In later years, his fears were amply justified—not in America, as he had originally feared, but back in France itself. Napoleon III, Bonaparte's nephew, had borne out in real life the specter of a "democratic despot" Tocqueville had envisioned in his gloomier dystopian predictions about America's possible future—a demagogue who claimed to want to extend equality to the disadvantaged, used the army to seize power, and then held a plebiscite in which the cowed masses voted him permanent absolute power.

But the spiritual fascination with the original Napoleon continued as well. Stendhal's novel *The Red and the Black* poses the question: What is an ambitious young man like Julien Sorel to do in the banal bourgeois world left behind by the departed emperor and his sullied glory? He cannot follow the emperor's colors and rise to a marshal's rank. All that is left to him is bourgeois materialism and the conversion of a warrior's ambition to success in the wars of seduction; Julien's only battle scars come from sliding too quickly down a ladder from a clandestine meeting in the bedroom of Mademoiselle de la Mole, the daughter of a wealthy businessman.

This sense of a vacuum for glory seeking did not escape the young United States. The same mixture of involuntary fascination and moral revulsion over Napoleon is evident in an essay by Emerson:

> Here was an experiment, under the most favorable conditions, of the powers of intellect without conscience. Never was such a leader so endowed and so weaponed; never a leader found such aids and followers. And what was the result of this vast talent and power, of these immense armies, burned cities, squandered treasures, immolated millions of men, of this demoralized Europe? It all came to no result. All passed away like the smoke of his artillery, and left no trace. He left France smaller, poorer, feebler, than he found it; and the whole contest for freedom was to be begun again.

It is out of this welter of conflicting sentiments that Napoleon and the other members of "the family of the lion" emerged in the American frontier town of Springfield, Illinois, through the idiosyncratic musings of an as yet largely unknown and impecunious backwoods lawyer.

Abraham Lincoln and the Soul of a Leader

At the beginning of this section, I described the blight of slavery as the poison root out of which all the branches of American life radiated during Lincoln's lifetime. Considering his role in its abolition, one might describe Lincoln's remarkably complicated personality as a hub in which many spokes, not only of American experience but of world experience, intersected. For now it is clearer that the Lyceum speech in heartland Illinois, seemingly so far away from the blood-soaked perturbations of Europe or even the more sophisticated intellectual culture of the original New England colonies, reflected a number of tumultuous quandaries surrounding the issue of democratic leadership in the modern world. Lincoln's attempt to think through the problem of honor demonstrates that the examples of Napoleon and the other members of the family of the lion had cut right into the heartland of the new democracy as it confronted its greatest challenge since the founding. Uncovering the soul of the leader in Lincoln requires us to circle around his character, reaching to grasp its core from diverse and shifting perspectives as his career unfolds toward its blood-soaked and redemptive zenith. His origins, his psychological shaping, his evolving political principles, his private life, his relationship to the founders and to the existing social strata of the America of his day—it is impossible to pinpoint any one of these as the defining arena of his greatness. Like a revolving wheel, the spokes of his life are separate yet move together to keep the center stable.

In the abolition of slavery, of course, Lincoln found the cause he had been searching for in the Lyceum speech. He was the savior of the republic, not the destroyer. In one specific sense he was a kind of domestic Napoleon: Whereas the French emperor waged war against the other nations of Europe to force them to adopt the modern principles of equality and the rights of man, Lincoln in effect waged war within America, against a huge portion of his own country, to extend freedom to all Americans. Moreover, just as Napoleon fought on behalf of egalitarian principles to topple the remaining feudal remnants of Europe, Lincoln made war upon what survived in America of something akin to the premodern, landed, and feudal aristocracy of the Old World.

One cannot, of course, push this comparison too far. Despite occasional flirtations with theories of feudalism by fringe ideologues during the Civil War, the American South remained stoutly loyal to the American Constitution and the rights of man *except* for the slavery issue. Indeed, a number of the founders, including Washington, Madison, and Jefferson, had come from the landed class of slave owners. Therefore the ideological divide between North and South, apart from slavery, was nothing like that between, say, Napoleonic France and tsarist Russia. Nevertheless, even apart from their clinging to slavery, there was something about the South that held back from the vision of a full-blown commercial republic of the kind that Madison and especially Hamilton had envisioned. Even before the Civil War, the South began to see the North, with its large cities and smoke-belching factories, as somehow too modern, too far from the soil of that virtuous "yeoman farmer" whom Jefferson, with his Rousseauan sympathies for the Arcadian state of nature, had romanticized as the backbone of the American body politic. In some ways the Civil War was an extension of the English battle between court and country, between commerce and landed gentry, and earlier between Roundhead and Cavalier. The Confederate general Stonewall Jackson, whom many lionized as a champion of the Jeffersonian ideal, believed the South was defending its old-fashioned agrarian way of life against "bank rule" and "the moneyed interest" in the North. The South was a courtlier, slower society that hearkened back to a simpler age. In embracing slavery to the point of secession and defeat, the southern states doomed forever that Arcadian vision of America and consolidated the triumph of Northern industry and commerce.

However this may be, the most important difference between Napoleon's war to modernize Europe and Lincoln's war to modernize his own country is that Lincoln undertook his mission with no trace at all of the personal glory seeking, bombast, and self-aggrandizement that saw the Corsican corporal affect to wear the imperial crown of Charlemagne, Constantine, and Augustus. Indeed, as Lincoln's mission unfolded, as his presidency wore on through the days of despair and carnage, every trace of personal self-interest or even mild enjoyment of his office was cauterized from Lincoln's soul. He became ever more saintlike in his self-abnegation and self-denial—a transformation vividly apparent to those around him. As his friend William Herndon wrote:

> Mr. Lincoln was the best man, the kindest, noblest, loveliest *since Christ*. He was better and purer than Washington, and in my mind he stands incomparable, grandly looming up. He is now the great central figure of American history. God bless Abraham Lincoln!

Herndon's judgment was not unusual: whether they knew Lincoln or not, many nineteenth-century Americans saw Lincoln in almost superhuman terms, especially after his death. Herndon again:

> [Lincoln was] a very sensitive, diffident, unobtrusive, natural-made gentleman; his mind was strong and deep, sincere and honest, patient and enduring, with a good heart filled with the love of mercy and with a conscience that loved justice, having no vices, only negative defects with many positive virtues; he is strong, self-reliant, honest, full of practical sagacities, manly, noble; he stands high in the foremost ranks of man in all ages, their equal, if not their superior, one of the very best types of free institutions and this Christian civilization; and if I were to deliver a eulogy freed from all rhetoric of extravagant eulogy, I say here was a man in his general life who thought strongly, willed firmly, and acted nobly, and in whose life and death the world is lifted to a higher plane of existence.

Here, too, we must note a cardinal difference between Lincoln and the would-be liberator of Europe. Lincoln, like almost every American of his time, grew up steeped in the cadences of the Protestant Bible. His parents belonged to a Baptist congregation that had split from their original church because the Lincolns' group were abolitionists, and his speeches are inconceivable without an immersion in the somber riches of the King James Version and its hard-grooved exhortations to righteousness before God. Tocqueville saw this attachment to faith as the unique good fortune of America. In Europe, and especially in France, democracy was staunchly opposed by religion, which regarded it as atheistic, and so democracy could prevail only by openly combating religion. Napoleon tolerated the church, but was as fiercely anticlerical as your average Jacobin in his promotion of the secular doctrine of the rights of man. American democracy, by contrast, grew directly out of the Protestant conviction that all men were equal in the sight of God and that we are placed on this earth to do God's work and advance the causes of justice and salvation, to build the shining city on the hill.

Lincoln's religiosity was a matter of great debate during and after his lifetime. After his death, some Christian clergymen tried to claim him for the fold. But those who knew him best, including Herndon and his wife, Mary Todd Lincoln, held unequivocally that Lincoln was never a believer in the Christian faith. His earliest associates in Springfield regarded him as a Deist in the tradition of Thomas Paine. It is said that Lincoln even wrote a pamphlet refuting the Bible and the main tenets of Christian revelation based on the claims of reason; a friend convinced him to destroy it lest it harm his future political prospects. The first drafts of neither the Gettysburg Address nor the Emancipation Proclamation contained any reference to God.

While he may have been a freethinker, however, Lincoln certainly respected the moral code contained in Christianity when stripped of its miraculous provenance. Whatever the precise character of his belief, he understood the deep faith of his countrymen, and his greatest speeches are deeply ingrained with the rhythms and imagery of the Old Testament. Lincoln knew that he could not advance his cause without the churches, which had often been the backbone of abolitionism. Nevertheless, at bottom Lincoln was a politician and an aspiring statesman. He was not content to aspire to do good; he was compelled to carry it out, on a national scale. And so we must recognize, as did his greatest biographer, Lord Charnwood, that, however saintlike his trials may have rendered him, Lincoln retained his strong desire for honor stretching back to his youth. Theodore Roosevelt, who shared with his forebear this passion to gain distinction through serving the common good—and who was far more open in his enjoyment of his high office—considered Lincoln a kindred spirit. He recognized that Lincoln, like the great-souled man of Aristotle's *Nicomachean Ethics* (and like Churchill in the next century), would never have excelled in peaceful and ordinary times, when his chances to serve would have been limited to more humdrum matters of domestic economics and vote getting:

> If there is not a great war, you don't get the great general; if there is not a great occasion, you don't get a great statesman; if Lincoln had lived in a time of peace, no one would know his name.

The historian Garry Wills has compared the Gettysburg Address with Pericles' Funeral Oration in the history of Thucydides. The cadences of Lincoln's speech are indeed both Periclean and biblical. This was hardly unusual: Edward Everett, the illustrious classical scholar and orator who preceded Lincoln that day, certainly modeled his address on that of Pericles. Everett spoke for two hours, but remarked afterward that Lincoln had said far more in two minutes.

All the themes we have been discussing seem to intersect on the podium at Gettysburg: ancient and modern understandings of honor, and how the new generation might add to the achievement of the Founding Fathers. Like the founders, Lincoln loathed populist demagoguery and revolutionary radicalism. He was no revolutionary but firmly endorsed the rights of property and the equality of opportunity for an earned inequality of result. Hadn't Lincoln's own rise shown what individual natural ability and hard work could achieve?

Yet Lincoln was very much a man of the common people, not a gentleman by birth or by education at prestigious schools. As he said in 1852 upon entering the Illinois legislature, "I was born and have ever remained in the most humble walks of life." He never sought military glory for himself as commander in chief—but he encouraged such ambition in his generals to give them further incentive to win the war and bring justice to the oppressed. His example taught them: All honor through serving the good, with no thought of material benefits for oneself.

This is how Lincoln was able to carry more ordinary men—and even men of exceptional ability, like his best generals, Ulysses S. Grant and William Tecumseh Sherman—to something much greater than themselves, a higher pitch of moral excellence. Those who served with him commonly observed, after he was gone, that for the rest of their lives they remained awestruck that someone so great had moved among them. Sherman never lacked for bravado or self-esteem, yet he felt humbled by Lincoln: "Of all the men I ever met, he seemed to possess more of the elements of greatness, combined with goodness, than any other." While in his youthful Lyceum speech he may have flirted, at least in his imagination, with the idea of the great man who enslaves rather than liberates, the argument he used to rout his opponent, Stephen A. Douglas, in the 1858 Senate race was that to tolerate the enslavement of anyone amounts to inviting the enslavement of everyone. And it was in taking this stand that he found his path toward a principled greatness.

The key to understanding Lincoln's soul as a leader is to trace how his personality and his politics intertwined and grew organically together. We begin by asking: What were Lincoln's political principles? During his rise to the presidency, and even a good ways into it, many of his contemporaries viewed him as an opportunist. The Abolitionists saw him as entirely too willing to compromise over slavery. A part of Emerson's understanding of the great man is that he must be a nonconformist. On the face of it, Lincoln would not have measured up to this definition, for he kept his true views to himself for many years. ("If I had eight hours to chop down a tree," he once quipped,

"I'd spend six hours sharpening my axe.") On the other hand, he did embody Emerson's maxim that "a foolish consistency is the hobgoblin of little minds." He readily and frequently shifted his tactics in order to steer his way through to his principled mission. In Burkean and British political terms, he was the ultimate "trimmer," tacking neither too far to the left nor the right so as to catch the best wind. As *Harper's Weekly* wrote in some amazement upon his election as president:

> Twenty months ago he was without a party. The copperheads hated him; the conservative republicans thought him too fast; the radical republicans thought him too slow; the war democrats were looking for the chance to return to political power. He held steadily upon his way. . . .

When we think about how Lincoln's personality and principles evolved together, it is instructive to compare him with Robert E. Lee. For it was Lee who was Lincoln's true antagonist—a comparably imposing figure, as opposed to the vexatious and overwhelmed Jefferson Davis. Lee was the closest living embodiment of the Founding Fathers; his ancestors were among the earliest settlers of Virginia, and his wife was descended from Martha Washington. Lee was personally admirable but politically blind, the unwitting defender of slavery because of his sincere love of the older American tradition of the yeoman farmer loyal to the soil of his home state. He was the incarnation of the inevitable logic of Douglas's defense of the right of the states to decide on slavery for themselves—an argument that hearkened back to the "anti-federalist" faction of dissidents during the ratification debate over the Constitution, who regarded each state as a "virtuous small republic" of the kind romanticized by Rousseau in his praise of the ancient city-states. Arguably the greatest soldier of his era, Lee was at bottom a patriot to the Commonwealth of Virginia, only secondarily to the Union. He was the great oak standing in the road to victory and emancipation.

Most mysterious of all, in its relation to Lincoln's virtues as a statesman, was his lifelong melancholy, his version of Churchill's "black dog." Lincoln's depression is intimately connected to the debate about his religiosity. For behind the modern medical term lies the older term *despair*—an existential category, and ultimately one of theology and faith. One's degree of despair must hinge on the degree to which one wonders whether man's hopes for justice and happiness are supported by reality, by the cosmos, and by a divine purpose in the universe. Among the observations Lincoln left us about the role of fate, and man's place in the universe, signs of what we might now term "depression" are often impossible to disentangle from religious reflections, or at least ruminations on the tenability of such reflections. As Lincoln's frequent companion and early biographer Colonel Ward Hill Lamon observed, Lincoln may not have been a conventional believer, but he certainly believed that man's fate was in the grip of higher powers:

> Lincoln was by no means free from a kind of belief in the supernatural. . . . He lived constantly in the serious conviction that he was himself the subject of a special decree, made by some unknown and mysterious power, for which he had no name.

Reading Lamon's astute description of the inner state of Lincoln's psyche, it is difficult to distinguish cause from effect. Did Lincoln's predisposition to a depression readily explained by real-life loss and trauma make him search out some mysterious force of fate that would root his melancholy in the impenetrable mystery of the world at large? Or was he predisposed to these cosmic ruminations in a way that exacerbated the sorrow caused by his real-life losses? Lamon continues:

> His mind was filled with gloomy forebodings and strong apprehensions of impending evil, mingled with extravagant visions of personal grandeur and power. His imagination painted a scene just beyond the veil of the immediate future, gilded with glory yet tarnished with blood. It was his "destiny" splendid but dreadful, fascinating but terrible. His case bore little resemblance to those of religious enthusiasts like Bunyan, Cowper and others. His was more like the fatalist conscious of his star.

Lincoln's melancholy also shaped his expectations from political life. As one of his close friends, the journalist Noah Brooks, recalled, "Mr. Lincoln had not a hopeful temperament, and, though he looked at the bright side of things, was always prepared for disaster and defeat." Colonel William Crook, the president's bodyguard, provides a particularly intriguing observation from their visit to Richmond after the surrender of the South: "Mr. Lincoln never looked sadder in his life than when he walked through the streets of Richmond and knew it saved to the union and himself victorious." What are we to make of this lack of joy at the very moment when his years of work and suffering had been crowned with triumph? Was he feeling sadness over the death and destruction it had required? No doubt. But might he also have felt a dawning sadness that his great mission, the work that had filled his life and compelled him to rise above his personal disappointments and innately gloomy temperament, was over? Perhaps he foresaw that he would now once again feel empty lacking such a challenge, and not only feel empty but have no burden to distract him from the sadness of his marriage and his other demons. One thinks of Churchill's depression resurfacing after World War II, a war whose conduct had kept his "black dog" at bay, summed up in a remark that so stunned his young granddaughter that she remembered it forever after. When asking her grandfather about his famous life, he replied, "I achieved a great deal to achieve nothing in the end." Yet there is a different possibility in Lincoln's case: that it was precisely his melancholy that gave him the inner strength to persevere as a statesman.

Lincoln's Political Principles

One of the great pleasures in studying leadership is the sheer number of great books on the subject. The best of these not only teach us about particular leaders, but themselves shape the very terms of discourse and the values through which we interpret history. Often, our only access to the personality of a leader is through biography, and that in turn shapes our expectations and judgments about leaders, present and future. Among the best of the twentieth century is Winston Churchill's 1935 *Great Contemporaries*, an unrivaled collection of short profiles of important political figures that manages to capture not only each leader's most important achievements but how his origins and temperament shaped those achievements and in turn evolved with them. One of Churchill's pithy essays—on Arthur Balfour, Leon Trotsky, T. E. Lawrence, Adolf Hitler—can teach us more about its subject than an entire book. In the same league are Duff Cooper's masterful biography of Talleyrand and Lord David Cecil's *Melbourne* (a favorite of John F. Kennedy).

The history of American politics has been blessed with a steady parade of great writers whose insight and eloquence have permanently influenced the way we view their subjects. Among these, one standout is the life of Lincoln published in 1917 by Lord Charnwood. While more information about Lincoln has come to light since it was written, in its combination of profound psychological insight, a shrewd understanding of American politics, and his gorgeous prose, Charnwood's biography, admired for generations, still offers lessons to students of Lincoln. Charnwood's *Lincoln* is marked by maturity and sober balance; he is neither a cheerleader nor a debunker. He is equally alive to Lincoln's greatness and to his capacity for opportunism and evasion. This evenhanded realism is in refreshing contrast to much of the writing about politics in our own era, which tends to veer between an easily purchased cynicism in which the vocation of politics is dismissed as corrupt if a leader can be accused of the slightest leaning toward personal self-advancement or compromise or, on the other hand, a kind of doe-eyed and naïve idealism that insists that a certain leader's motives are as pure as the driven snow, absolutely selfless and devoid of any desire for honor or advancement. Both viewpoints are pure cant, the mark of an inexperienced and immature grasp of life that cannot accept that, in order to achieve good through politics, you *must* achieve power, which means that you must occasionally compromise, and that you do in fact want honor and to rise in life.

Charnwood's subtly nuanced portrait of Lincoln reminds students of history to avoid both cheap moralizing and cheap cynicism. Above all, he shows a remarkable instinct for how Lincoln's heroic wartime leadership intersected with the darker and more obscure elements of his psyche, as well as his lifelong drive for honor and recognition. Like the best of the foreign writers about America, including Tocqueville and Lord Bryce, Charnwood was an admirer of things American but unwilling to overlook faults and defects where he sees them. Americans usually respond positively to such outsiders because, not being native Americans themselves, they see America in a fresh and different way, excited precisely because it is new to them, careful and observant because they are afraid of getting something wrong and do not want to be unpleasant guests. Thus, at their best, books by people like Tocqueville and Charnwood can become a mirror in which America can see itself, but in a different light and perhaps with different contours revealed.

CHARNWOOD RECOGNIZED THE core of Lincoln's mission as a statesman: "There is thus no escape from Lincoln's statement: 'If slavery is not wrong, nothing is wrong.'" From this core principle a number of corollaries radiate, when viewed against the realities of Lincoln's era, his own personality, and the circumstances of his life:

> It does not follow that the way to right the wrong was simple, or that instant and unmitigated emancipation was the best way. But it does follow that, failing this, it was for the statesmen of the south to devise a policy by which the most flagrant evils should be stopped, and, however cautiously and experimentally, the raising of the status of the slave should be proceeded with. It does not follow that the people who, on one pretext or another, shut their eyes to the evil of the system, while they tried to keep their personal dealing humane, can be sweepingly condemned by any man. But it does follow that a deliberate and sustained policy which, neglecting all reform, strove at all costs to perpetuate the system and extend it to wider regions, was [a] criminal . . . policy.

In Lincoln's time, it was possible to view him as either a flaming radical or a timid gradualist, and both views of him were widespread.

Both pure abolitionists and southern defenders of states' rights excoriated him. Tocqueville had predicted that the tyranny of majority opinion in the United States, while it might not result in outright political oppression, could produce an insidious spiritual corrosion that leveled all distinctions of rank and merit and left no room for extraordinary men. Anyone wishing to get ahead must conform to the average and the mediocre. Charnwood viewed the age of Jacksonian democracy, during which Lincoln's political career was launched, as the realization of Tocqueville's vision. While mid-century British politics became more flamboyant, peopled by the likes of Benjamin Disraeli, American politics became less so.

Outwardly, Lincoln could appear to be a typical timeserving conformist:

> In forming any judgement of Lincoln's career, it must, further, be realized that, while he was growing up as a statesman, the prevailing conception of popular government was all the time becoming more unfavorable to leadership and to robust individuality. The new party machinery adopted by the Democrats under Jackson, as the proper mode of securing government by the people, induced a deadly uniformity of utterance; breach of that uniformity was not only rash, but improper.

In these early years, evidently, Lincoln was often considered a venal political hack, unwilling to act on principle. As Charnwood notes, it was a plausible perception:

> Very soon the question whether a proposal or even a sentiment was timely or premature came to bulk too large in the deliberations of Lincoln's friends. The reader will perhaps wonder later whether such considerations did not bulk too largely in Lincoln's own mind. Was there in his statesmanship, even in later days when he had great work to do, an element of that opportunism which, if not actually base, is at least cheap? Or did he come as near as a man with many human weaknesses could

come to the wise and nobly calculated opportunism which is not merely the most beneficent statesmanship, but demands a heroic self-mastery.

However, the conformism of the Jacksonian era provided Lincoln with protective coloration for his core mission. What may have appeared to be opportunism proved in the long run to be a prudent consistency in hewing to the main course—the end of slavery—while refusing to be distracted into expending influence on side issues, or rushed into proclaiming the goal openly before he could build the support he needed to bring it off. In this sense, the conformism of American politics at the time was a good thing for Lincoln, enabling him to camouflage his patience as middle-of-the-road mediocrity. Being underestimated allowed Lincoln to throw others off the scent of his long-range aim. As Charnwood observes:

> [I]t was a happy thing for him and for his country that his character and the whole cast of his ideas and sympathies were of a kind to which the restraint imposed on an American politician was most congenial and to which therefore it could do least harm. He was to prove himself a patient man in other ways as well as this. On many things, perhaps on most, the thoughts he worked out in his own mind diverged very widely from those of his neighbors, but he was not in the least anxious either to conceal or to obtrude them.

As the historian Doris Kearns Goodwin has observed, Lincoln listened politely to all views, but he rarely changed his mind on fundamentals. During his presidency, his cabinet members claimed that they were rarely if ever convened. Having decided early in life to combat slavery, but without knowing precisely how or when, he could bide his time and let events develop. (In 1864, well into his presidency, he claimed that he could "not remember a time when" he did not "think and feel" that slavery was wrong.) It was America itself that came to a point where it could no longer live with the contradiction between slavery and the principles of a free society, not Lincoln—he had already resolved it in his own mind. When America was ready to come to him, he had been in the same place morally for years, waiting for his countrymen to join him there. He could truly say, had he chosen to, what Pericles had said to the democracy of Athens: "I am the same—it is you who have changed."

Moreover, as we have seen, Lincoln believed that most of life's great issues were in the hands of a mysterious and unfathomable fate. This might have been the result of his melancholy, or it might have been the wisdom earned through the interaction of his pessimistic temperament with the challenges of public and private life. You did everything you could and then let fate determine the outcome. As Charnwood says, Lincoln had "a sort of fatalistic confidence in the ultimate victory of reason, and saw no use and a good deal of harm in political agitation for them." He was willing to forgo a passionate declaration of his opposition to slavery in order to avoid alienating anyone who might be kept on his side or eventually won over.

To those idealists who were willing to proclaim their moral beliefs at the cost of middle-of-the-road supporters or the undecided, this could make Lincoln look opportunistic. Lincoln once observed that morally vexatious questions like slavery "must find lodgment with the most enlightened souls who stamp them with their approval. In God's own time they will be organized into law and thus woven into the fabric of our institutions." "This seems a little cold-blooded," Charnwood concedes in describing Lincoln's caution, "but perhaps we can already begin to recognize the man who, when the time had fully come, would be on the right side."

In any event, it's possible to discern an unexpected and paradoxical connection between Lincoln's sometimes almost crippling depression and his effectiveness as a leader. The despair that might have dragged him under if it had been purely personal was transmuted by the endless quandaries of public affairs into an inexhaustible *patience*. Precisely because he did not assume that reason and justice would inevitably or easily triumph, but at the same time thought it impossible that ignorance and evil could hold them permanently at bay,

Lincoln strove with every fiber of his being to maintain his goal, and then allowed destiny to work out the precise time and degree to which that aim would be fulfilled.

A LETTER TO his intimate friend from youth, Joshua Speed, written five years before ascending to the presidency, is the only time, as Charnwood puts it, that "Lincoln opened his heart about politics" in an unguarded way. Speed came from a prominent Kentucky family and went west to make his fortune. He and Lincoln became friends in Springfield in the 1830s when Lincoln was starting out as a lawyer. In the letter, Lincoln makes a rare confession of that intense ambition that he expressed in public only once, in the Lyceum speech, but whose fires still banked within: "I have no doubt it is the peculiar misfortune of both you and me to dream dreams of Elysium far exceeding all that anything earthly can realize." In Greek mythology, the Elysian fields were reserved for the souls of those who had been great conquerors and statesmen in life—that is, for the tribe of the eagle Lincoln had described at Springfield. Here is confirmation that Lincoln included himself among such men. Since the Lyceum speech of all those years before, however, he has come down to earth: he foresees a life of earthly political work, within the bounds set for him by America and its burgeoning crisis over slavery.

The rest of Lincoln's letter to Speed sets forth his inner political compass. He begins by acknowledging their disagreement about slavery. Speed, according to Lincoln, admits "the abstract wrong of it," but defends the legal right of slave owners to their property and would rather "see the union dissolved" than have that right abrogated. Lincoln claims he is not asking Speed or any other slave owner—by which we must understand him to mean any *current* slave owners—to give up that right. "I also acknowledge your rights and my obligations under the Constitution in regard to your slave." This, then, is the Lincoln who so far only opposes the extension of slavery to new territories. Where established already, although a moral evil, slavery will remain, hopefully to wither away with time. At this point, he essentially embodies the same position as the Union's future great battlefield foe Robert E. Lee and his ancestor Thomas Jefferson. He is nothing like the firebrand abolitionists would have preferred.

Most remarkable, however, is the purely personal cri de coeur that Lincoln permits himself in the letter over the suffering of the slave, a horror that seared him from youth. "I confess I hate to see the poor creatures hunted down and caught and carried back to their stripes and unrequited toil," he tells his old friend, "but I bite my lips and keep quiet." This was a pang of conscience that Lincoln would not allow himself to indulge in public, lest he alienate fluid and undecided opinion that might eventually be won over or at least not actively support the pro-slavery side.

In this connection, Lincoln goes on to recall a steamboat trip from Louisville to St. Louis that he and Speed had taken in 1841. The ship was also carrying a dozen shackled, miserable slaves being transported for delivery to the market in human chattel. "That sight was a continual torment to me, and I see something like it every time I touch the Ohio or any other slave border." Here we have a window into the burning sense of injustice that sickened Lincoln when he was even in the physical proximity of a slave state. It is consistent with a story, widespread but never verified, that as a young man of twenty-two while visiting New Orleans Lincoln had trembled with rage at his first sight of a slave market. "By God, boys . . . if I ever get a chance to hit that thing, I'll hit it hard!" he reportedly told his companions. We must wonder whether his sympathy for the wretched human cargo on the steamboat to St. Louis was not heightened by the helpless vulnerability he felt from his own childhood, when his widowed father abandoned his family to woo a new wife and returned six months later to find his miserable children in rags and malnourished. Lincoln may well have been traumatized at an early age by the shattering revelation that a person can be cast adrift in life and become absolutely helpless; that human goodness and decency cannot be taken as givens. Having known as that ragged and abandoned child what it meant to feel helpless and utterly powerless, he must have had a keen fellow feeling for that vastly worse oppression to which the slaves on that steamboat were subjected all their lives.

Lincoln tells Speed that he is wrong to think that only slave owners like himself have an "interest" in the issue as property owners, and that nonowners should butt out and mind their own business. Lincoln gently chides Speed for not realizing that there are other interests beyond property interests—including the interest of conscience:

> It is not fair for you to assume that I have no interest in a thing which has, and continually exercises, the power to make me miserable.

Lincoln goes on to confess his revulsion at the fact that his public career has forced him to compromise in *any* way over slavery in the United States. Limiting his public objections to the extension of slavery is a sacrifice of his own best instincts, one he makes in order to preserve the Union that both he and Speed love. He extends his own ambivalence to the North as a whole, using Christian imagery to liken the North's tolerance of existing slavery to the crucifixion of its conscience on behalf of a patriotic desire to preserve the Union:

> You ought rather to appreciate how much the great body of the northern people do crucify their feelings, in order to maintain their loyalty to the constitution and the union. I do oppose the extension of slavery, because my judgement and feelings so prompt me, and I am under no obligations to the contrary. If for this you and I must differ, differ we must.

In other words, what Speed sees as intolerable meddling in southern and states' rights, and abolitionists see as a vacillating middle ground, Lincoln defends as a realistic compromise that exerts a great psychological toll on those who must put up with it: "I now do no more," he concludes this train of thought, "than oppose the extension of slavery." Is the qualifying "now" a harbinger of the future?

Finally, Lincoln addresses an issue for which he was frequently taken to task—his support of, or at least refusal to repudiate, the Know-Nothings, a xenophobic movement opposed to new, non–

Anglo Saxon emigrants and to Catholics. He disavowed sharing their beliefs, but he also sought not to alienate their support. In terms of political tactics, the issue was clear. The Know-Nothings were largely drawn from the old stock—ethnically Anglo-Saxon and fiercely Protestant—of the original settlers of the thirteen colonies. Proud of their historical preeminence and deeply hostile toward the Catholic creed of many of the newer immigrants, they tried to maintain their status and exclude the newcomers. Yet many of these same people were among the staunchest abolitionists: The same fundamentalist Protestantism that animated their ugly anti-Catholicism and diatribes about popish encroachment also fueled their hatred of slavery with the uncompromising morality of the Old Testament prophets. As far back as the 1700s, pious believers—such as the Quaker moralist John Woolman—had preached tirelessly for the eradication of this moral blot on the righteous God-fearing people of the new Jerusalem. Lincoln simply could not afford to alienate these people.

As to his being a Know-Nothing himself, as he pleads to his old friend, "how could I be? How can anyone who abhors the oppression of Negroes be in favor of degrading classes of white people?" If Lincoln believes in the equality of black Americans, how can he not believe in the equality of Irish Catholics and Jews? The founders had been bad enough—Lincoln goes on in a very rare criticism of the fathers—for declaring in effect that " 'all men are created equal except Negroes.' " If the Know-Nothings "get control, it will read, 'all men are created equal, except Negroes, foreigners and Catholics.' " Before this happens, he declares, he would emigrate to a country like Russia, where despotism "can be taken pure, and without the base alloy of hypocrisy."

THE ENDGAME OF the old Union began with Justice Taney's majority decision for the United States Supreme Court in the *Dred Scott* case in 1857 that the exclusion of slavery from *any* state or territory was unconstitutional, *regardless* of whether local majorities wanted it or not. This went far beyond the position of Stephen Douglas—whom Lincoln debated in 1858 in a Senate campaign—that the states and territories should decide the matter for themselves, a view already implied by the repeal of the Missouri Compromise three years previously. It lent weight to John C. Calhoun's argument that the southern states effectively constituted a separate nation whose right to own slaves was beyond the purview of the federal government. It would now be the law of the land that the federal authority of the Union must enforce the right of owners to keep slaves everywhere. A key part of the Taney decision was its finding that black slaves were not human beings at all, but property, and that the right to acquire and possess property was universal and could admit of no exceptions. As Madison had written, echoing John Locke, it was the "first object" of legitimate government.

Whereas abolitionists wanted to purge this inconsistency by making slaves explicitly free and equal like all other Americans, Taney wanted to purge it by making slaves explicitly and permanently unfree, maintaining that they were neither American nor, strictly speaking, human. As many astonished observers said at the time, the Taney decision obviously violated the intent of the founders and the understanding of their contemporaries about how the Constitution was meant to work. After all, at the very time Taney declared that blacks could not be citizens and have citizen rights, in many states they had been exercising such rights fully for decades. The Taney decision violated all such precedent and tore the Constitution into pieces. As Charnwood put it:

> [I]t is enough to say this much: the first four presidents— that is, all the presidents who were in public life when the constitution was made—had all acted unhesitatingly upon the belief that Congress had the power to allow or forbid slavery in the territories.

The *Dred Scott* decision abundantly confirmed what Lincoln had seen as the inescapable logic of Douglas's defense of local majorities deciding on slavery, and threatened to make it the law of the land. If it was truly within a territory's legitimate authority to decide by popular vote whether other human beings can be enslaved, then it only follows that a popular majority could decide to enslave *anyone*—free black citizens or white people. This must follow from the fact that, in truth, black Americans are human beings like other Americans. If they can be reduced to the nonhuman, so, therefore, can any group.

The ensuing crisis found its savior in Lincoln's long-standing inner conviction. As Charnwood concludes, "it was at this late period of bewilderment and confusion that the life-story of Abraham Lincoln became one with the life-story of the American people." Lincoln's moment had come.

It was a striking irony that the increase in the extension of slavery made possible by both the repeal of the Missouri Compromise and the *Dred Scott* decision, which made Lincoln's earlier middle ground less tenable, finally paved the way for him to pursue the authentic object of his ambition: the eventual complete abolition of slavery. Like Aristotle's great-souled man, Lincoln flourished only in crisis. His talents came fully to the fore in the same proportion as compromise became less possible. As Charnwood writes of Lincoln,

> He has himself recorded that the repeal of the Missouri Compromise meant for him the "sudden revival in a far stronger form" of his interest in politics, and, we may add, of his political ambition. The opinions which he cherished most deeply demanded no longer patience but vehement action.

After crossing the moral Rubicon provided by the repeal, Lincoln's public pronouncements grew exponentially in both fervor and rigor. He unflinchingly associated Judge Douglas with the odious views of Taney:

> [Douglas] has no very vivid impression that the Negro is a human; and consequently has no ideas that there can be any moral question in legislating about him. In his view, the question of whether a new country shall be slave or free, is a matter

of utter indifference, as it is whether his neighbor shall plant his farm with tobacco.

Charnwood offers the following instructive gloss on Lincoln's evolving understanding of American public opinion and how it took on firmer shape and substance at this time:

> "Public opinion on any subject," he said, "always has a 'central idea' from which all its minor thoughts radiate. The 'central idea' in our public opinion at the beginning was, and till recently has continued to be, 'the equality of man'; and, although it has always submitted patiently to whatever inequality seemed to be a matter of actual necessity, its constant working has been a steady and progressive effort towards the practical equality of all men." The fathers, he said again, had never intended any such obvious untruth as that equality actually existed, or that any action of theirs could immediately create it; but they had set up a standard to which continual approximation could be made.

In Lincoln's interpretation of the American founding, in other words, equality is not understood as a current description of *fact*, but as an *ideal* continually to be striven for. Was this actually the case? Or is Lincoln showing how a visionary statesman can radically alter a nation's course without appearing to violate—indeed, appearing only to revive—its founding principles? As we observed in Part One, the best political rhetoric aims to bring a nation to improve itself by convincing citizens that they are not making a bold departure from the past but merely living up to its highest existing potential. It was a bit of a false leap for Lincoln to argue that, since the founders could not have believed that equality actually existed, they must have intended it as a goal for continual future striving. What they probably actually intended is closer to this: Human beings have certain inalienable rights, such as life, liberty, and the pursuit of happiness. They can delegate some of their rights to a representative government, whose officers will exercise their authority on their behalf. That government will maintain the rule of law to protect everyone. But it will also refrain from intruding upon the basic civil liberties of free speech, freedom of worship, freedom of association, and property rights.

In other words, Enlightenment students that they were, the founders did not see equality as a *goal* so much as a *minimum*, a starting point: We are all equal by nature. For government to function and protect us from one another's aberrant behavior, we must delegate our rights of self-protection to an authority we elect. In turn, we obey that legitimate authority and enjoy our other liberties as best we may. The founders, in fact, explicitly rejected the attempt to achieve an actual equality of condition as dangerously radical and the enemy of merit. They believed in the equality of opportunity for an earned inequality of result. Lincoln took their definition of equality much further, pledging something like continual political action to work toward actual equality of condition. Although he may not have imagined this project extending to all spheres of life—to literal economic equality, for example—it was important to adopt a radical formulation of the principle in order to portray slavery as an intolerable violation of the original compact.

As the Lincoln biographer Harry Jaffa argues, it was indeed a second American Revolution. In order to prevent the impression that he was blaming the founders too severely, Lincoln maintained that they acquiesced to slavery out of a pressing need to create a unified government and not squander the fruits of their victory over Britain: "They yielded to slavery what the necessity of the case required, and they yielded nothing more." In Lincoln's view, the founders assumed that the establishment of freedom for the former colonies would extend steadily toward freedom for the slaves: "The fathers place slavery where the public mind could rest in the belief that it was in the course of ultimate extinction." Instead, it had grown in a way the founders could never have anticipated—and thus the statesmen working to abolish it, or at least forbid its extension, were not reversing the founders' intention but bringing it to fruition: "to put slavery back where the fathers placed it."

Here is Charnwood's trenchant summing up of the dilemmas crowding around Lincoln as he approached the presidency:

The difference of which people grown accustomed to slavery among their neighbors thought little, between letting it be in Missouri, which they could not help, and letting it cross the border into Kansas, which they could help, appeared to Lincoln the whole tremendous gulf between right and wrong, between a wise people's patience with ills they could not cure and a profligate people's acceptance of evil as their good. And here was a distinction between Lincoln and many Republicans, which again may seem subtle, but which was really far wider than that which separated him from the abolitionists. Slavery must be stopped from spreading into Kansas not because, as it turned out, the immigrants into Kansas mostly did not want it, but because it was wrong, and the United States, where they were free to act, would not have it.

According to Aristotle's teaching about ethics, virtue is a mean between two extremes, but closer to one extreme than the other. In these terms, then, Lincoln at this juncture represents a mean between the extremes of immediate abolitionism and limitless slaveholding, but closer to the abolitionist extreme. Lincoln opposed the spread of slavery to Kansas not because Kansas didn't happen to want it, but because the Union *could not tolerate* its moral stain spreading further. Here is as complex a syllogism as has ever faced an American leader. Justice Taney took the stance that slavery *could not* be restricted, regardless of what local majorities believe. Judge Douglas took the stance that, while he personally did not approve of the existence of slavery, the states must be allowed to decide yes or no for themselves. The pure abolitionists, the opposite of Taney, argued that slavery must not be allowed anywhere, North or South, old state or new. Lincoln's view was that, for now, it must be tolerated where it is already established, but that it must not be extended further regardless of the opinion of the new territories. As is often the case with great statesmen, it was an early measure of his final triumph that Lincoln managed to dissatisfy everyone in equal measure.

As Charnwood sums up Lincoln's search for the mean between extremes:

> Two things we can say with certainty of his aim and purpose. On the one hand . . . whatever view he had taken of the peril to the union he would never have sought to avoid the peril by what appeared to him a surrender of the principle which gave the union its worth. On the other hand, he must always have been prepared to uphold the union at whatever the cost might prove to be. To a man of deep and gentle nature, war will always be hateful, but it can never, any more than an individual death, appear the worst of evils.

In this same spirit, Winston Churchill recognized in his great predecessor a classic "trimmer," ready to change tactics as required by circumstance in order to flexibly pursue the long-range purpose. As he wrote of Lincoln:

> Anxious to keep the ship on an even keel and steer a steady course, he may lean all his weight now on one side and now on the other. His arguments in each case when contrasted can be shown to be not only very different in character, but contradictory in spirit and opposite in direction; yet his object will throughout have remained the same. . . . [W]e cannot call this inconsistency. The only way a man can remain consistent amid changing circumstances is to change with them while preserving the same dominating purpose.

The logic of enslavement, Lincoln repeatedly insisted after the repeal of the Missouri Compromise, now extended to everyone. The principle of slavery's limitless extension was, at bottom, as true of Douglas's position as it was of Tancy's, for Douglas's position also allowed slavery to be extended, and would allow a local state or territorial majority that today forbade slavery to change its mind tomorrow. As Charnwood sums up Lincoln's views:

> The proposed principle could, as Lincoln contended, be reduced to this simple form—that, if one man chooses to enslave another, no third man shall have the right to object.

And further:

> The "central idea" which had now established itself in the intellect of the southerner was one which favored the enslavement of man by man "apart from color." A definite choice had to be made between the principle of the fathers, which asserted certain rights for all men, and that other principle against which the fathers had rebelled and of which the "divine right of kings" furnished Lincoln with his example.

So the Civil War would in effect continue the American Revolution; where the antagonist once was Britain, now it was the South. Yet the deeper struggle was against that part of the original founding still insufficiently egalitarian. In effect, the Civil War continued not only the American Revolution but its predecessor, the Glorious Revolution, which had begun to establish the rights of man and responsible government in Britain. In this sense it would revive the English civil wars between Protestant Roundhead and royalist Cavaliers. While the North would revive the role of the Protestant reformers, the Cavalier spirit would be epitomized by the man who emerged as the South's most formidable champion, Robert E. Lee.

The Great Antagonist: Robert E. Lee

Having lived there for a year and visited many times, I have always been charmed by the city of Washington, D.C. I know that people complain about the crime, the lack of a nightlife, the nine-to-five and early-to-bed mentality, the two-hour drive into three surrounding states to find an affordable house. But, for a foreign visitor, the city has a kind of Roman imperial magic. The marble, the domes, the Palladian staircases—the influence of Jeffersonian classicism is everywhere, a deliberate echo of that older republic that trails down through the ages to the American republic, a combination of Roman dedication to the rule of law with democratic opportunity and the compassion of the Abrahamic faiths. There was a spot I always looked forward to reaching on my daily walk from the row house we were renting on a cobblestoned street near the Folger Library to my office in the old Smithsonian building. It was when you walked past the Capitol toward the Arboretum that the National Mall swung into view from a height, a succession of Greek and Roman columns and pediments massed in the distance, ending in Washington's soaring obelisk at the other end. It sounds silly, but it really looked like an enormous and convincing set of imperial Rome in one of those great old epic films like *Cleopatra* or *The Robe* that had fired my childhood imagination about the ancient world.

In the year I spent there, as a visiting fellow at the Woodrow Wilson International Center for Scholars, I happened to occupy an office on the top floor of one of the gothic turrets of the old redbrick "Castle" at the Smithsonian Institution, where the center was housed at the time. Ensconced in my aerie, I had a sweeping view of the Mall from the mullioned windows. I was writing a book about statesmanship in the thought of Plato, and, corny though it may have seemed, I took inspiration from the idea that I was writing about the ancient republics with the splendid buildings of today's Rome visible all around me.

One beautiful spring day, with the smell of blossoms on the air, I took the Metro to Arlington National Cemetery. As I walked up the long winding hill, I confronted the somber and appallingly long rows of military gravestones. This much I expected. What I did not anticipate was that at the summit of the hill I would come across the home of Robert E. Lee. I had seen its columns peeking out through the trees in the hills above the Potomac when driving around the city below, and knew vaguely that it was open to visitors. But I didn't know it would offer itself as a part of my visit to the cemetery.

There was something enchanting about the house and its setting.

It was a weekday and there were no other visitors; I stood alone on the large Greek Revival front portico, with its forest of enormous white columns, and looked out over the scene. The modern city of Washington largely vanished beneath the treetops all around. Standing there alone in the quiet, washed by a balmy breeze, the smell of blossoms and the buzz of cicadas all around, one could easily imagine being transported back to the days when Lee lived here, and "Washington City" was still a parcel of muddy tracks and newly surveyed land.

It was the view from the house of a patrician member of the old planter aristocracy of Virginia, a descendant through marriage of George Washington. For a moment, the old antebellum America seemed to live beneath me—the America of the original Federalist and Democratic-Republican ruling class, often educated gentry with landed wealth, not unlike the gentlefolk of middling position in Jane Austen's novels. The interior of the house was all dark oak and creaking floorboards, with the wonderful smell of old wood and oiled furniture. The rooms were hushed, lovingly redecorated and furnished in the precise style of when the Lees lived there, before the house was abandoned and trashed during the war. I stood in the parlor where Lee spent his famous long night of the soul, agonizing with his wife over Lincoln's offer to take supreme command of the Union Army. It was there that Lee finally concluded that, much as he abhorred the thought of the Union breaking up, he could not make war against his first and real "country," the Commonwealth of Virginia.

I had been fascinated by Lee all my life, ever since my parents gave me a picture book about the American Civil War when I was a boy. I loved the smart gray uniforms of the southern soldiers, a somehow more aristocratic color than the Union blue, the cavalier dash and swagger of the Confederate troops, Lee's gentlemanly calm and effortless elegance and breeding—though I knew, even at that age, that Lincoln and the Union cause were 100 percent right, the South 100 percent wrong. It was my first experience of the possibility that justice and beauty do not always coincide. Also, I felt there was something about Lee that placed him above his fellow Confederates. Although his face in photographs was always composed and serene, when you looked at the eyes, you saw how extraordinarily worn they were, as if envisioning a terrible prospect for a very long time and internalizing the suffering of his people. But the eyes also spoke of confusion, of not quite understanding how it had come to this terrible pass in the world's most decent country.

Lee has often been granted a special and striking exemption by Americans, even in the North, from the opprobrium and disgrace visited upon the other main Confederate leaders. It was as though everyone sensed how painful his choice had been, and sensed his lack of hatred toward his enemies. Within a few years of the war, he was one of the most admired men in the United States, although he remained mostly out of the spotlight and refused to exploit his experiences for profit. Instead, entirely in keeping with his atavistic character, Lee became the much-loved president of a small liberal arts college in Virginia, ending his life in seemly repose, much like a character in an Austen novel. He worked tirelessly to improve the college's academic standing and declared its "one rule" to be "that every student is a gentleman." He maintained that young men bent on a military career have a particular need to be liberally educated. In the course of Lee's life, and this concluding reflection, there is something of the ancient world, of the attempt of a Scipio Africanus to balance his martial ambition with his devotion to family, country, and higher learning. Of course, it may also be that Lee was simply hiding himself from the world in the aftermath of fighting for a cause he knew in his heart had been wrong.

To generations of American military men, Lee remained the epitome of honor and breeding in the service of war, the perfect gentleman warrior. Arlington Cemetery is the ironic proof of this veneration. The Union general Montgomery Meigs deliberately chose the land around Lee's abandoned house for burying the northern dead, intending it as a desecration and an insult. Instead, the legend of Lee embodied visibly in the splendid old house merged with the aura of sanctity that has surrounded the final resting place for generations of American soldiers, as if his memory and theirs honored one another. Far from being desecrated, the nearby graves sanctified the house and

Lee's reputation. In death, he became the great general for both the North and South.

Lincoln's biographer Charnwood aptly describes the two cultures of North and South at the outbreak of the Civil War. In the North, "the stirring intellect of America old and young was with the Republicans." Powerful voices in literature, politics, and the press, crystallized by Horace Greeley's *New York Tribune*, gathered around the abolitionist cause, or were at least fighting to preserve a Union where slavery would extend no further. In contrast with the intellectual world, polite society sympathized with the South, from which most of the founders had sprung and which still set the tone for fashion and gracious living. "Fashion and that better and quite different influence, the tone of opinion prevailing in the pleasantest society, inclined always to the Southern view of every question." Lee epitomized what fashionable society preferred about the South. But that would have been the case whether there had been a Lincoln presidency or not. By contrast, Lincoln, the frontier boy who did not know what color gloves to wear to the opera when he visited New York as president, became the unexpected avatar of the best and the brightest among the intellectual classes of the Northeast, young idealists like the classics professor Joshua Chamberlain of Maine, who played a heroic role at the Battle of Gettysburg, or the poet Walt Whitman, for whom Lincoln was "my captain." An analogous irony took place a century later when the progressive Boston Brahmins aiding Jack Kennedy found themselves serving the uncouth Texan Lyndon Johnson, who through the Civil Rights Act brought to full fruition an agenda toward which his predecessor had made only gracious gestures of intention. It took the rougher-hewn and more pragmatic man to bring about in reality the greatest step forward in civil rights since Lincoln himself.

Firsthand descriptions of Lee often echo those of Washington's innate nobility. As Charnwood details:

> The epithet Cavalier has been fitly enough applied to Lee. . . . To quote from a soldier's memoirs, Wolseley calls Lee "one of the few men who seriously impressed and awed

me with their natural, their inherent greatness"; he speaks of "his majesty," and of the "beauty" of his character, and of the "sweetness of his smile and the impressive dignity of the old-fashioned style of his address." "His greatness," he says, "made me humble."

This sounds exactly like the man described by his son in his recollections of his childhood. On a personal level, Lee was a conscientious husband and family man, always attentive to his invalid wife, Mary Custis, devoted to his sons and daughters, writing to them constantly from the front and taking a minute interest in their every activity. Like Jefferson among his forebears in the Virginia gentry, he took a keen interest in the gardening and decor of his houses—even his tent while away at war was tastefully accoutered. His life manifested a level of calm and wholeness that Lincoln's nervous energy and abstemious, ruminating temperament altogether prevented.

In the early stages of the war, under Lee's direction, the South was able to inflict a series of devastating defeats or stalemates on the North that seemed to make light of the North's overwhelming superiority in munitions and manpower. This stemmed in part from the incompetence of Lincoln's generals, but also from the culture and traditions of the South. As Charnwood reports, Southerners of the time were "bred to an outdoor life" and accustomed to living frugally. "Above all, all classes . . . were still accustomed to think of fighting as a normal and suitable occupation for a man; while the prevailing temper of the north thought of man as meant for business, and its higher temper was apt to think of fighting as odious and war as out of date."

Lee embodied the atavistic qualities of the Jeffersonian "yeoman farmer." He, not Jefferson Davis or the other politicians, was the South's natural leader. Charnwood writes:

> He could have been dictator of the Confederacy had he chosen . . . but it was not in his mind to do anything but his duty as a soldier. The best beloved and most memorable by far of all the men who served that lost cause, he had done nothing

to bring about secession at the beginning, nor now did he do anything but conform to the wishes of [Davis].

Ultimately, Lee was neither of the North nor even entirely of the South; he fought for Virginia. But herein lies his tragedy: He was forced to divorce justice from loyalty. While Lincoln was firmly fixed on ending slavery, flexible only as to timing and tactics, Lee chose a false middle ground. He was neither pro-slavery nor pro-secession. But he was not antislavery or pro-Union either. Like his Virginia predecessor Thomas Jefferson, Lee owned slaves while regarding the institution of slavery as a sin. In a letter to his wife in 1856, he wrote: "There are few, I believe, in this enlightened age who will not acknowledge that slavery as an institution is a moral and political evil." But its abolition, he went on, can only come about by the slow spread of enlightened opinion and the favor of God, "with whom a thousand years is but a single day." He opposed Virginia's secession from the Union, but would not accept command of the Union forces. Through these ambiguities, he tried to preserve his personal honor and integrity at the sacrifice of moral principle, standing aside from the great debate in which he was better equipped than most to participate, and in which he would have had enormous influence in the South. Like the pious and moderate Athenian general Nicias in Thucydides' account of the Peloponnesian War—whom he resembles in breeding and personal probity—Lee sought an illusory middle ground that preserved his own self-respect but sacrificed what was best for his country.

While justice requires this exacting judgment, one still tarries with Lee's personal grace on the eve of the great conflagration that would render his world "gone with the wind." Lee was the perfect expression of a personally noble character and a stainless reputation for courage, honor, gallantry, love of family, and respect for higher learning. He was more balanced, more integrated, than Lincoln, aesthetically more pleasing. In photos, Lincoln is all angular, black, bony and creased, slightly disheveled, as if he couldn't be bothered smoothing himself out for the camera in the brief pause between sleepless nights and endless, grinding dispatches to the front. Lee is compact, self-possessed, rounded and composed, his white hair and beard fatherly and protective. The scarf swept around his neck behind his epaulettes has a slightly jaunty air, the attention to a dashing appearance that an old cavalry man is permitted to allow himself. In eyewitness accounts of his appearances before the troops or the public, he was always magnificently mounted, erect, unsmiling but unfailingly gracious, touching his hat to the ladies, never raising his voice even in anger, his gentlest reproof a source of long agony to the young officer who had failed him in some point of conduct. He refused to castigate the enemy—indeed, even to mention them by name, as if too fastidious to admit the existence of a political cause behind the war, or as if it would be vulgar to stoop to arguing about right and wrong. Even in battle, he referred to the Union simply as "those people." Was he unable to bring himself to admit that they were his fellow Americans, or face the possibility that he no longer was one of their number? Calling Lincoln's armies "those people" made it sound as if they were faceless inexplicable raiders who had dropped from the sky.

Where Abraham Lincoln was all nervous energy, zeal, compassion, and woe, Robert E. Lee was all balance, seemly reserve, gravitas, and courtesy. Lincoln wanted to convince you, to shoulder your burden and entreat you to share his. "In his company," Frederick Douglass recalled, "I was never in any way reminded of my humble origin, or of my unpopular color." Lee believed it would be indelicate to presume that you need to hear his view about the conflict: Gentlemen do their duty; that is enough. But his moderation was of the kind that ultimately did a disservice to his country. Like Nicias, he allowed his love of peace, his concern with his own reputation and roots, to render him neutral in a cause where no thoughtful man could be neutral. They were wrong for diametrically opposite reasons: Nicias should have done everything in his power to prevent war, while Lee should have done everything to help Lincoln win it. But their errors stemmed in both cases from a faulty notion of moderation—from the delusion that personal integrity can be separated from what is right.

It was not enough that Lee opposed secession, that he regarded slavery as an evil, that he wished slavery would fade away, that he opposed its extension. His middle ground was an illusion, because it allowed radical slavers to rise to power and almost win out. He was a beautiful man, but innocent in a way that served corruption, though he himself was not corrupt. His nobility was at its worst a failure of moral imagination, a benign but naïve wish to live and let live when tolerance could only mean consigning millions to slavery and torture. The scenes his son sketches of his domestic life, the love of his children, his tender devotion to his crippled wife, the orderliness of his daily routines and attention to the gracious details of decor and table—it is as if we are transported to the world of Jane Austen, a green Augustan world of white-pillared houses, picnic expeditions, and the hunt—not a world in which half a million men soaked the fields with their blood in a carnage never before known in modern military history, to remove an institution that consigned millions of men, women, and children to be whipped and branded as chattel livestock. Lee lives on in an older America when that America is doomed to pass away in an ocean of blood, overdue payment for the crime it tried to overlook and hide from itself for so long.

When Lincoln, through the intermediary Francis Blair, offered Lee the chance to direct the Union Army, Lee thanked him politely, conveyed his compliments to the president, and returned the few miles to his great plantation house, where he spent the night talking it over with his wife, Mary. Imagine how different things would have been if he had said yes—if Lincoln could have counted on the brilliance Lee was to display at Second Bull Run, Fredericksburg, and Chancellorsville, battles that earned him comparison to Caesar and Alexander, such that cadets from the great military academies of the Old World attended his battlefields to observe the master firsthand. Imagine if Lincoln could have had a Lee in the opening days of the war, rather than the preening plume-hatted McClellan, who drilled and drilled and drilled his shiny columns, lost in his resentment of a president whom he considered his social inferior, dreaming of being an American Napoleon but unwilling to fire a shot. Lee's refusal, however sincerely intentioned and painfully felt, arguably cost thousands of lives by prolonging the war.

As Julian Hawthorne has observed, the first Union defeat at Bull Run shocked Lincoln and the Union forces into showing more resolve, but its immediate impact was to buoy up the Southerners, convincing them that their bravery and élan trumped the North's greater numbers, factories, and money. Lee allowed his troops to persevere in this delusion. His stunning victory at Chancellorsville, where he lured and encircled a much larger Union Army and shattered it, entered the history books along with Cannae and Austerlitz. Lee sent his troops roaming the valleys of the Shenandoah mountains, darting forth and striking as far north as Pennsylvania—a political strategy meant to terrorize the politicians in Washington and force a truce; the gambit came very close to working. Lee knew very well that the South would lose a prolonged war through attrition, no matter how bravely its men fought; the North's superiority in manpower and munitions was growing exponentially. In the short term, however, this very insight made his men believe that he and they together were invincible—that fighting spirit could overcome any mere material disadvantage.

Lincoln may have lacked Lee's personal grace and polish. As mentioned above, he was once laughed at in New York and ridiculed in the city's press for wearing the wrong-colored gloves to a performance of Verdi's *A Masked Ball*. Lee would have known such things without even remembering how he knew them. But, for Lincoln, all such externals had to be sacrificed, had to be burned away, in the cold fire of moral resolve. That is why Lincoln overshadowed Lee as the greater man. Without ever fully realizing it, Lee was outflanked at every turn by Lincoln's moral syllogism: If slavery isn't wrong, then all the things Lee most abhorred—cowardice, indelicacy, libertinage, coarseness, disrespect for education—weren't wrong either. If you could own a fellow human being, why couldn't you be a coward, a rapist, and a scoundrel? Lee's way of life was built on sand. He rode like a great cavalier off the field at Appomattox, rode into history and legend, gracious and modest to the end, saving his one remaining clean uniform for the ceremony of surrender. He was visibly moved when Grant insisted he keep his most treasured sword with its golden scabbard. As he rode back to the southern lines the Confederate men ran after him weeping, calling him "Daddy Lee" and touching his uniform as he passed. Tears streaming down his cheeks, he told them to go home in peace. Refusing to express bitterness, later he told the South: "Abandon your animosities and make your sons Americans." With him went the old America, as it must. Robert E. Lee, the landed aristocrat, was more like the founders than any other man living, certainly more so than Lincoln—but only if one discounts their love of justice, which was more important to the founders than their cultivation and breeding.

If one could be a gentleman without being just, then Lee was the most perfect gentleman who ever lived. Yet it was his Virginia forebear Thomas Jefferson who had observed of slavery: "I tremble for my country when I reflect that God is just; that his justice cannot sleep forever." In a war fought within America to preserve slavery, Jefferson foresaw, "the Almighty has no attribute which can take side with us in such a contest." These were among Lincoln's favorite words from the Founding Fathers. Lee loved his country, but not enough. He hated almost no one, but slavery needed to be hated.

The Inner Lincoln

As the crisis of secession and the Civil War unfolded, the interaction between Lincoln's personality and his burdens as president gained in depth and intensity, fusing them into an increasingly legendary whole. Lincoln inspired a remarkable range of responses in other people, including those who knew him well, or at least had met him in person, as well as distant observers in America and abroad. Even Karl Marx, ever cynical about the merits of what he dismissingly called "the bourgeois republic," could not suppress some awe about Lincoln. He begins by depicting him as a plain, unimaginative figure with a prosaic mind, motivated by no high principles:

> Lincoln is a *sui generis* figure in the annals of history. He has no initiative, no idealistic impetus . . . no historical trappings. He gives his most important actions always the most

commonplace form. Other people claim to be "fighting for an idea," when it is for them a matter of square feet of land. Lincoln, even when he is motivated by an idea, talks about "square feet."

Marx, whose main constituency was a library carrel, obviously misunderstood Lincoln's genius for reducing complex issues of morality, war, and peace to a seemingly homespun lexicon that ordinary men and women could easily grasp. He even more obviously misunderstood the complex psychology revealed by the Lyceum speech, misjudging Lincoln's commanding presence in American life to be unwilling and unwitting on the president's part:

> He sings the bravura aria of his part hesitatively, reluctantly and unwillingly, as though apologizing for being compelled by circumstances "to act the lion."

Lincoln was not acting. Homespun on the outside, he was lionlike within himself—in his tenacity to save the Union, or split it apart if that was what it took to purge it of the crime of human servitude. Marx goes on to complain about the uninspiring language of Lincoln's decrees, failing to realize that, in a republic of laws deriving its authority from the people, clear language is prized over flowery declamations, while legislative and executive decrees may go no further, owing to legal precedent, than the precise issue in question:

> The most redoubtable decrees—which will always remain remarkable historical documents—flung by him at the enemy all look like, and are intended to look like, routine summonses sent by a lawyer to a lawyer of the opposing party, legal chicaneries, involved, hidebound actiones juris.

For all his woodedheadedness about Lincoln's character, however, Marx recognized the full import of the Emancipation Proclamation before even some Americans, including some on the Union side. As Marx notes, the proclamation was the death of the original American social compact:

> His latest proclamation, which is drafted in the same style, the manifesto abolishing slavery, is the most important document in American history since the establishment of the Union, tantamount to the tearing up of the old American Constitution.

Others were more discerning about Lincoln's character. It is surprising to note that Ralph Waldo Emerson cannot be counted among them. Though he met Lincoln and afterward deemed him worthy of praise, he plainly missed the man's true greatness and genius. Instead, Emerson seems to have been taken in by the public image of "Honest Abe," the backwoods boy who proved that any decent man could rise to the highest office. Others understood how much this public image, perfectly true in its outlines, was a simplification of a far more complicated man. While Lincoln was certainly not ashamed of his origins, as Doris Kearns Goodwin observes, he was in no hurry to recall them—marred as they were by memories of poverty, neglect, and bereavement.

Lincoln knew how far he had come and how extraordinary he was. He was the living proof of what Jefferson had termed the "naturally best," the natural aristocracy. American democracy, Jefferson had argued, would be based not on inherited privilege but on a level playing field that would allow those endowed by nature with superior intelligence and character to excel and rise. Who better than Lincoln demonstrated this principle of equality of opportunity for the earned inequality of result? At the same time, Lincoln did genuinely believe in the natural decency and moral energy of the American people when led toward their better instincts. His gift for leadership did not, in his own eyes, make him essentially superior to his fellow citizens. Yet Emerson seemed to miss these nuances: His surprisingly modest assessment seems slightly tinged with the condescension of the New

England patrician toward his rough-hewn countryman from the frontier: Emerson is pleasantly surprised that Lincoln is not "vulgar":

> The president impressed me more favorably than I had hoped. A frank, sincere, well meaning man, with a lawyer's habit of mind, good clear statement of his facts, correct enough, not vulgar, as described, but with a boyish cheerfulness. . . .

One wonders how many people underestimated Lincoln in this way, and how it must have fueled his steady political rise to have potential opponents continually caught off guard, so that he was easily able to confound their aims and push past them. In this respect, his public image as an ordinary, plainspoken, and prosaic man helped him both to relate to the public and to camouflage his depth of purpose. The image of Lincoln as a kind of Everyman hero was widespread, as expressed by the *New York Times* in 1865: "Everything which made Abraham Lincoln the loved and honored man he was, it is in the power of the humblest American boy to imitate." Imitate, perhaps, but succeed in imitating?

None of this is to suggest that the public image of Honest Abe was a fake. On the contrary, it was drawn from instincts and experiences bred deep within him by his background. He really was an unaffected, straightforward man, as many of those closest to him repeatedly aver. But he was able to build layers of more sophisticated experience and insight achieved from his progress through life and his native intellect on the solid grounding of those humble origins. Many who knew Lincoln admired his intellectual flexibility and freedom from moralistic cant and dogma. "He was no fanatic, wedded to one idea," wrote Charles Hodge in the *Princeton Review* at the height of the war. "If one plan would not do, he would try another." This assessment recalls what Garry Wills said of FDR, reminding us again that tactical flexibility in the service of a core moral aim is a hallmark of great leadership.

Of course, there have been some—yesterday and today—who regard this flexibility as opportunism and a compromising attitude toward abolitionism. Others were struck by his lack of outright hatred toward the South, as opposed to a deep sadness that their actions had brought the war to pass and a firm resolve to defeat them. According to the extraordinary Elizabeth Keckley, a freed slave who founded a school for the poor and became a close friend of Mary Todd Lincoln, "Mr. Lincoln was generous by nature, and though his whole heart was in the war, he could not but respect the valor of those opposed to him." By one account, he reacted to the news of Lee's surrender by throwing open the window and asking the marine band, which was practicing on the White House lawn below, to play "Dixie." Turning back to those in the room, he said that it was "one of the best tunes I have ever heard." Had he lived longer, Lincoln would have taken a less punitive attitude toward the postwar South—at the risk of offending the more zealous abolitionists or Union soldiers looking for revenge.

Many who met Lincoln were struck by his instinctive natural breeding, an innate gentlemanliness stemming from his decency toward people that more than made up for his lack of polish. "There is about him," wrote the British journalist Edward Dicey, "a complete absence of pretension, and an evident desire to be courteous to everybody, which is the essence, if not the outward form, of high breeding." House Speaker Schuyler Colfax paid tribute to Lincoln's lack of rancor in debate and quiet firmness in maintaining his views: "Criticized ever so unjustly, he would reply with no word of reproof, but patiently and uncomplainingly, if he answered at all, strive to prove that he stood on the rock of right." This unpretentious dignity made a powerful impression on many he encountered. Although open-minded and generous in debate, he was no pushover. "Lincoln had great respect for the superior knowledge and culture of other persons," the Union general Carl Schurz recalled. "But he did not stand in awe of them." Harriet Beecher Stowe, whose novel *Uncle Tom's Cabin* did much to inflame public opinion against slavery—and who was therefore a kind of distant partner in Lincoln's mission—was particularly sensitive to the inner steel in Lincoln, which enabled him to be outwardly fair and flexible.

As she perceived, he was willing to adjust his means, but never his end. That is why his quiet inner resolve was sometimes mistaken for infirmity of purpose; in reality, he did not need fiery speeches or flamboyant gestures, for his purpose was immovable. "Lincoln is a strong man, but his strength is of a peculiar kind; it is not aggressive so much as passive, and among passive things, it is like the strength not so much of a stone buttress as of a wire cable." Finally, and at bottom, Lincoln was enigmatic. There were parts of himself that no one could probe—as those closest to him sensed most vividly. "He was a stranger to deceit, incapable of dissembling, seemed to be the frankest and freest of conversationalists," wrote one of his political allies, Alexander McClure, "and yet few understood him reasonably well, and none but Lincoln ever thoroughly understood Lincoln."

How, FINALLY, TO summarize the character of Lincoln? Fundamentally, his soul as a leader was driven by contradictory impulses—by a burning ambition for distinction, and by a melancholy sense of loneliness and separation from the world at large. Satisfying the ambition was meant to fill the hole of the loneliness, and in large measure it may have done so. But Lincoln's sense of life's fragility, of its largely forlorn and doomed hopes for peace and repose, prevented his ambition, once met with success, from becoming merely venal, vain, or satisfied by superficial fame. Success deepened him as a statesman, and eventually his absorption in his own solitariness was transmuted into a compassion for the frailty of his fellow Americans and his fellow human beings.

Perhaps the answer is to be found in Lord Charnwood's reflections about his subject's early ambition. For Charnwood, one of the most important lessons of Lincoln's life was that one cannot advance the cause of justice through statesmanship without first experiencing a hunger for honor. To deny this, he felt, would be either naïve or hypocritical. Far from controverting the values of Christianity—insofar as Christianity adjures us to advance God's justice in the world—a legitimate ambition to serve one's country is itself a Christian virtue:

We must accept without reserve Herndon's reiterated assertion that Lincoln was intensely ambitious; and, if ambition means the eager desire for great opportunities, the deprecation of it, which has long been a commonplace of literature, and which may be traced back to the Epicureans, is a piece of cant which ought to be withdrawn from currency, and ambition, commensurate with the powers which each man can discover in himself, should be frankly recognized as a part of Christian duty.

As Lincoln himself put it in his first try for the Illinois state legislature: "Every man is said to have his peculiar ambition. Whether it be true or not, I can say for one that I have no other so great as that of being truly esteemed of my fellow men, by rendering myself worthy of their esteem." This craving for the honor of his fellow citizens was compounded by Lincoln's sense of being an outsider from the world of the establishment. His humble origins exacerbated his purely innate psychological sense of loneliness and alienation, which he would likely have possessed even had he been born on Beacon Hill. This mood of solitariness enabled him—as it has enabled other leaders, for both ill and good—to feel a unique sense of connection with the public at large, transcending the intermediary bonds of birth, family connections, schools, and inherited status to fuse with the entire nation:

> I was born and have ever remained in the most humble walks of life. I have no wealthy or popular relations to recommend me. My case is thrown exclusively upon the independent voters of this country.

Lincoln's sense that he was able to bond directly with the American people as a whole was likely a source of his celebrated rhetorical abilities. As Thucydides was the first historian to explore, skill at oratory is a requirement for any leader in a democracy, where policy cannot be confined to private negotiation within ruling circles but must be settled with the consent of the public. A feeling of isolation such as Lincoln's may have heightened his sense that he had no bond more important than the one he felt with the entire nation—and that, in turn, may have enhanced his capacity to speak directly from the mind and the heart to his people. Lincoln was not always a brilliant speaker: as befit his legal training, he often confined himself to a narrow parsing of the matter at hand. Tocqueville had already predicted that inasmuch as equality before the law was the most important American social value, more important than any inherited status or attachment to caste and clan, lawyers were likely to emerge as the most influential source of political leadership and the legal mind as the model for clear, straightforward exposition of policy of a kind suited to a democratic temperament that distrusted elaborate rhetorical contrivances. As Charnwood writes:

> If we credit [Lincoln] with occasional manifestations of electric oratory—as to which it is certain that his quiet temperament did at times blaze out in a surprising fashion—it is not to be thought that he was ordinarily what could be called eloquent. Some of his speeches are commonplace enough, and much of his debating with Douglas of a drily argumentative kind that does honor to the mass meeting which heard it gladly.

Daniel Webster, a pillar of early American jurisprudence, set forth what he thought should be the kind of rhetoric suitable for an American statesman: Plain and unadorned on the surface, but moved by an "inner fire" of sincerity and moral conviction.

> Clearness, force and earnestness are the qualities which produce conviction. True eloquence, indeed, does not consist in speech. It cannot be brought from far. Labor and learning may toil for it, but they will toil in vain. Words and phrases may be marshaled in every way, but they cannot compass it. It must exist in the man, in the subject, and in the occasion.

By all accounts, Lincoln fit the bill. This observation goes together well with Lincoln's belief, attested to by many who knew him, that a special destiny, both inspiring and terrifying, hung over him and drew him on. That is what endowed him with the "inner fire" praised by Webster. Charnwood writes:

> [T]he greatest gift of the orator he did possess; the personal- ity behind the words was felt. "Beyond and above skill," says the editor of a great paper who heard him at Peoria, "was the overwhelming conviction imposed upon the audience that the speaker himself was charged with an irresistible and inspiring duty to his fellow man.

Charnwood contrasts Lincoln's speeches with the style pursued in the British Parliament, where the speakers strove to keep the listeners "pleasantly expectant rather than dangerously attentive," so that, even if the arguments "might prove unsubstantial," the audience could be sure that "it all leads in the end to some great cadence of noble sound." Lincoln's style was the exact reverse, as the Gettysburg Address il- lustrates so well. Its most ornamental language comes at the begin- ning, so as to engage the audience's attention; by the ending, Lincoln's words are simple and plain, with no rousing peroration, moving in a direct way, but lacking beautiful contrivances or bravado. Charnwood continues:

> In Lincoln's argumentative speeches the employment of beautiful words is least sparing at the beginning or when he passes to a new subject. It seems as if he deliberately used up his rhetorical effects at the outset to put his audience in the temper in which they would earnestly follow him and to chal- lenge their full attention to reasoning which was to satisfy their calmer judgement.

Charnwood connects Lincoln's well-known melancholy and fa- talism to his statesmanship. It was not a crusade whose idealism is so pure that it cannot compromise with the best opportunity in the given situation, the lesser of evils:

> It is not to be supposed that any undue hopefulness, if he felt it, influenced his judgement. He was of a temper which does not seek to forecast what the future has to show, and his melancholy prepared him well for any evil that might come.

But Lincoln's inner sense of life's frailty or mutability was not only the source of a Stoic fortitude in facing the constant likelihood of adversity and reverses. It also enabled him to identify personally with the uncertain and imperiled destiny of his country, and its as yet unresolved relationship to its Creator or whatever divine force it was that held sway over the universe. America's uncertainties and his own mirrored each other. As Lincoln put it in 1839:

> If ever I feel the soul within me elevate and expand to those dimensions not wholly unworthy of its mighty architect, it is when I contemplate the cause of my country, deserted by all the world beside, and I standing boldly alone and hurling defiance at her victorious oppressors.

As Charnwood notes, after Lincoln achieved his titanic aim of preserving the Union and freeing the slaves, he went unthanked in many quarters; many flattered themselves that they, too, could have done it as readily and perhaps sooner. Charnwood also records how disappointed Lincoln's followers were at first by what they considered his overly cautious and halting progress:

> Above all, in that point of policy which most interests us, we shall witness the long postponement of the blow that killed Negro slavery, the steady subordination of this particular issue to what will not at once appeal to us as a larger and higher issue. All this provoked at the time in many excellent and clever men dissatisfaction and deep suspicion; they longed for

a leader whose heart visibly glowed with a sacred passion; they attributed his patience, the one quality of greatness which after a while everybody might have discerned in him, not to a self-mastery which almost passed belief, but to a tepid disposition and a mediocre if not low level of desire.

As the war wore on toward its final victorious and blood-soaked conclusion, however, Lincoln's earlier willingness to compromise slipped steadily away. He grew sadder, more distant, darker but also deeper and stronger, and soared above even the most selflessly motivated honor toward something like saintliness:

> It seems to be above all true that the exercise of power and the endurance of responsibility gave him new strength. This, of course, cannot be demonstrated, but Americans then living, who recall Abraham Lincoln, remark most frequently on how the man grew into his task. And this perhaps is the main impression which the slight record here presented will convey, the impression of a man quite unlike the many statesmen whom power and the vexations attendant upon it have in some piteous way spoiled and marred, a man who started by being tough and shrewd and canny and became very strong and very wise, started with an inclination to honesty, courage and kindness, and became, under tremendous strain, honest, brave and kind to an almost tremendous degree.

A World Imperial Republic?

In his Lyceum speech, the young Abraham Lincoln called for a political religion to reinvigorate citizen commitment to the ideals of American justice. Ironically, with his immortalization after death, he became the icon in this civil religion—the larger-than-life figure in the marble memorial on the National Mall with which we began this section, the martyr whose creed is "a new birth of freedom." Lincoln would not have seen himself in such superhuman terms. But he might well have understood the value of being seen this way by others, since he had always known the value of joining his own mission to that of the founders, whose select band he came to inhabit. In the panegyrics that followed his death, as his full accomplishment sank in, Lincoln finally joined the tribe of the eagle he had celebrated at the Lyceum.

Even as he was hailed as a successor to the heroes of the ancient republics, Lincoln was also rechristened as the instrument of God's plan. In an 1865 tribute, the renowned Congregationalist minister and abolitionist Henry Ward Beecher placed Lincoln in a line of succession going back to Moses and David:

> And now the martyr is moving in triumphal march, mightier than when alive. The nation rises up at every stage of his coming. Cities and states are his pall-bearers, and the cannon beats the hours with solemn progression. Dead, dead, dead, he yet speaketh! Is Washington dead? . . . Is David dead? Is any man that ever was fit to live dead? Disenthralled of flesh, and risen in the unobstructed sphere where passion never comes, he begins his illimitable work. His life now is grafted upon the infinite, and will be fruitful as no earthly life can.

Thirty years later, Henry Watterston, once an ambivalent supporter of the Confederacy, placed Lincoln squarely in the ranks of the heroes of the ancient world while at the same time comparing him to Christ:

> Where shall we find an example so impressive as Abraham Lincoln, whose career might be chanted by a Greek chorus as at once the prelude and the epilogue of the most imperial theme of modern times? Born as lowly as the Son of God, in a hovel; reared in penury, squalor, with no gleam of light or fair surrounding; without graces, actual or acquired; without name or fame or official training, it was reserved for him to have command at a supreme moment of a nation's fate.

Lincoln's other legacy to America was to cast the Civil War and the abolition of slavery as a direct continuation of the original American Revolution. As a result, it was not only the perpetuation of American freedom that hinged on the just outcome of that conflict, but the prospects for freedom around the world. Just as Jefferson had appealed to "the opinions of mankind" in extolling the young democracy, Lincoln could now offer the eighty-seven-year-old experiment in self-government as mankind's "last, best hope." In explaining why it was crucial that the North win the Civil War, Lincoln explicitly claimed that its significance went far beyond America's own borders: "This is essentially a people's contest—a struggle for maintaining in the world that form and substance of government whose leading object is to elevate the condition of men." He hated slavery not only "because of the monstrous injustice of slavery itself," but "because it deprives our republican principle of its just influence in the world."

By the beginning of the twentieth century, some forty years later, the United States was becoming one of the world's leading military and economic powers, and it brought this sense of a moral mission to its dealings with other nations. At the Republican Convention in 1900—which nominated William McKinley as its candidate, with Theodore Roosevelt as his running mate—the prominent Republican senator Alfred Beveridge delivered a keynote address that caught the heady mood of America's destiny at the opening of the new century.

America's history, Beveridge declaimed, demonstrates that she was designed to be the "master nation" of the world from her earliest Puritan origins:

> It is the "divine event" of American sovereignty among the governments of men for which these forces have been working since the Pilgrims landed on the red man's soil.

No nation would henceforth make war without America's consent—a source of pride for Americans, but also for the good of all mankind:

This is a destiny neither vague nor undesirable. It is definite, splendid and holy. When nations shall war no more without the consent of the American Republic—what American heart thrills not with pride at that prospect?

As American power continued to grow militarily, no government would any longer be able to oppress its own people:

> When governments stay the slaughter of human beings because the American Republic demands it—what American heart thrills not with pride at that prospect? And yet to-night there sits in Constantinople a sovereign who knows that time is nearly here.

When America came to dominate world trade, economic prosperity would be fostered for the entire planet. American military and economic might would both serve America's self-interest and advance freedom for all peoples:

> When the commerce of the world on which the world's peace hangs, traveling every ocean highway of earth, shall pass beneath the guns of the great Republic—what American heart thrills not at that prospect? . . . When any changing of the map of the earth requires a conference of the powers, and when, at any congress of the nations, the American Republic will preside as the most powerful of powers and the most righteous of judges—what American heart thrills not at that prospect?

Did Beveridge turn out to be right? In some cases—the two world wars—definitely. On other occasions—Korea and Vietnam—the benefits have been questionable when weighed against the costs in blood and treasure. However good the intentions behind these forays, they have sometimes been sullied by greed for profit or political opportunism. These sober reflections, thrown into relief by that fin de siècle zenith of optimism that America could be "the most powerful of powers and the most righteous of judges," take us full circle back to Part One of this book and the saga of the modern American presidency. They also raise a broader question: Can a democracy achieve imperial power without endangering its core value of freedom, whether at home or abroad? That question, in turn, takes us further back in time—to the very first democracy, ancient Athens, the original and in some ways still the clearest illustration of the contradictions between freedom and empire.

PART III

The First Democracy

Pericles, Athens, and the Challenge of Freedom

Imagine the following: A great democratic empire that prides itself on its freedom and affluence decides to invade a faraway country whose size and resources it consistently underestimates, dismissing it in effect as "a piss-ant little country." It begins the war with a united front, but at length the conflict opens up fissures in domestic politics. Those who begin with silent misgivings about the morality of foreign wars gradually become outright opponents. They identify the government's projection of military power abroad with the capacity for violence against themselves at home. At the same time, the government finds it must expand its power enormously in order to conduct the war more vigorously—and this increases its power at home. It may be tempted to use this power to quell its opponents. This exacerbates the dissidents' fears that the power needed to win the war abroad threatens democratic freedom at home—that the chief magistrate will become, in effect, an imperialist. At length, the democracy turns against the kind of men who would not have flinched at taking the measures needed to win the war, driving them from office when the power they acquired through expanding the war threatens internal freedom.

The description clearly resembles the American war in Vietnam, culminating in the premature end of two presidencies heavily involved in it. For many, it may also carry hints of the current conflict in Iraq, where a well-intentioned plan to extend democracy to another country kindled widespread dissent at home and undermined another commander in chief. Yet, uncannily, every word of the description also applies to Thucydides' account of the Athenian invasion of the island of Sicily during the Peloponnesian War of 431 to 404 B.C. That invasion was precipitated by the same underestimation of the enemy; led to the same exacerbation of domestic tension; and ended with the main leader of the war party, Alcibiades, being stripped of his authority and forced into exile.

As the historian of the West's first superpower conflict, Thucydides unforgettably explains and anticipates the recurring dilemmas of democracy and empire, generating lessons as powerful as ever for the world after 9/11, the world the next American president will face. The relationship between democracy and empire is one of the oldest themes in the history of statesmanship, and still one of the most relevant. Are democracies especially likely to embark upon imperial expansion? Does the pursuit of empire undermine the civic virtues needed for good government at home? Is the use of force against other countries ever morally justified? Is amassing imperial power abroad likely to increase the danger of tyranny at home? Thucydides is the original and enduring source for reflecting on these questions.

The tensions first uncovered by Thucydides resonate down to the present, for our dilemmas are much the same. Not literally, of course. But the leadership types and challenges form consistent patterns. Hawks versus doves, youth versus age, the importance of rhetoric in a democracy—where public opinion must be won over and shaped—accompanied by the corresponding danger of demagoguery. These patterns were first observed by Thucydides and rediscovered and embellished by every generation down to the Renaissance writers on statecraft, the American founders (who were often both statesmen and political thinkers), Napoleon's far-reaching reforms and tarnished glory, and Lincoln's fascination with the tribe of the eagle. The patterns continue throughout Churchill's driving ambition to safeguard the West from Hitler (an updated version of the despotic aggressor fought off by Athens) and FDR's determination to wage war against the enemies of democracy abroad while rescuing the American economy at home. After that, the cold war against the totalitarian successor to Nazism, the passing of the torch to JFK and his pledge that America would pay any price to defend freedom around the world, down to the mixture of good intentions and miscalculations in the recent American occupation of Iraq.

The traits of temperament, the virtues and character flaws that Thucydides first uncovers in leading figures of the Peloponnesian War like Pericles, Alcibiades, Nicias, and Archidamus reemerge, like a shifting kaleidoscope, in new combinations in response to different constellations of circumstance. Thucydides enables us to see the enduring contradiction and dynamism in the pursuit of empire abroad and the threat it may pose to freedom at home. The original conflict between the martial ambition of Alcibiades and the civilian authorities in Athens over the planned conquest of Sicily repeats itself in a long list of insubordinate, hotheaded, overly sanguine, or incompetent generals vying with their civilian overseers: Caesar versus the Senate, Napoleon versus Talleyrand, McClellan versus Lincoln, Patton versus Eisenhower, MacArthur versus Truman, Westmoreland and LBJ. President Bush's relationship with Secretary of Defense Rumsfeld offers another variation: the aggressive civilian manager of the military overwhelming a civilian commander in chief who tends to avoid the details of planning. Often, although not invariably, this tension between civilian and military authority has been tragic, because the mulish subordinate is sometimes right about how to achieve victory, just as Thucydides says that Alcibiades' war strategy before his recall was as good as could be desired. But the exercise of boldness needed to bring victory about can come at too high a price to the rights of citizens and the authority of elected officials.

Thucydides is also the first to see the mixed motives in a democracy's pursuit of empire that recur throughout the Roman and British empires and the rise of America to world power status marked by the Spanish-American War, the two world wars, and the wars in Korea, Vietnam, and Iraq. None of these wars was undertaken solely out of idealism or materialism alone. The Bush administration's war in Iraq was not "all about oil," but profit was not irrelevant either. So it has been in all of democracy's wars. The recurrent divisions between hawks and doves, between expansionism and isolationism, so familiar from British and American foreign policy debates, so troubling to the founders and in Lincoln's youthful ruminations on the permissible outlet for glory in a democracy, are already visible in the competition between the young hawk and expansionist Alcibiades and the moderate older peace negotiator Nicias. To be sure, much has changed in the world since Thucydides. With each passing century, the technological capacity to wage war has grown inexorably to the point where much of the world could be devastated. But it is therefore all the more striking how consistent the dilemmas of statesmanship remain, and the importance of the human factors of character, prudence, and resolve in coming to grips with them. The fundamental tension between democracy and empire remains in many ways as Thucydides first diagnosed it, so that even as I write these words in the summer of 2008, the clash between noble intentions, profit seeking, and a democratic citizenry uneasy with imperial power has hobbled another American president and saddled his future successor with an unresolved crisis. A new president will emerge to lead the nation and the world into a future marked, as much as ever, by the temptations and challenges of empire.

As WE'LL SEE, Thucydides' judgment about Athenian democracy and its imperial ambitions was complex, and would probably displease both hawks and doves during modern times. On one hand, he makes it clear that the war could very likely have been won had domestic dissent not forced Alcibiades, the man best equipped to achieve victory, from office. Nor was the war necessarily or in every respect unjust; that judgment depends on how one views human nature, our tendency to aggression, the geopolitical sphere, and how much power a country needs to protect its way of life. In this sense, Thucydides was neither a devotee of the ideal of peace—of the possibility that peace can be permanently established everywhere—nor a defender of Kissingerian realpolitik, the notion that international affairs can be conducted purely on the grounds of rational actors who pursue their self-interest as they perceive it. What might put off both sides about Thucydides is his very complicated proposition that the exercise of power is itself always and indivisibly a moral issue. It is not a question of the pursuit of power in contrast with the pursuit of morality, of realism versus idealism. Instead, it is a question of the more or less moral or immoral pursuit of power. Thucydides, for instance, could never have agreed with Jimmy Carter's description of the campaign to reduce energy consumption as "the moral equivalent of war," a phrase suggesting that war in itself could never be moral. Certain kinds of war can be pursued at least in part for a moral purpose, others not at all.

It is possible, Thucydides invites us to consider, that even a democratic regime may have to expand its influence simply in order to keep what it has—and, furthermore, that it is possible for a democracy in particular to promote freedom both at home and abroad while increasing its imperial power. This, at least, was the Athenian claim during that democracy's ascendancy, and Thucydides (himself an Athenian) does not dismiss it out of hand. The war, he tells us, was not a disaster simply or primarily because it was immoral, but because of the very nature of democratic politics. The democratic empire of Athens gives full flower to individualism, ambition, personal freedom, technical innovation, culture, and prosperity. Its greatest statesman, Pericles, praised all these aspects of Athenian society in his famous Funeral Oration that inspired so many succeeding generations of statesmen down to Lincoln's fellow speaker at Gettysburg. But the pursuit of empire at the same time subverted the common good by creating a tension between the individual and the state (in this case, the city-state). The individual's pursuit of open-ended prestige, wealth, and power through imperial expansion may undermine loyalty to the common good. This is neither entirely a factual nor entirely a value judgment, but simply what happens when events collide with personalities. And this tension between democracy at home and empire abroad has overwhelmingly important practical results as well as moral and psychological ones.

Thucydides, for these reasons, stands above both vulgar realpolitik and unworldly moralizing. He himself contends that the lessons in his account render it "a possession for all time," for human nature will never change. The tensions between empire and democracy—which produced great leaders like Pericles and opportunistic ones like Alcibiades—may not repeat themselves precisely. But similar tensions will recur, and analogous leadership personalities will continue to emerge. What Lincoln called the tribe of the eagle will always be with us, for good or for ill, if not always in the same manner.

This is why reading Thucydides can be both sobering and refreshing: In our own time, we tend toward either a pragmatism that ignores morality or a striving for moral purity that disdains what human nature and the conditions of life can realistically sustain. In this light, the ancient writings can seem grimmer and less hopeful than our own pretensions of selfless morality, which proclaim that unconditional peace, equality, and prosperity are both desirable and possible. At the same time, the last century saw millions slaughtered and uprooted in the name of these same fair words—peace, purity, and idealism—and the current century shows no signs of parting with terrorism and genocide carried out on behalf of an allegedly higher cause of faith, patriotism, or world peace. Perhaps, therefore, we might learn something from a writer like Thucydides, who believed that power is inseparable from its moral effects, and that no ideal can be divorced from the capabilities and limits of human nature.

Thucydides distinguishes himself from Homer and the other ancient Greek poetic sources by claiming to be an empiricist: He is describing a real conflict, one that he lived through personally, and he has made every effort to be accurate. Little is known about him from contemporary sources. Born in 460 B.C., he tells us that he was appointed a general in the eighth year of the war. After losing a battle with the Spartans, however, he was exiled for twenty years. We can really know him only from his single masterpiece, which, according to a story that may be apocryphal, was discovered abandoned after Thucydides' death and saved from oblivion by Xenophon, another Athenian general and a companion of Socrates. Some of the lessons Thucydides draws from the war were explored earlier in the ancient Greek tradition: How much honor seeking is appropriate? Where should the line be drawn between encouraging a constructive ambition to serve the common good and giving leeway to potential tyrants disguised as benefactors? Abraham Lincoln would grapple with these same problems in his Lyceum speech of 1838: Is it possible to find a middle ground where a man's belligerent impulses and love of fame can be educated, sublimated, and directed away from tyranny and pointless war making into the honor that comes from serving one's fellow citizens in a republic of laws?

The Homeric tradition was ambivalent about this very issue. In a sense, Homer holds up Achilles as the eternal model for Greek youth. Yet Achilles was deeply insubordinate, withdrawing his services from his allies during the Trojan War out of a purely personal vendetta against their leader, Agamemnon, after a fight over a woman and other perceived slights and insults. The problem is that the tyrant and the leading citizen might, at bottom, share some of the same darkly hubristic, aggressive qualities. The chorus in Sophocles' play *Oedipus the Tyrant*, performed during the Peloponnesian War and very likely an allegorical meditation on its moral ambiguities, express this quandary when they pray that God will protect them from tyrants while at the same time helping the man ambitious to serve his country. This is one part of the tragedy of that play: that, in their subconscious anxiety, the Thebans are not sure which category Oedipus himself falls into—and neither is he. They begin:

> *Insolence breeds the tyrant, insolence*
> *if it is glutted with a surfeit, unseasonable, unprofitable,*
> *climbs to the roof-top and plunges*
> *sheer down to the ruin that must be,*
> *and there its feet are no service.*

But then they qualify their condemnation of ambition:

But I pray that the God may never
abolish the eager ambition that profits the state.
For I shall never cease to hold the God as our protector.

Sophocles is suggesting that the difficulty of distinguishing between the self-professed protector of the state and its would-be tyrant is a permanent quandary of civic life—while hinting between the lines that his fellow Athenians face this very same riddle with their own leaders right now.

These are profound reflections on the soul of a leader, and Thucydides sets them squarely within the context of real life. He asks: Are democracy and empire compatible? Do expansion and economic success necessarily undermine the character of citizens at home, leading to hedonistic self-indulgence and inviting the rise of men so ambitious that they will sacrifice the best interests of the democracy to maximize their own power and glory? Thucydides explores a further quandary: Are democracies not only especially likely to be harmed by acquiring an empire but at the same time especially likely to embark on doing so? A regime that promotes the well-being and affluence of the individual may not be able to satisfy the expectations it encourages within its own borders. It may need the wealth that only an expansionist foreign policy can bring—while awakening the desire for individualism in the nations with which it comes into contact.

According to Thucydides, sometimes freedom must be defended by force. Athens would not have risen to empire had she not first been compelled to defend herself and the other Greek city-states against the overwhelming might of Persia, by far the most advanced and powerful regime of that era, a vast, well-ordered, and affluent multinational empire of millions of subjects, capable of fielding a standing army of perhaps two hundred thousand well-equipped and trained men. Athens was the first to discover what Britain found out after the defeat of Napoleon and America after the victory in World War II: It is not so easy to renounce the geopolitical power that can suddenly fall into a nation's hands after an immediate peril recedes. The nation that has a tiger by the tail, in other words, may not be able to let it go—and may not want to.

EVER SINCE THUCYDIDES' history reappeared in the West in Lorenzo Valla's Latin translation in 1452 , it has exercised a profound and continuing influence on modern assessments of democracy and leadership. The English political thinker Thomas Hobbes, who made the first translation of the work into English in 1650, was forcefully struck by Thucydides' bleak account of the horrors of civil war engendered by the conflict between Athenian democracy and Sparta's oligarchical rule. This ideological struggle between the two superpowers undermined the internal political harmony of their allies, leading extreme partisans on each side to usurp local authority and wield it exclusively on behalf of its own faction to the detriment of the other. Hobbes saw a direct parallel between these horrors and those of the English civil wars of his own era. In his view, Thucydides' account offered historical evidence that only an absolute monarch can restrain the potential terrors of human nature when the authority of law lapses—can prevent the "war of all against all," driven by the natural striving for power, wealth, and prestige.

Hobbes felt that Thucydides' account also proved that democracy was the worst possible form of government, the most prone to factional strife, demagoguery, and mob rule. In its promotion of individualism and the free expression of opinion, it came closer than any other particular form of government to the sheer license and anarchy of the state of nature itself, mirroring on a daily basis the war of all against all. The brief brilliant interval when Athens was led by Pericles—a man who put what was best for Athens ahead of his personal ambition—only confirmed this view. According to Hobbes, Pericles was a monarch in all but name; he was the exception that proved the rule about the usual excesses of democracy. Later Enlightenment thinkers like Locke and Montesquieu, and their American devotees, including Alexander Hamilton, did not share Hobbes's preference for absolute monarchy. But they did echo his deep distrust of undiluted popular sovereignty, and its potential for factional strife and majoritarian tyranny. They also shared Hobbes's view that a soundly ordered government was a far more reliable guarantee of social peace and personal liberty than the rare and accidental emergence of brilliant and farsighted statesmen like Pericles. Their new democratic experiment, the United States of America, was to be a government of laws—in which, as Madison put it, ambition would counteract ambition and honor seeking would be directed into the tangible rewards of peaceful commerce.

As modern representative governments like Britain and America prospered and achieved power in the world, later democratic statesmen trying to reconcile free government at home with imperial power abroad continued to be influenced by Thucydides' narrative, the first great history of an expansionist democracy. Lincoln, for instance, established through military force the authority of a liberal democratic empire based in the North over a retrograde oligarchy in the South, with its own class of oppressed Helots. Some historians, including Garry Wills, have argued that there are formal similarities between Lincoln's Gettysburg Address and a number of famous ancient Greek orations, including Pericles' Funeral Oration and works by Plato and Demosthenes. Others, such as James MacPherson, doubt that any direct connection existed, because Lincoln knew neither Latin nor Greek and was less influenced by the classics than by the Bible and Shakespeare.

What does seem clear is that Lincoln's speech at Gettysburg was shaped by the broader Greek revivalist spirit of nineteenth-century America, which included an interest in Thucydides and other classics. In that sense, at least, Thucydides was present on the podium with Lincoln at Gettysburg. Indeed, Edward Everett's two-hour encomium to the fallen, which preceded Lincoln's two-minute masterpiece, was deliberately modeled on Pericles' Funeral Oration. It could be argued that Everett embodied the Greek Revival in America. A Unitarian minister, Harvard classics professor, and political leader, he was the first American to receive a Ph.D. (in Germany, then the world's leading center of classical studies). Emerson, who had written that it was natural even in a democracy to believe in great men, had studied under Everett at Harvard and revered him throughout his life. It gives one pause that a man who consciously modeled his own Gettysburg speech on Pericles—and who taught the man who promoted the importance of great men in history—should have shared the stage that day with Lincoln, whose speech is remembered as rivaling the ancient Periclean model, and who fulfilled Emerson's criteria for greatness perhaps more than Emerson himself realized.

Unlike Lincoln, Theodore Roosevelt had a thorough grounding in the classics. According to his correspondence, he read Thucydides in the original Greek on at least two occasions, including when he was president for his evening reading in the White House. He qualifies his praise for Thucydides by remarking that, like Tolstoy's novels, his history was great but "unmoral"—an interesting insight to which we'll return, for it raises questions about how relevant Thucydides' exploration of democracy and empire are to the modern American experience in all respects.

Winston Churchill, the leader of a great league of free governments against the threat of invasion and oppression by the tyranny of Hitler, was also touched by Thucydides—although how directly is also the subject of some speculation. As noted earlier, Churchill did not attend university but read voraciously to educate himself in the classics. Since Churchill could not read Greek, his former headmaster at Harrow, Thomas Welldon, who remained interested in his development in later years, recommended that he read Thucydides in the Hobbes translation. Churchill's biographer Martin Gilbert does not say whether he read that translation, but it seems likely. Michael Valdez Moses, a professor of English literature at Duke University who has lectured on Churchill, believes it would have been difficult for Churchill to avoid Thucydides in the course of his reading projects. He points to Churchill's book *The River War* as evidence that Churchill and his Victorian contemporaries may have learned something from Thucydides about empire building. Another scholar, James Muller at the University of Alaska, has detected what he believes may be an unreferenced gloss on Thucydides in Churchill's history of World War I, *The World Crisis*. The most tangible and most satisfying connection is recounted by Churchill himself in his memoirs of World War II. During 1942, when the war was at a particularly low ebb for the Allies and Nazi Germany was seemingly unbeatable, Churchill's great friend Lord Beaverbrook, a press baron, wrote to him with a quotation from Thucydides to bolster his morale. The quote is from an unnamed leader on the Athenian side (most likely Cleon) urging the Athenians never to negotiate with Sparta. In his memoirs, Churchill recalls Beaverbrook's letter with the quote from Thucydides without further comment on its source, simply using the name "Thucydides" without a qualifier like "the famous historian," suggesting that Churchill understood both the context of the quote and the parallel to his own situation.

FOR READERS OF Thucydides today, however, the Vietnam parallel is the most eerie and vivid. Just as the war in Vietnam was widely considered to be a debacle for the liberal interventionist and containment policies originating in the 1950s, Thucydides presents the cataclysmic Athenian defeat in Sicily, in which the flower of its fleet and land forces were utterly demolished, as the fatal final blow to its joint ambition of expanding its empire while preserving democracy at home and spreading it abroad. (The Athenians apparently convinced themselves that partisans of democracy on Sicily would rise up against the island's oligarchies to support the invasion—an Athenian "hearts and minds" campaign, and another parallel with both Vietnam and Iraq.)

In order to understand the Sicilian expedition, its disastrous conclusion, and what it reveals for Thucydides about Athenian democracy, we must consider two pairs of events. The first is Pericles' Funeral Oration, which was followed by a plague that devastated the city—a pair of events that culminates in Thucydides' evaluation of Pericles and his successors, especially with respect to the Sicilian expedition. The second pair of events is the so-called Melian Dialogue and the Sicilian expedition that followed. The Melian Dialogue, in which a group of Athenian generals lecture a weaker people on the cold-blooded realities of realpolitik, is the first and still classic statement of the maxim "might makes right." It embodies Athenian hubris at its zenith, while the ensuing expedition and the defeat of Athens is often taken to represent the tragic nemesis of this hubris.

There is certainly something to this. Thucydides is indeed a kind of tragedian who uses real-life events to impart the lesson that overweening ambition rides for a fall. He lets us hear the speeches of the leading political actors and feel the emotion of the crowd. The opposite of today's value-neutral "objective" historian, Thucydides is a moral historian who culls the full range of psychological and didactic richness from real-life events without feeling limited to the facts he could verify directly. Still, it's important not to conclude that Thucydides' presentation of the Melian Dialogue and the Sicilian expedition prove that he believes expansionism and power seeking are always morally wrong as well as dangerous. Thucydides wasn't arguing that peace is normal, attainable, or even always desirable in international relations, or that the Athenians were necessarily punished for their evildoing.

To understand why, let us look more closely at the first pair of events—the Funeral Oration followed by the plague—and how they shape what Thucydides means us to draw from the second pair, the comeuppance of those who believed that might makes right.

PERICLES GAVE HIS famous Funeral Oration to commemorate the Athenian soldiers and sailors killed in the first year of the war, when casualties were as yet fairly light. He wanted to bolster morale and shape public opinion decisively now, before the strain of prolonged combat and death began to wear down the Athenians psychologically. He ended his speech with a solemn adjuration to the Athenians to do their duty—but only after detailing how every individual Athenian benefits from the city's power. As citizens, he tells them, they can combine the merits both of Athens and of Sparta: while the internal life of Athens celebrates high culture, tolerance, relaxation, and personal ease, they are able to Spartanize when needed and toughen themselves rapidly for war:

> Where our rivals from their very cradles by a painful dis-
> cipline seek after manliness, at Athens we live exactly as we
> please, and yet are just as ready to encounter every legitimate
> danger.

Unlike the Spartans, who resent any departure from their austere collective morality and believe that individual freedom and pleasure seeking undermine patriotic vigilance, Athens glories in its open-mindedness, prosperity, and diversity:

> We do not feel called upon to be angry with our neighbor
> for doing what he likes. We celebrate games and sacrifices all
> the year round, and the elegance of our private establishments
> forms a daily source of pleasure and helps to banish the spleen;
> while the magnitude of our city draws the produce of the world
> into our harbor.

Far from sapping patriotism, according to Pericles, the pleasures of individual freedom that Athenian life provides for every citizen create a strong personal incentive to protect what they have jointly achieved:

> If I have dwelt at some length upon the character of our
> country, it has been to show that our stake in the struggle is not
> the same as theirs who have no such blessings to lose.

In sum, Pericles is urging his fellow citizens always to remember that they have many strong reasons for fighting on Athens's behalf. They should "feast their eyes . . . from day to day" on the splendor of the city and her magnificent buildings, he exhorts them, stirring them to heights of patriotism "until love of her fills your hearts." Significantly, we never hear a similar public speech by a Spartan leader.

There is no need for such a speech in Sparta, whose laws mold the citizens from birth to regard the common good as superior to that of the individual. They are not encouraged to speculate about *why* Sparta is good for them on a personal level.

One of Thucydides' priceless insights into the soul of a leader is that leadership is shaped by the character of the regime—the laws, the constitution, the mores and way of life—which fosters certain kinds of character traits to the exclusion of others. No one regime can combine every character type and every way of life, despite Pericles' belief in the example of Athens. A war driven initially by self-interest and power seeking will inevitably become a conflict of values in which one regime will try to convert others to its way of life. At the same time, the shocks of war will threaten to unravel that distinctive way of life at home. The war between Athens and Sparta steadily escalated into a war not only about material interests but between two political principles—democracy versus oligarchy, or individualism versus collectivism.

As the two sides sought allies, they wanted converts not only for pragmatic reasons but to justify their cause and the superiority of their way of life. At the same time, both regimes were threatened inwardly as the war intensified. After the death of Pericles, Athens was endangered by the rise of politicians who urged the expansion of the war to serve their own selfish ambitions for military and political power. Sparta was endangered because the need to fight abroad threatened to destabilize her rigid way of life at home, inviting the Athenians to subvert Sparta's slave class of Helots to rebel and overthrow their Spartan masters and tempting individual Spartans to behave arrogantly abroad in their capacity as viceroys in a way that would not have been tolerated at home. As the war unfolds, the two regimes start to interact and blend. After the death of Pericles, certain Athenian leaders, such as Cleon, imitated what they perceived to be Sparta's admirable discipline, ruthlessness, and distrust of public debate. For their part, the Spartans tried to imitate what they saw as Athens's enviable dynamism and flexibility as epitomized by their mighty roving fleet—a mission so successful that they eventually scored some surprise naval victories over Athens late in the war.

The Two Superpowers: Athens and Sparta

These two archetypal regimes are introduced very early in Thucydides' account, and their values shape much of what unfolds. Each of the two embodied a different interpretation of what it meant to be Greek. The distinction was not primarily ethnic but one of values. Sparta was the original definer of archaic Greek morality, the embodiment of the Homeric code of manly honor. A self-governing aristocracy dedicated to a common good preserved by its laws, Sparta was, according to Thucydides, the first city-state to strike a balance between anarchy and tyranny. Living on a level social playing field, avoiding the temptations and trappings of luxury, the Spartans sublimated ambition in favor of simple manners and conformity to the law:

> A modest style of dressing . . . was first adopted by the [Spartans], the rich doing their best to assimilate their way of life to that of the common people.

Founded by the legendary Lycurgus, their laws remained fixed for centuries.

> At a very early period it obtained good laws, and enjoyed a freedom from tyrants which was unbroken; it has possessed the same form of government for more than four hundred years, reckoning to the end of the late war, and has thus been in a position to arrange the affairs of other states.

In a passage every modern reader will find haunting, Thucydides remarks that Sparta had no great buildings and was not outwardly splendid like Athens. Future travelers, he writes, will find that all that remains there are empty fields and traces of huts, yet in some ways Sparta at her height was as great as or greater than Athens with its splendid Parthenon.

> For I suppose if [Sparta] were to become desolate, and the temples and the foundations of the public buildings were left,

that as time went on there would be a strong disposition with posterity to refuse to accept her fame as a true exponent of her power. And yet they occupy two-fifths of the Peloponnese and lead the whole, not to speak of their numerous allies without. Still, as the city is neither built in a compact form nor adorned with magnificent temples and public edifices, but composed of villages after the old fashion of Hellas, there would be an impression of inadequacy. Whereas, if Athens were to suffer the same misfortune, I suppose that any inference from the appearance presented to the eye would make her power to have been twice as great as it is.

The ironic insight of Thucydides' remark becomes clear when Pericles ends his Funeral Oration by exhorting the Athenians to "feast their eyes" on the splendor of Athens and her buildings for inspiration to fight on her behalf. Was he suggesting that Pericles was deluding the Athenians about the extent of their real power by focusing on these visible splendors—that Sparta in a way had tougher morale, despite achieving no such material adornments? One is easily put in mind of Gibbon's melancholy reflections on seeing the ruins of Rome and the disjunction between the magnificence of those buildings and her terrible downfall at the hands of barbarians. The same effect is produced today by viewing the imposing government buildings of the British Raj in New Delhi, a powerful synthesis of Mogul and Hindu architecture meant to imply that both previous ruling traditions had been superseded and absorbed by the British, the scale of whose buildings clearly meant they intended to stay forever. By the same token, can one visit New York's Ground Zero without contemplating how the Rome of the modern West was penetrated and wounded by men whose models had acquired their fanaticism fighting on foot against the tanks and bombers of the Soviet Union in Afghanistan?

The visible signs of affluence and civilization do not always coincide with an inner strength of purpose—indeed, to the extent that we are enthralled by those outward signs, it may signify that we are hiding from ourselves just how much we have lost the original moral vigor by which they came to be created as a testament to the rewards of virtue. Indeed, a visit to the ruins of Athens and of Sparta today confirms Thucydides' predictions: the Parthenon still shines and enchants, while all that remains of ancient Sparta are pastures and a few scattered low walls and humble foundation stones. It's no surprise that the Athenians managed to convince themselves that a cityscape of eternal buildings would preserve their way of life forever.

The Spartans, Thucydides tells us, were harsh toward their own slave class of Helots and toward other peoples. A closed society, they discouraged foreign visitors and tried to keep innovation at bay. Their economy was agrarian and discouraged urban commerce. The wealth of the ruling aristocracy was entirely landed. The limited economy offered no real opportunity for upward mobility by a merchant class and no need for immigrant traders. The Spartans distrusted the flowery and elaborate oratory that enthralled the Athenians: Just as "spartan" came to mean "ascetic," the term "laconic," derived from their actual name for their homeland, Lacedaemonia, came to refer to one who spoke little and directly to the point. It suggested an aristocratic refusal to explain oneself to inferiors, and a tendency to trust breeding, a gift of the few and fortunate, over intellect, which anyone might possess. In many ways, the Spartans were extremely unpleasant to outsiders. Yet among themselves they displayed a fierce love of liberty and patriotism, a willingness for total sacrifice for one another. This is one place where the comparison between Athens and modern America is imperfect: The Spartans might fairly be likened to early colonial patriots like Nathan Hale, but in the twentieth century, at the height of the Pax Americana of the 1950s, the United States was more kindred to the liberal empire of Periclean Athens.

The democratic Athens described by Pericles embodied a very different version of Greek identity—lively, trendy, chatty, cosmopolitan, and lots of bling:

> The Athenians were the first to lay aside their weapons and
> to adopt an easier and more luxurious mode of life. Indeed, it is
> only lately that their rich old men left off the luxury of wearing

undergarments of linen, and fastening a knot of their hair with
a tie of golden grasshoppers, a fashion which spread to their
Ionian kindred, and long prevailed among the old men there.

Athens doubtless owed its cosmopolitan character in part to its
status as a naval power and active trading hub rather than a strictly
agrarian economy: She had a window on the world. Yet the difference
was also a matter of temperament. Athens welcomed the whole world
into her teeming harbor at Piraeus—new ideas, new religions, new
ways of life. Foreigners were welcome as businessmen and as teachers
of rhetoric and natural science, free to trawl for fee-paying students.
Foreign nationals could sometimes serve in the military. Because the
fleet was needed to build a commercial seafaring economy and to fight
the Persians, the old landed aristocracy of knighthood gave way over
time to the mass of men who manned the oars. Having manned the
trade routes and won the war, they could not be denied the franchise.
Spartan politics took place out of public view, restricted to a small
council of elders and ephors elected by an assembly of the peers. By
contrast, Athenian politics were conducted openly, in the agora or
public forum. The "assembly" included the entire male citizen body.
Its debates were raucous and tumultuous. Even war strategies were debated directly by the people in the assembly. Generals could be recalled
and stripped of their commissions if they lost a battle or displeased the
people some other way, like not retrieving the dead for burial. The
Athenian people could be loving toward their leaders or could turn on
them suddenly and lethally—as Thucydides knew full well himself.
Above all, oratory was respected. Rhetoric was absolutely necessary
to get ahead, to promote a policy or one's own interests, because the
majority had to be convinced.

Thucydides' account of the two regimes is vividly cinematic.
Sparta is quiet, bucolic, silent in her fields. Her armies move word-
lessly, relentlessly toward their aim. Debates are hidden, eloquence is
distrusted. Athens by contrast is a wild, noisy melee of clashing voices,
the bustle of the streets, shops, hawkers, the crowded agora roaring
with laughter, approval, or disdain as one or another brash speaker

struggles to make his voice heard, his cadences roll. The Spartans distrust change. The Athenians embrace it—whatever will make more money, whatever will win in war. The Spartans are brutally straightforward; they want nothing but to preserve their own way of life, and they will fight only to protect it. They do not want to meddle in the affairs of others or to have others meddle in theirs. The Athenians are subtle, clever, often indirect, sly, sometimes outright liars. They welcome newcomers and are eager to expand their influence and power. They will take whatever they can get, and do it with a genial smile. *After all*, they know, *there are far worse masters than ourselves.*

The Proxy War: Corinth Versus Corcyra

Like many of history's worst and most extensive wars—such as World War I, to cite just one example—the decades-long superpower conflict between Athens and Sparta began as a local brushfire between their smaller allies, one that only gradually sucked in the two larger city-states. The original dispute laid bare long-simmering tensions between the two major powers, and when they finally surfaced the conflict mushroomed into a conflagration that swept the entire Greek world.

How did a war of such magnitude begin? One key to understanding politics, Thucydides notes, is to understand the difference between speech and deed, between the openly professed justice of a cause and the material motivations that may underlie that cause. Just as material self-interest can weaken a claim of pure justice by making both parties in a conflict reluctant to risk prosperity through war, a strong claim of justice can lead to such zealous self-righteousness that war is undertaken even at the threat to one's own wealth and power.

In probing the causes of the Peloponnesian War, Thucydides offers a case study in the role that political oratory can play in leadership. He begins by reviewing the *prophasis*—the "grounds of complaint and points of difference" that the parties to the conflict *claimed* to be the root of the conflict. Yet he makes it clear that these publicly advanced positions were shaped by underlying matters—the true ground or *aitia* of the conflict:

The real cause I consider to be the one which was formally most kept out of sight. The growth of the power of Athens, and the alarm which this inspired in Sparta, made war inevitable. Still, it is well to give the grounds alleged by either side, which led to the dissolution of the treaty and the breaking out of the war.

The conflict began when the city of Epidamnus deposed its oligarchy and the exiled oligarchs joined the barbarians menacing Epidamnus from nearby to attack their own native city. The Epidamnians appealed to Corcyra, their mother country, for help. (Many Greek city-states sent out colonies that eventually became independent states, but remembered their historical connection to the mother country.) But Corcyra, seeing nothing in it for them, refused to get involved. Epidamnus called in turn on Corcyra's mother country, Corinth, for protection. The people of Corinth thought they had a duty to protect the Epidamnians—their grandchildren, as it were. But they also had a second motive—to gall the Corcyraeans:

Believing the colony to belong as much to them as the Corcyraeans, they felt it to be a kind of duty to undertake their protection. Besides, they hated the Corcyraeans for their contempt of the mother country. Instead of meeting with the usual honors accorded to the parent city by every other colony at public assemblies such as precedence at sacrifices, Corinth found herself treated with contempt by a power which in point of wealth could stand comparison with any even of the richest communities in Greece. . . . All these grievances made Corinth eager to send the promised aid to Epidamnus.

So the original conflict between Epidamnus and its deposed oligarchs allied with barbarian forces boiled over into a more serious conflict between Corinth and its colony Corcyra.

In the opening round of hostilities, Corcyra scores an early victory by winning a naval battle against Corinth. The Corinthians react to this setback by building up their ground and naval forces for an eventual counterattack. But the war widens as both sides try to draw in the two superpowers, Athens and Sparta:

> Corinth, exasperated by the war with the Corcyraeans, spent the whole of the year after the engagement and that succeeding it in building ships and in straining every nerve to form an efficient fleet. . . . The Corcyraeans, alarmed at the news of their preparations, being without a single ally in Greece, decided to repair to Athens in order to enter into alliance and to endeavor to procure support from her. Corinth also, hearing of their intentions, sent an embassy to Athens to prevent the Corcyraean navy being joined by the Athenian. An assembly was convoked and the rival advocates appeared.

The Corcyraeans send a delegation to warn Athens that Corinth has enlisted Sparta on its side. The Corcyraeans claim that Sparta fears the growing power of Athens and wants to strike at Athens through her perceived ally, Corcyra. War is inevitable, the Corcyraeans argue to the Athenian assembly; we might as well get the jump on our foes, as delay will only give Sparta and Corinth time to build their forces. They speak as follows to the Athenians gathered in the agora to hear the debate:

> If any of you imagine that the war is far off, he is grievously mistaken, and is blind to the fact that Sparta regards you with jealousy and desires war, and that Corinth is powerful there—the same, remember, that is your enemy, and is even now trying to subdue us as a preliminary to attacking you. And she does this to prevent our becoming united by a common enmity, and her having us both on her hands, and also to insure getting the advantage over you in one of two ways, either by crippling our power or by making its strength her own. In fact, we ought to form plans against her instead of waiting to defeat the plans she forms against us.

Of course, Corcyra's contention about the inevitability of war is heavily influenced by the Corcyraeans' own self-interest in gaining the Athenians' help in defeating Corinth. Moreover, at the ensuing congress in Sparta it becomes clear that the Corcyraeans have exaggerated the extent of the pact between Sparta and Corinth in order to win over Athens; in truth, Sparta has yet to commit. Moreover, they may be exaggerating the extent to which the Spartans, at this point, assume that Athens and Corcyra are allied, since no formal alliance has as yet been concluded.

A Corinthian delegation, in turn, tries to make its case for Athenian neutrality in their conflict with Corcyra. We have the right to punish rebellious allies just as you do, they tell the Athenian assembly. If our allies, such as Corcyra, are allowed to flout our authority and rebel, yours may as well. So you should defend our rights in this regard—or at least agree not to interfere—because it will reinforce your own authority over your allies.

> Every power has a right to punish its own allies. Why, if you make it your policy to receive and assist all offenders, you will find that just as many of your dependencies will come over to us, and the principle that you establish will press less heavily on us than on yourselves.

This line of reasoning is not entirely plausible, however—not least because Corcyra was actually *not* an ally of Corinth (the fact that Corinth was Corcyra's mother country entailed no such formal alliance), so there was no agreement for Corcyra to abrogate in the first place. Corinth merely resents the fact that Corcyra, her upstart colony, now rivals her in wealth and power. The Corinthians add an even sharper and more menacing argument: Despite Corcyra's claims, they contend, war is not inevitable. But it will *become* so if you support Corcyra and take their side against us. You may be eyeing their fleet greedily. But making an enemy of us will trump any short-term gain in that department. It is better for you to remain neutral and let us handle the problem:

Not only is the straightest path generally speaking the wisest, but the coming of the war which the Corcyraeans have used as a bugbear to persuade you to do wrong is still uncertain, and it is not worth while to be carried away by it into gaining the instant and declared enmity of Corinth. . . . And do not be seduced by the prospect of a naval alliance. Abstinence from all injustice to other first-rate powers is a greater tower of strength than anything that can be gained by the sacrifice of permanent tranquility for an apparent temporary advantage.

In making this case for neutrality to the Athenian assembly, however, the Corinthians never address Corcyra's charge that Corinth was trying to draw Sparta into the conflict, or whether Sparta was considering using the conflict as a proxy war to pave the way for a full-scale assault on Athens. Later, this proves to be the Athenians' primary consideration as they debate the arguments presented by the two delegations. For it turns out that the Athenians themselves have felt all along that war with Sparta was on the horizon.

Rejecting Corinth's plea for neutrality, the Athenians decide to form a defensive alliance with Corcyra:

There was a manifest disposition to listen to the representations of Corinth in the first meeting. In the second, public feeling had changed, and an alliance with Corcyra was decided on, with certain reservations. It was to be a defensive, not an offensive alliance. It did not involve a breach of the treaty with Peloponnese. . . . For it began now to be felt that the coming of the Peloponnesian War was only a question of time.

The Athenians' own motives are mixed and not entirely straightforward. They are certainly not motivated by an altruistic regard for Corcyra's cause or belief in its intrinsic justice. They are eager to see Corcyra's recently victorious naval fleet preserved from harm by Corinth, so that the fleet will pass into Athenian control intact for their own use in the coming conflict with Sparta.

Moreover, they figure that they can calibrate their assistance to Corcyra so as to let Corcyra and Corinth bleed each other, letting neither win a decisive victory.

> No one was willing to see a naval power of such magnitude as Corcyra sacrificed to Corinth—though if they could let them weaken each other by mutual conflict, it would be no bad preparation for the struggle which Athens might one day have to wage with Corinth and the other naval powers.

But as so often happens in war, diplomatic calculations and gradualist military strategies unravel under the impact of actual combat. For the Corinthians win the next naval engagement with Corcyra, leading to a significant escalation of the war. Athenian naval forces accompany the Corcyraeans as observers, but in the heat of the battle they begin engaging the Corinthians themselves:

> Seeing the Corcyraeans hard pressed, the Athenians began at length to assist them more unequivocally. At first, it is true, they refrained from charging any ships. But when the rout was becoming patent, and the Corinthians were pressing on, the time at last came when everyone set to, and all distinction was laid aside, and it came to this point, that the Corinthians and Athenians raised their hands against each other.

At this point, reluctant to take on the Athenians by themselves, Corinth prudently calls a halt to the action.

> The next day the thirty Athenian vessels put out to sea, accompanied by all the ships that were seaworthy, and sailed to the harbor where the Corinthians lay, to see if they would engage. The Corinthians put out from land, and formed a line in the open sea, but beyond this made no further movement, having no intention of assuming the offensive. For they saw reinforcements arrive fresh from Athens and themselves con-

fronted by numerous difficulties. . . . What they were thinking more about was how their voyage home was to be effected. They feared that the Athenians might consider that the treaty was dissolved by the collision which had occurred, and forbid their departure.

The Conference at Sparta and the Widening Conflict

The months that follow see both a "phony war" and an intense round of diplomatic jockeying for alliances. The Corinthians encourage all the Greek states with complaints about Athens to pressure Sparta to act. This leads to Sparta convening a special conference to which all of Athens's foes are invited. Mounting a diplomatic counteroffensive against Corcyra's alliance with Athens, Corinth tries to inflame the sluggish Spartans and goad them into joining the war to check the burgeoning power of their great antagonist, Athens. Corinth is willing to fan the flames of a world war in order to strike back at Corcyra.

The passages that follow offer a window into the Spartan psyche as revealing as the earlier portrait of Athens as it weighed the arguments of the Corinthian and Corcyraean delegations. The Corinthians try to shame Sparta into action. *You Spartans are sluggish, homebound, isolated*, they charge. *You have no idea what is going on in the outside world.*

Spartans! The confidence which you feel in your constitution and social order, inclines you to receive any reflections of ours on other powers with a certain skepticism. Hence springs your moderation, but hence also the rather limited knowledge which you betray in dealing with foreign politics. Time after time was our voice raised to warn you of the blows about to be dealt us by Athens, and time after time, instead of taking the trouble to ascertain the worth of our communications, you contented yourselves with suspecting the speakers of being inspired by private interest.

The Corinthians accuse the Spartans not just of letting their allies down but of endangering themselves by allowing Athens to outstrip their power:

> For all this you are responsible. It was you who first allowed them to fortify their city after the war with Persia, and afterwards to erect the long walls.

Up until now, the Corinthians continue almost tauntingly, the Athenians simply thought you were unable to understand what they were up to. Now, however, you risk convincing them that you're not merely unobservant, but afraid:

> We know what are the paths by which Athenian aggression travels, and how insidious is its progress. Athens may feel a degree of confidence from the idea that your bluntness of perception prevents your noticing her. But it is nothing to the impulse which her advance will receive from the knowledge that you see, but do not care to interfere.

You Spartans may pride yourselves on being disciplined and united, the Corinthians charge, *as opposed to the self-indulgent Athenians*. Yet in fact, they argue, the Athenians are the more disciplined people, always looking for ways to improve themselves and get ahead.

> The Athenians are addicted to innovation, and their designs are characterized by swiftness alike in conception and execution. You have a genius for keeping what you have got, accompanied by a total lack of invention, and when forced to act, you never go far enough. Again, they are adventurous beyond their power, and daring beyond their judgement, and in danger they are sanguine. Your habit is to attempt less than is justified by your power, to mistrust even what is sanctioned by your judgement, and to fancy that from danger there is no release.

The Spartans' disinclination to change their ways or learn about the outside world, according to the Corinthians, leaves Athens free to run circles around them:

> There is promptitude on their side against procrastination on yours; they are never at home, you are never away from it, for they hope by their advance to extend their acquisitions, while you fear by your advance to endanger what you have left behind. They are swift to follow up a success and slow to recoil from a reverse. Their bodies they spend ungrudgingly in their country's cause, their intellect they jealously husband to be employed in her service.

The Corinthians press on about Athenian dynamism and Sparta's need to recognize it:

> Thus they toil on in trouble and danger all the days of their life, with little opportunity for enjoyment, being ever engaged in getting, their only idea of a holiday is to do what the occasion demands, and to them laborious occupation is less of a misfortune than the peace of a quiet life. They were born into the world to take no rest themselves and to give none to others.

In the course of their propaganda campaign to persuade Sparta to join their fight against Athens, then, the Corinthians unwittingly portray the Athenians just as Pericles had in the Funeral Oration— ever dynamic, ever bold and innovative on behalf of their empire. Yet, as we know from the context of the speech and Thucydides' characterization of their way of life, the Athenians are in fact rather addicted to luxury and ease. Pericles is very concerned that he must appeal to their self-interest to motivate them to do what is necessary, and fears the effects on their collective resolve of individual envy toward the meritorious.

The Corinthians tell the Spartans bluntly: You want to stay within your own borders, keep to yourselves, mind your own affairs, and avoid the taint of outside contact. But the world doesn't work that way. Peace and domestic life aren't permanent possibilities, only temporary intervals in a never-ending struggle for power and enrichment. The Athenians are always looking for technical improvements to enhance and project their power. The rest of us simply must keep up with them or risk being overwhelmed.

> Your idea of fair dealing is that if you do not injure others, you need not risk your own fortunes in preventing others from injuring you. Now you could scarcely have succeeded in such a policy even with a neighbour like yourselves. But in the present instance, your habits are old-fashioned as compared with theirs. It is the law as in art, so in politics, that improvements must ever prevail, and though fixed usages may be best for undisturbed communities, constant necessities of action must be accompanied by the constant improvement of methods. Thus it happens that the vast experience of Athens has carried them further than you on the path of innovation.

Once again, Thucydides reveals how leaders can shape public speeches to suit their unstated purposes. In Athens, the Corinthians preached moderation and adherence to the status quo because they didn't want Athens to tip the scale in favor of Corcyra. Here, for the same motive—prevailing over their enemy—they take the opposite rhetorical tack, preaching boldness and calling for expansion. Their self-interest, which requires a different strategy in each situation, dictates the shift in rhetoric.

Still, the events that follow suggest that this latest version of Corinthian rhetoric at the conference in Sparta does in fact come close to reflecting the reality about Athens. For an Athenian delegation happens to be present in Sparta on other business during the conference, and when it learns of the Corinthians' arguments it requests to be heard. The Athenians' presence is entirely accidental, a fact that seems to prove the Corinthians' warning that the Athenians are always in motion, traveling everywhere to advance their interests. Moreover, given that they are here by chance and had no way of knowing what the Corinthians were hatching, the Athenians prove united and remarkably persuasive in their arguments; they appear completely comfortable speaking to important foreign policy matters on behalf of their fellow citizens without any prior consultation, summoning up impressive arguments on the spot to protect their great city's interests. This confirms the Corinthians' warning that the Spartans are wrong to consider themselves the only Greek people capable of resolute collective action, and to dismiss the Athenians as divided and concerned only with their personal welfare and pleasure.

The case the Athenians present is another masterful illustration of the tension between speech and deed. They claim that their motive in speaking is to prove that they have a just title to their possessions—that their empire is legitimate. Yet behind the rhetoric, according to Thucydides, their motive is to remind the Spartans of just how much power they wield, and thereby to cow the Spartans into preferring the current detente to the risk of war.

The Athenians begin by reminding the Spartans—as one suspects they have done many times before—that they saved Greece from Persian conquest at the battles of Marathon and Salamis when the Spartans hung back. Athens gained power and allies, they argue, only because they fell into her lap as the sluggish Spartans withdrew too soon.

> Receiving no reinforcements from behind, seeing everything in front of us already subjugated, we had the spirit, after abandoning our city, after sacrificing our property, instead of deserting the remainder of the league or depriving them of our services by dispersing, to throw ourselves into our ships and meet the danger, without a thought of resenting your neglecting to assist us.

The Athenians' willingness at a moment of dire national peril to abandon their ancestral soil and live at sea until the Persian invasion was repulsed confirms the Corinthians' account of the Athenians' boldness, lack of fixed ties, dependence on mobility, and advanced naval technology. They continue:

The empire we adopted by no violent means, but because you were unwilling to prosecute to its conclusion the war against the barbarian, and because the allies attached themselves to us and spontaneously asked us to assume the command. And the nature of the case first compelled us to advance our empire to its present height; fear being our principal motive, though honor and interest afterwards came in.

We gained our empire first out of a healthy fear of the Persians, the Athenians are arguing; surely that is a matter of simple human nature. Admittedly, once we possessed this empire, we strove to preserve it, out of both honor and self-interest. But what is wrong with that? After all, you Spartans control the entire Peloponnesian mainland. We concede that as your sphere of interest; we do not contest it or begrudge it. Why is it any worse for us to want the same?

> You, at all events, Spartans, have used your supremacy to settle the states in Peloponnese as is agreeable to you. . . . It follows that it was not a bizarre action, or contrary to the common practice of mankind, if we did accept an empire that was offered to us, and refused to give it up under the pressure of three of the strongest motives—fear, honor and interest.

You Spartans, the Athenians imply, never complained about us before now. Now you say we're being unjust, simply because you feel we threaten your interests. But no one appeals to justice unless he cannot achieve his aims by others means.

> Besides, we believed ourselves to be worthy of our position, and so you had thought us till now, when calculations of interest have made you take up the cry of justice—a consideration which no one ever yet brought forward to hinder his ambition when he had a chance of gaining anything by might.

In fact, they continue both disarmingly and menacingly, we could be a good deal *more* aggressive toward your interests if we wanted to. Yet we refrain, even when we have the power to do so, a generosity on our part that deserves your respect.

All praise is due to all who, if not so superior to human nature as to refuse dominion, yet respect justice more than their position compels them to do.

In other words, watch your step. Things could get a lot worse.

As for our allies, the Athenians argue, the truth is that we treat them so decently that they take us for granted—forgetting how much they owe us, how much worse we could be to them. They carp about the slightest inconveniences:

[A]ny defeat whatever that clashes with their notions of justice when it proceeds from the power which our empire gives us, makes them forget to be grateful for being allowed to retain most of their possessions, and more vexed at a part being taken, than if we had from the first cast law aside and openly gratified our covetousness.

This is the thanks we get for being such nice guys!

But this contention points to a gaping hole in Athenian logic: After all, could Athens's leaders treat their *own* subjects, their fellow citizens, this way? And would ordinary Athenians allow themselves to be treated at home the way they treat their allies abroad, satisfied to know that their lot is pretty bearable given their lesser status? In presenting the Athenians' justification of their empire, Thucydides is reminding us of the dangerous potential conflict between how a democracy's leaders treat other peoples and how their own people will expect to be treated. This moral contradiction will prove to undermine the cohesion of Athenian democracy at home as its post-Periclean leaders are tempted to turn the tyranny they exercise abroad (however benignly) against their own citizenry.

The Athenians' speech, apparently so straightforward, is actually a blend of half-truths and clever evasions, one that justifies the Corinthians' warnings about the Athenians. The Athenians profess to act as if they are no different from the Spartans by nature. Their purported aggressiveness is merely the product of necessity and circumstance, they claim: Anyone would do the same in such a situation. First fear of oppression, then honor and self-interest, compel us all to seek power and dominate others, whether in Athens or Sparta. That is the Athenian thesis about human nature—but it's not the whole story. Even as they profess a willingness to live and let live, to leave the Spartans' sphere of influence intact, the Athenians are trying to disarm the Spartans psychologically by playing upon their unvoiced fear of Athens's might. Their spoken message may be *We should each keep our share*, but the unspoken message is clear: *Go up against us and we'll cream you.*

As we'll see, the Spartans do tend to believe that human nature is the same everywhere. But the flip side of the Athenian claim that fear made them dominate their allies is that anyone strong enough to do so will oppress the weak and take advantage of them. Conquer or be conquered—that's the way of the world. If that is true, how can one expect justice in international affairs? There can be no lasting détente, much less true peace, only a wary interval between conflicts. If it is a matter of prevailing over your foe before your foe prevails over you, preemptive aggression may seem the most rational policy.

The Athenians do speak with refreshing candor; they make no attempt to disguise their power seeking behind preachy moralizing about the purity of their motives. In a bluff and manly way, they admit openly that, having gained an empire, they have no intention of giving it up. Their arguably criminal posture comes across as worldliness and frankness, a belief in the notion that all states, as "rational actors" mindful of their mutual self-interest, are capable of respecting each other's dominions without worrying about ethics. Indeed, for an empire, Athens does display a certain mildness, even generosity, toward allies and foreigners. The Athenians avoid wanton cruelty or haughtiness toward those under their sway, asking only that their client states provide what they want and need, and offering in return peace and prosperity under their protection. The Athenians claim to understand entirely, and accept, the Spartans' desire to dominate the surrounding land mass and their slave class of Helots. If power seeking is inevitable and unavoidable, these relatively benign and candid imperial qualities may be virtues. If it is not, they are mere sophistries disguising a lust for conquest.

Despite the Athenians' evident attempt to intimidate the Spartans with an unspoken reminder of their increasing power, their arguments have the opposite effect. When they withdraw to deliberate, Thucydides reports, the majority of Spartans had reached "the same conclusion: the Athenians were open aggressors and war must be declared at once."

Whether due to the warnings from Corinth, or to the fear that they had let the Athenians get away with too much, the Spartans finally came to regard them as sheer aggressors who must be put down. This outcome is in striking contrast with the earlier Athenian assembly, which was inclined to temporize and stay on the sidelines after hearing the Corcyraeans ask Athens for assistance. We learn from this that no regime is always true to form: the Athenians can be cautious, the Spartans bold.

Yet the Spartan king, Archidamus, fears the disastrous consequences of an all-out war for his country, and he makes a last-ditch effort to talk his people out of war. According to Thucydides, the Spartans considered Archidamus a wise and moderate leader. His speech gives us a crucial insight into the psyche of Spartan statesmanship—one that holds great importance for the struggle that follows, and which has a counterpart in Athenian public opinion itself that becomes increasingly visible as the war expands. For just as the cold war between America and the U.S.S.R. revealed that each side harbored its share of hawks and doves alike, so does the Peloponnesian War reveal that each Greek regime boasted both a war party and a peace party. Neither side can act with total unanimity.

Archidamus entreats his fellow Spartans not to rush into war, but rather to negotiate:

> None need think it cowardice for a number of confederates
> to pause before they attack a single city. The Athenians have

allies as numerous as our own, and allies that pay tribute, and war is a matter not so much of arms as of money, which makes arms of use.

We cannot defeat Athens at sea, he argues—and Athens, as a seafaring power, does not care about protecting its land as much as we do. In making this last point, he seems to have been persuaded by the Corinthians' speech about the ever-mobile Athenians and the Athenians' reminder that they were willing to abandon the city in their ships during the war with Persia. They have much more money to arm their forces than we do, Archidamus adds. At the same time, he rebuts the Corinthians' accusations that the Spartans are sluggish, naïve, and slow to respond to danger. While we cannot defeat the Athenians in an open war at present, he maintains, neither can they fundamentally harm us or threaten our interests here in the heart of the Greek mainland. We remain united and strong at home. Our way of life, bred into us by our ancient traditions, is one of manly fortitude and moderation. We are neither insolent in victory nor easily crushed by disappointments. The laws breed us to an equal collective level of honor and bravery; this has always been our surest safeguard.

As Archidamus argues, the Spartans need not embrace the Athenians' addiction to innovation. No matter how daring you are, no matter how sophisticated your plans and weapons, some freak chance or unanticipated fate can defeat you. He appears to share the view of Homer and the other tragic poets that life is governed by an unfathomable necessity and cycles of fate that make a mockery of all human pretensions to cleverness and skill. The best weapons are caution, discipline, and solid preparation, not bold adventurism. Relying on individual brilliance is a dubious enterprise, not as dependable as the collective severity, toughness, and self-reliance of the Spartan culture.

We have nothing to be ashamed of in this way of life, Archidamus insists, despite the Corinthians' charges:

> The slowness and procrastination, the parts of our character
> that are most assailed by their criticism, need not make you

blush. If we undertake the war without preparation, we should by hastening its commencement only delay its conclusion. A free and famous city has through all time been ours.

We know from tradition that the kind of daring our Corinthian critics admire in the Athenians can go badly awry. We prefer to go slowly:

> The quality which they condemn is really nothing but a wise moderation. Thanks to its possession, we alone do not become insolent in success and give way less than others in misfortune. We are not carried away by the pleasure of hearing ourselves cheered on to risks which our judgement condemns. Nor, if annoyed, are we any the more convinced by attempts to exasperate us by accusation. We are both warlike and wise, and it is our sense of order that makes us so.

Where Pericles praised Athens as "the school of Greece," able to combine imperial power with intellectual sophistication and culture, Archidamus praises the Spartans for not overeducating its citizens to the point where it would distract them from their duty or make them arrogant:

> We are warlike, because self-control contains honor, and honor bravery. And we are wise, because we are educated with too little learning to despise the laws, and with too severe a self-control to disobey them, and are brought up not to be too knowing in useless matters, but are taught to consider that the schemes of our enemies are not dissimilar to our own, and that the freaks of chance are not determinable by calculation. Nor ought we to believe that there is much difference between man and man, but to think that the superiority lies with him who is reared in the severest school.

In many ways, Archidamus's view of the world parallels that presented by the Athenian tragic poet Sophocles in his great drama *Oedipus the Tyrant*, with its allegorical warning to the Athenians of his day that their imperial hubris, and determination to master the world through brains and daring, would lead to their downfall. As the war unfolds and Athenian fortunes waver, we learn that many Athenians quietly share Archidamus's view that arrogance and imperial ambition will be the death of them.

Despite their respect for Archidamus, however, the Spartans remain resolved to take on Athens. The final verdict is pronounced by the ephor Sthenalaidas, who points to the justice of their cause—and, for the first time in the conflict, invokes the gods. As the simmering cold war heats up, each side's rational calculation of its own self-interest is complicated by the emotional conviction that its side has divine backing. As diplomacy gives way to bloodshed and struggle, this religious zeal fuels their patriotism:

> Vote, therefore, Spartans, for war, as the honor of Sparta demands, and neither allow the further aggrandizement of Athens, nor betray our allies to ruin, but with the gods let us advance against the aggressors!

Ultimately, however, Thucydides maintains that fears of Athenian domination, rather than religious zeal, were behind the Spartans' decision.

> The Spartans voted that war must be declared, not so much because they were persuaded by the arguments of the allies, as because they feared the growth of the power of the Athenians, seeing most of Greece already subject to them.

It appears that the Athenian thesis may have been right after all: If relations between states are destined to go one of two ways—domination or fear, conquer or be conquered—the Athenians were right to keep their empire and the Spartans are right to try to reduce it. The Athenians did succeed in appealing to the Spartans' self-interest by stirring their fears. The irony is that the Spartans drew the opposite conclusion from the one the Athenians intended: War now, without delay.

The History of the Cold War

At this point, having shown how positions harden as the proxy war grows into a full-scale conflict, Thucydides abruptly shifts his narrative, taking us back forty-three years to the rise of Athenian power and the first stirrings of tension with Sparta. In doing so, he implies that the spoken and unspoken motives of the actors in the contemporary crisis are not sufficient to explain the circumstances and the full range of options for statesmanship. We need a deeper historical dimension. This is a recurring theme in the annals of statecraft. As we saw in Part One, in order to understand the deeper causes of the cold war between America and the Soviet Union one must go back to the end of World War II. The distrust and hostility between the two superpowers, the psychology of their leaders, and the evolution of their policies is only fully explained by that moment when, having vanquished the Nazi aggressor, America and the Soviet Union stood triumphant as victorious allies—until the common danger uniting them passed and they began eyeing each other warily. In like fashion, after joining forces to vanquish the Great King of Persia, Athens and Sparta stepped back to reassess each other in the cold light of victory. Just as leaders like Truman, JFK, Nixon, and Reagan cannot be fully fathomed without considering the formative experiences of the postwar era, and the influence of figures like Acheson and Kissinger in shaping their attitudes toward what they perceived as the Soviet threat, Thucydides implies that the mutual distrust between the Athenians and the Spartans traced back to the great Athenian wartime leader Themistocles and his Spartan counterparts like Pausanias—a great democracy allied with a great oligarchy. History, in other words, is essential for the understanding and practice of democratic statesmanship. Without reaching into its pulse and patterns, the underlying motivations and worldviews of the principal leaders of today will always remain partially hidden to us, like marionettes substituting for real people. Historical cycles sometimes repeat themselves, but sometimes they do not: We need to understand the backgrounds and motivations of leaders like Pericles and Alcibiades—not only because similar types may appear again but also to help us recognize how other leadership personalities may sharply differ.

The mutual suspicion between the erstwhile allies began when Athens announced that it wanted to build a wall to create a fortified corridor between the main city and the harbor, the source of trade and home for the fleet. The Spartans resisted the idea, which would make Athens more difficult to menace by land (Sparta's only means of projecting military force), while allowing Athens to retain her overwhelming superiority at sea. The Spartans expressed no public objection to the plan; instead they urged that *no* Greek state build walls, because of the danger that the Persian king might return and capture one of these walled cities to use as an impregnable base for further operations in Greece. Moreover, some of the other Greek states were already pleading with the Spartans to help them counter the increasingly overbearing power of Athens. Thucydides writes:

> Perceiving what they were going to do, the Spartans sent an embassy to Athens. They would have themselves preferred to see neither her nor any other city in possession of a wall, though here they acted principally at the instigation of their allies, who were alarmed at the strength of her newly acquired navy, and the valor which she had displayed in the war with the Persians. They begged her not only to abstain from building walls for herself, but also to join them in throwing down the walls of other cities.

As usual, the publicly stated position and the unstated motive were somewhat at variance:

> The real meaning of their advice, the suspicion that it contained against the Athenians, was not proclaimed. It was urged so that the barbarians, in the event of a third invasion, would not have any strong place for a base of operations.

In modern terms, building the wall was roughly analogous to Ronald Reagan's attempt to create a defensive shield against nuclear attack. The U.S. government claimed that the Strategic Defense Initiative (SDI) was a purely defensive program, not designed to attack others. The Soviets, however, professed to see SDI as America's attempt to shield itself against retaliation for a potential future attack of its own. Why would America need such a shield if it wasn't entertaining the possibility of surviving such a retaliatory blow? In such circumstances, even a defensive weapon can be destabilizing.

Even without menacing Sparta directly, in building his walls Themistocles might have been preparing to shield Athens from military retaliation for some future aggression of its own. Yet the Spartans were slow to perceive such motives in Themistocles' plans. In Thucydides' account, they remain grateful to Athens for previous military assistance in saving Greece from the Great King, and willing to give her the benefit of the doubt—showing the very slowness and unworldliness of which Sparta's Corinthian allies would complain some forty years later.

The Spartans do, however, send a delegation to Athens to express their qualms about the wall. In a breathtakingly shabby deception, Themistocles holds an audience with the Spartans, detaining them indoors until the walls are complete—at which time he announces it to them as a fait accompli that nothing can reverse. "Athens was now fortified sufficiently to protect its inhabitants," they were told. The Spartans, who are brutal warriors but incapable of such an outright deception in diplomacy, are dumbfounded by this sophistry and trudge home.

By reaching back to remind readers of Themistocles' ploy, Thucydides casts a new light on the Athenians' defense of their empire in Sparta decades later, when they claimed that they had acquired their empire out of fear and defended it out of honor and self-interest. The earlier story makes clear that, perhaps even before the conflict with Persia had been fully concluded, Themistocles had resolved on an imperialistic policy. To be sure, he and his followers were genuinely afraid of the continuing threat posed by Persia. But they also wanted a great sea empire for its own sake. As the Corinthians will bitterly complain years later, after the other Greek states trusted Athens to lead them against the Persian despot's attempted invasion, Athens herself then became like the Great King over the rest of the Greeks.

In Thucydides' depiction of the struggle against Persia and its aftermath, Themistocles and the Spartan commander in chief Pausanias are the two most impressive leaders to have emerged to date. The extraordinary danger of the Persian threat summoned equally extraordinary qualities in each man—qualities that might have lain dormant in a more ordinary period of domestic political affairs. In this respect, they foreshadow the trend we have noted with respect to modern leaders like Lincoln, Churchill, and FDR.

The contrasting careers of Pausanias and Themistocles offer an important perspective on the two regimes and the kind of statesmanship possible within each. The Spartans ordinarily shunned contact with the outside world, and avoided foreign entanglements precisely because they foster the kind of individual ambition that their collectivist institutions discourage. When its leaders did go abroad, they tended to be corrupted by the new and intoxicating experience of personal power in foreign lands. At home, they could never act with the kind of impetuosity and absolute authority that was available to them as commanders abroad.

Among these was the Spartan general Pausanias. In Thucydides' telling, Pausanias behaves like a corrupt and brutal fool when he involves Sparta in the affairs of the other Greek city-states. His fatal blend of inexperience and xenophobia prompts the allies in the common front against Persia to ask Athens to be their arbiter. In this way, Sparta itself opened the door to Athens's rise.

> The violence of Pausanias had already begun to be disagreeable to the Greeks, especially to the newly liberated populations. They resorted to the Athenians and requested them as their kinsmen to become their leaders, and to stop any attempt at violence on the part of Pausanias. The Athenians accepted their overtures and determined to put down any attempt of the kind and to settle everything as their interests might seem to demand.

The Spartan government at length recalls Pausanias, removing him from command for his excesses. Yet upon his return he is treated mildly for his blunders and outrages abroad; his fellow Spartans are more concerned about the psychological strain he has suffered than about the toll he has exacted on Sparta's allies:

> His recall came at just the time when the hatred which he had inspired had induced the allies to desert him and to range themselves by the side of the Athenians. On his arrival at Sparta, he was censured for his private acts of oppression, but was acquitted on the heaviest counts and pronounced not guilty. . . . They feared for those who went out a deterioration similar to that observable in Pausanias. Besides, they desired to be rid of the war with Persia and were satisfied with the competency of the Athenians for the task, and of Athens' friendship at this time toward themselves.

Whatever his savagery toward foreign allies abroad, at home Pausanias remains loyal to Sparta, and his countrymen respond with forgiveness; they care little for the feelings of other peoples, and regard only fellow Spartans as their friends. Moreover, upon his return Pausanias promptly abandons his arrogant posture and folds himself back into the collective—a testament to the regime's internal stability and its power to inspire loyalty at home. Sparta is much to be admired as a collective; its great weakness can be found in its individual leaders, who are often unskilled or go off the rails when dealing with other countries.

In this respect, the Athenian democracy is the opposite of the Spartan collective. Themistocles is a brilliantly successful leader both at home and abroad—tough, smart, flexible, persevering, and eloquent. He is a shrewd bargainer with the allies without being violent or intimidating like Pausanias. Yet the Athenians fear his ambition and eventually—on the word of the Spartans!—condemn him to death in absentia for treason, without giving him the chance to defend himself. They end up hating their greatest benefactor because they fear his power over them. Where they need him as a leader, he needs them only as the basis for his own glory, wealth, and stature. Athens produces brilliant individual leaders, but in the long run it lacks a capacity for unity and sober deliberation. The very qualities that are most admirable in their leaders as imperial statesmen make them threatening to democratic equality at home: The pattern set by Themistocles recurs with Pericles and his successors Cleon, Alcibiades, and Nicias: Imperial success abroad prompts the fear of tyranny at home.

At the end of the day, Athens acquires her empire largely because Sparta lets it happen, distracted from foreign imperatives by its full-time devotion to domestic affairs. The allies want the continuing security and comparative mildness of Athenian leadership. And, quite apart from any continuing fear of the Persian threat, Athens wants this supreme position. Themistocles consolidates Athens's dominance when he very cannily sets a pattern of accepting payment from the allies in lieu of actual military service—a gambit that lulls the allies into abandoning their own military preparedness while handing Athens enormous monetary resources, which it uses to expand its fleet, further tightening its control over their allies. Thucydides remarks:

> For this the allies had themselves to blame. The wish to get off service made most of them arrange to pay their share of the expense in money instead of in ships and so to avoid having to leave their homes. Thus while Athens was increasing her navy with the funds which they contributed, a revolt always found them without resources or experience for war.

In drastic contrast with Athens, Sparta wants done with war as quickly as possible. The Spartan government is concerned about the corrosive and destabilizing effects of ruling abroad on the regime's internal stability—the danger that the absence of Spartan forces from the country and general instability across Greece might encourage the oppressed class of Helots to rise up and overthrow the collective, and also the danger that fellow citizens like Pausanias might have corrupting "heart of darkness" experiences while exercising absolute power in foreign lands.

Ultimately, the lesson of the cold war between Sparta and Athens—and the key to understanding the hot war that finally erupts between the two superpowers four decades later—is that domination is not compelled but chosen. Whatever its claims to the contrary, states like Athens do not acquire empires solely or even primarily out of fear. Athens became an empire because her people wanted it.

Pericles' Funeral Oration and the Plague

Having filled in the context for the war as a whole, we return to the first pair of defining events mentioned above: Pericles' Funeral Oration and the plague that followed it. The funeral address brings to light the problem of the individual versus the city, for in many (although not all) ways Athens is a flawed polis. Its main defect, in contrast with Sparta, is the elevation of the interests of the individual over that of the country as a whole. This is most clearly manifest in Pericles' emphasis on the problem of envy: He warns his listeners in advance of the dangers of heaping too much praise on those fallen in war (a warning that would never have been necessary in Sparta):

> He who is a stranger to the matter may be led by envy to suspect exaggeration if he hears anything above his own nature. For men can endure to hear others praised only so long as they can severally persuade themselves of their own ability to equal the actions recounted. When this point is passed, envy comes in and with it incredulity.

In his speech, Pericles tries to balance self-interest and public duty. Given on the occasion of a comparatively minor skirmish in the war's opening months, the speech addresses far grander themes than its context suggests. Pericles urges his listeners to assume the proper attitude toward war now, before the fighting gets worse and individual self-preservation puts a greater strain on collective duty. This speaks to one of the cardinal lessons of statesmanship—the need for foresight. Leaders must think ahead; the time to build character and resolve in your fellow citizens is at the beginning of a serious crisis, and the way to do it is to be frank about both rewards and risks, rather than improvising one's justification as events unfold, as many would contend the Bush administration did to explain the war in Iraq.

Still, Pericles' pitch for a spirit of common sacrifice is problematic. He deliberately avoids mentioning that individual Athenians must die. Their death will be "in common" and "unfelt" in the heat of combat, while the glory will be individual. Furthermore, the dead will never be envied; rather, they will be honored universally, since they no longer pose any competitive threat to their countrymen:

> Surely to a man of spirit, the degradation of cowardice must be immeasurably more grievous than the unfelt death which strikes him in the midst of his strength and patriotism! The living have envy to contend with, while those who are no longer in our path are honored with a goodwill into which rivalry does not enter.

The main solution to the tension between the individual and the common good is for them all to become "lovers" of Athens in her splendor:

> You must yourselves realize the power of Athens, and feed your eyes upon her from day to day, till love of her fills your hearts.

Pericles argues as if the individual could never gain more glory for himself than by doing what is best for Athens.

> For this offering of their lives made in common by them all they each of them individually received that renown which never grows old.

But what if the individual and the city do not always have the same interests? Notably, Thucydides presents Pericles' oration, destined for fame throughout the ages, with no endorsement of his own. Apart from the speech itself, he presents not a shred of evidence that Athens was as Pericles describes. Indeed, Pericles himself may have considered it a vision of an ideal Athens, of what the city *must* be in order to survive the coming challenges. As noted earlier, the purpose of rhetoric is to inspire and exhort citizens to their best behavior: In Pericles' oration, as in Lincoln's Gettysburg remarks and Churchill's "never surrender" speech, the speaker presents an idealized vision, and—implicitly or explicitly—promises his citizens that they need only draw upon their own native virtues in order to realize it.

Yet Pericles' oration was followed immediately by the plague—revealing how precarious the balance can be when there is no binding common good, when duty toward the whole is premised on benefits for the individual and individual efforts prove unable to avert disaster. As the city is powerless to save the individual, the distance between the common good and the good of the individual widens to the breaking point.

The plague, which wiped out as much as a third of the city, was intensified by the unsanitary conditions that were created when large numbers of Athenians moved within the walls of Athens from the countryside for protection from a Spartan land invasion. Leaving the countryside also meant leaving the family hearth, where, in archaic Greek religion, the ancestors were worshipped. Finally, pious Athenians recalled an old saying that starting a war with Sparta would bring a plague to Athens as punishment, and they blamed Pericles for making this come true. To many Athenians, therefore, the plague appeared to be divine retribution for Athenian hubris, for precisely the blend of boldness, freethinking, and pleasure that Pericles praises in his great oration. Athens appeared to have given up its old ways in the pursuit of empire and affluence—the old code of self-restraint and piety that they once shared with the Spartans—and, many felt, brought on the pestilence as the gods' chastisement.

As people perish in countless scenes of agony and suffering, Pericles' lesson is undone. Personal selfishness and vice, not virtue on behalf of the common good, become the keys to survival. Despite their noble efforts to help others, the virtuous suffer the most. Pericles' vision of "unfelt" individual death pales next to Thucydides' narration of grue-some individual suffering:

> On the one hand, if they were afraid to visit each other, they perished from neglect. On the other, if they ventured to do so, death was the consequence. This was especially the case with such as made any pretensions to goodness. Honor made them unsparing of themselves in their attendance in their friends' houses, where even the members of the family were at last worn out by the moans of the dying and succumbed to the force of the disease.

There is a complete breakdown of the social fabric:

> The bodies of dying men lay one upon another, and half-dead creatures reeled about the streets and gathered round all the fountains in their longing for water. The sacred places in which they had quartered themselves were full of corpses of persons that had died there, just as they were. For as the disaster passed all bounds, men, not knowing what was to become of them, became utterly careless of everything, whether sacred or profane. All the burial rites before in use were utterly upset. Sometimes they tossed the corpse which they were carrying on top of another that was burning, and so went off.

As life becomes cheaper, people grow coarser and more shameless in their pleasures. Like the revelers during the Black Death in Boccac-cio's *Decameron*, they enter a grotesque bacchanal of revelry, enjoying every pleasure while they still can:

> Men now coolly ventured on what they had formerly done in a corner, and just as they pleased, seeing the rapid transitions produced by persons in prosperity suddenly dying and those who before had nothing succeeding to their property. So they resolved to spend quickly and enjoy themselves, regarding their

lives and riches alike as things of a day. Perseverance in what men called honor was popular with none, it was so uncertain whether they would be spared to attain the object. But it was settled that present enjoyment and all that contributed to it was both honorable and useful.

Exhausted and demoralized by the plague, the Athenians want to give up the war with Sparta:

They began to find fault with Pericles as the author of the war and the cause of all their misfortunes, and became eager to come to terms with the Spartans, and actually sent ambassadors there, who did not however succeed in their mission. Their despair was now complete and all vented itself upon Pericles.

By juxtaposing the plague with Pericles' immortal speech, Thucydides shows how fragile an appeal to self-interest can be, as a basis for civic loyalty, when that loyalty is not fortified by tradition, law, and the consolation of religion. In the plague, as in war, individual survival and self-interest come first. Natural disasters can therefore teach a moral lesson—as the Bush administration learned when the cataclysmic suffering unleashed by Hurricane Katrina in Louisiana made its victories over Saddam Hussein and the Taliban, already bogging down, appear useless when juxtaposed with its failure to protect ordinary Americans at home.

In a later speech, following the plague, Pericles tries to address the Athenians' dissatisfaction with his policies. In this second speech—far less beautiful and inspiring than the Funeral Oration—Pericles drops his stirring call for citizens to become "lovers" of Athens in all her splendor. Instead, he argues that the *only* purpose of the common good is its naked utilitarian value for serving the individual. It is a strict appeal to the rational calculation of self-interest: You will *always* be better off belonging to a city, he argues, than being left to fend for yourself. Never mind the common good—think about our "common safety." He elaborates:

A man may be personally ever so well off, and yet if his country be ruined he must be ruined with it, whereas a flourishing
commonwealth always affords chances of salvation to unfortu-
nate individuals. Since then a state can support the misfortunes
of private citizens, while they cannot support hers, it is surely the
duty of everyone to be forward in her defense, and not like you
to be so confounded with your domestic afflictions as to give up
all thoughts of the common safety, and to blame me for having
counseled war and yourselves for having voted for it.

Pericles also upbraids his fellow citizens for their fickleness and
changeability, contrasting it with his own steadiness:

I am the same man and do not alter, it is you who change,
since in fact you took my advice while unhurt, and waited for
misfortune to repent of it.

He plays on their concern for the safety of the state and their collective survival:

Born as you are citizens of a great state, and brought up, as
you have been, with habits equal to your birth, you should be
ready to face the greatest disasters and still keep unimpaired the
luster of your name. . . . Cease then to grieve for your private
afflictions and address yourselves instead to the safety of the
commonwealth.

Most strikingly, Pericles drops all pretensions that Athens's allies
appreciate the mildness of her rule over them. Who knows how they
might treat their former master if Athens's grip over them slackened?
Maintaining control over an empire, he argues, is like holding a tiger
by the tail:

For what you hold is, to speak somewhat plainly, a tyranny.
To take it perhaps was wrong, but to let it go is unsafe.

Pericles' second speech reveals once more how statesmen must shift their rhetoric under less favorable circumstances: Though he advances the same goal—convincing every individual Athenian that it is in his best interest to serve Athens—in each speech, once the plague has exposed the weakness of the social fabric he becomes steely and realistic. Though he does not flinch, does not apologize, he adjusts his expectations downward.

AT THIS POINT in the narrative, Thucydides finally offers his own assessment of Pericles as a leader. Pericles would not have endorsed the Sicilian expedition, he tells us—but only because he thought it would strain the city's resources. In itself, the invasion was not immoral, unless Athens's entire previous rise to empire and all the benefits of its way of life extolled in the Funeral Oration were immoral. Moreover, he ventures, the invasion could have succeeded: Alcibiades' conduct of the war before he was recalled "was as good as could be desired." The invasion was an error of expediency, and that is why Pericles would have avoided it. He was no pacifist and he favored the existence of the empire. He knew that Athens was, put bluntly, despotic in its relations with its allies, and that her citizens' loyalty depended on the rewards this power exercised abroad brought them:

> He told them to wait quietly, to pay attention to their fleet, to attempt no new conquests and to expose the city to no hazards during the war, and doing this, promised them a favorable result.

However, Thucydides goes on with reference to the impending disaster in Sicily:

> What they did was the very contrary, allowing private ambitions and private interests, in matters apparently quite foreign to the war, to lead them into projects unjust both to themselves and to their allies—projects whose success would only conduce

to the honor and advantage of private persons, and whose failure entailed certain disaster on the country in the war.

While he was alive, Pericles' unique blend of personal qualities
made it impossible for selfish politicians to drive the state in disastrous directions in order to increase their own power and reputation.
Because he gained no selfish personal advantage from leading them,
because his own authority and dignity did not hinge on continuous
further expansion, Pericles was in a position to use both encouragement and fear as needed to curb excessive despondency and excessive
confidence. He was not afraid to tell them they were dead wrong.

The causes of this are not far to seek. Pericles indeed, by his
rank, ability and known integrity, was enabled to exercise an
independent control over the multitude. In short, to lead them
instead of being led by them. For as he never sought power
by improper means, he was never compelled to flatter them,
but, on the contrary, enjoyed so high an estimation that he
could afford to anger them by contradiction. Whenever he saw
them unseasonably and insolently elated, he would with a word
reduce them to alarm. On the other hand, if they fell victim to
a panic, he could at once restore them to confidence. In short,
what was nominally a democracy became in his hands government by the first citizen.

The problem with the course pursued by Athens after Pericles'
death lay in the core dynamic of its politics—the tension between
democracy and empire. Once the uniquely prudent Pericles passed
from the scene, his successors reflected the perils of that dynamic. Individuals elevated themselves above the city and its collective interests.
Cleon, Alcibiades, and Nicias all confirmed the danger that Pericles
tried to alleviate in his Funeral Oration, and which the plague laid
bare. Even in assessing Pericles' cumulative record, it's worth noting,
Thucydides praises only his sober and measured conduct of the war—
not the shining image of Athens he paints in the Funeral Oration.

Pericles' approach to governance was one of moderate imperialism; he favored a schedule of conquests that was carefully calibrated to the city's resources. He wanted the Athenians to avoid undertaking adventures their resources could not support. From the moment of his emergence as the city's leading statesman, the successor to Themistocles, he takes a cautious approach to the coming war, warning against big risks. His tone recalls that of Archidamus—except that Archidamus wanted Sparta to avoid war altogether. Pericles, in contrast, knows his people and their addiction to affluence and easy living, and he advises prudent means for pursuing imperialistic ends. In his first recorded speech—in contrast with the later and much better known Funeral Oration—he says nothing of the splendor of the empire. Instead, he presents Athens as a beleaguered nation forced to fight against its will. This is probably meant to sober the people up, to curb any excessive enthusiasm or delusion that victory will come easily. He tries to inoculate his people against giddy overconfidence, suggesting a bit of the Spartans' bleak view that life is governed by necessity and individual striving can achieve only so much.

In remarks that parallel Archidamus's review of Athenian resources, Pericles tells the Athenians in an analysis of the enemy's resources that Sparta cannot win the war on her own; with its extraordinary seapower, Athens is like an impregnable island. By the same token, though, he concedes that it would be foolhardy to engage Sparta and her allies in an all-out land war, where Athens would be outnumbered. Rather, he argues, Athens must win the war by sitting tight. She can lose the war only through impetuous excitement—the kind of exuberance that leads to error.

> The rule of the sea is indeed a great matter. Consider for a moment. Suppose that we were islanders. Can you conceive a more impregnable position? Well, this in future should be our conception of our position. Dismissing all thought of our land and houses, we must vigilantly guard the sea and the city. No irritation that we may feel for the former must provoke us to a battle with the numerical superiority of the Peloponnesians. A

victory would only be succeeded by another battle against the same superiority; a reverse involves the loss of our allies, the source of our strength, who will not remain quiet a day after we become unable to march against them.

This cautious, slightly Spartanesque advice for safeguarding the empire goes against the usual impetuous Athenian grain, but Pericles has the authority and charisma to bring his listeners along. By the time of the Funeral Oration, however, the war is seriously under way—and Pericles emerges in all his greatness in a rhetorical masterpiece that recognizes that, come what may, Athens is now engaged for the long haul in a life-and-death struggle with a formidable foe. Victory is the only option. After all, Pericles *was* an imperialist. That is why Socrates, judging politics from the purest and most selfless standpoint, regarded him as a bad ruler, ethically no better than Alcibiades in his desire for Athens to expand. Pericles knew Athens was tyrannical in its foreign policy and that her citizens' loyalty depended on the material rewards achieved by empire. He argued tirelessly that the individual should identify his own good with that of the city, but by "good" he meant "having more," as the more nakedly shameless generals will proclaim in the Melian Dialogue, which Thucydides presents later. Although Pericles counseled moderation as a tactic, like the Athenian regime in general he did not embrace a moderate view of human nature and existence. Serving Athens, he argued, would get you all you could possibly want of prosperity and honor.

In this, Pericles and his successors disagree—in that they put their own good ahead of what was expedient for Athens. In a way, however, such self-interested leadership could be justified on the logic of imperialism itself, which Pericles himself accepted: If having more is best, after all, why shouldn't a leader have more than his fellow citizens? That was the direction in which Alcibiades took Athenian leadership. By the same token, if the city as a whole aims at having more, then wouldn't a policy of accepting less go against the common good? In this sense the later Athenian leader Nicias, who reflected the hidden Spartan and Sophoclean conservative strain in Athens, and who was genuinely against war and imperialism and would prefer Athens to look inward and moderate its desires, was as much an enemy of the common good defined in Periclean terms as was the more open and obvious selfishness of Alcibiades.

It is likely no accident that Thucydides offers his assessment of Pericles directly after his account of the plague. Why? Because, as an extreme case, the plague reveals something that may be true at any time in an expansionist democracy like Athens: that the individual may derive more benefits by acting in his own interest than by serving the common good. Moreover, just because Pericles was able to satisfy his desire for honor by steering Athenian imperialism on a moderate course doesn't mean that everyone would or that Thucydides himself thinks everyone would or even should. Pericles was wrong to think that his successors would follow his lead, finding more glory in serving Athens than in dominating her to pursue their private interests.

> With his successors it was different. More on a level with one another, and each grasping at supremacy, they ended by committing even the conduct of state affairs to the whims of the multitude. This, as might have been expected in a great and sovereign state, produced a host of blunders, and amongst them the Sicilian expedition, though this failed not so much through miscalculation of the power of those against whom it was sent as through a fault in the senders in not taking the best measures afterwards to assist those who had gone out, but choosing rather to occupy themselves with private cabals by which they not only paralyzed operations in the field but also first introduced civil discord at home. . . . Nor did they finally succumb till they fell victims of their own intestine disorders. So superfluously abundant were the resources from which the genius of Pericles foresaw an easy triumph in the war over the unaided forces of the Peloponnesians.

Pericles was unique because his desire for honor and influence was satisfied by serving Athens and encouraging her not to expand the empire if she did not possess the resources to do so. Through his blend of imperialism and prudence, he for a time embodied Athens in his own person. After his death, the two parts of this synthesis fly apart, revealing two opposed layers of opinion in Athens that had been concealed by his prominence. Whereas Pericles managed to combine imperialism with caution, after his death, Athenian politics are increasingly driven apart into a war party and a peace party. The war party wants endless expansion, while the peace party is troubled by the arrogance and immorality of imperialism and wants a return to the good old days of simple decency before Athens began her rise. None of Pericles' successors are able to recapture his middle ground. Instead, they exaggerate one extreme or the other—overweening imperial ambition or an unrealistic wish to shed the burdens of power and turn back the clock to more innocent times.

Neither Nicias, the leader of the peace party, nor Alcibiades, the champion of greater expansionism, found that his individual interest matched that of the city, as had Pericles. But Nicias and Alcibiades were more typical of Athens than Pericles. Indeed, together they embody the central contradiction of the Athenian thesis—the wish to combine virtuous self-government and equality at home (Nicias) with domination and exploitation abroad (Alcibiades).

Historically speaking, Hobbes was right: Pericles was a happy accident, not a real solution. His successors pulled apart what he had held together. Alcibiades is preceded by the coarse and violent Cleon, Nicias by the cautious Diodotus. None is able or even willing to restore the Periclean balance. Alcibiades was the incarnation of everything most hubristic about the democratic empire: He was daring, innovative, young, licentious, profligate, and impious. He enthusiastically urged the further uprooting of the old countryside shrines to the gods and the ancestral villages to concentrate the city's power within its walls. He was in favor of limitless expansionism, even *beyond* Sicily into Africa itself. His creed—summed up in the Melian Dialogue—was that might makes right the world over. Nicias, on the other hand, embodies the less obvious "silent majority" of pious moderates who favored a withdrawal from world affairs—many of them people shocked by the plague into thinking about the gods and their uprooted traditions. Despite Pericles' shining example, then, Thucydides' history suggests that the private and public interests were irreconcilable in Athens.

Ultimately, it was this tension that led both to the expansion of the Peloponnesian War—because Alcibiades needed more money and had a lust for supreme fame—and also to its failure. Wary of Alcibiades' thrusting ambition, the Athenians tried to balance the dynamic by handing control of the Sicilian expedition over to Nicias—precisely the wrong kind of man to carry out so bold a scheme. The Athenians were trying to have their cake and eat it too: If we agree with Pericles that the common good of Athens is inconceivable without the empire, then Nicias's conduct as an individual could not have been in harmony with the common good. If, on the other hand, we agree with Sophocles and the "silent majority" that the good of Athens requires returning to a nonaggressive peace and an absorption in domestic self-government, then Alcibiades could not have been in harmony with the common good. As the book unfolds, Thucydides appears to move closer to the second alternative.

Dealing with Allies: The Revolt of Mitylene

With the revolt of an important Athenian ally, Mitylene, Athenian statesmanship finally begins to fragment and forsake the Periclean middle ground, revealing even more about how Athens and Sparta, with their opposing models of statecraft, deal with their alliances and with rebellion.

The Athenians are enraged when the Mitylenians try to defect, because Mitylene is a privileged ally—it pays no tribute in money, and runs its own fleet. Furious at what they perceive as ingratitude, the Athenians vote to have all the men killed and the women and children enslaved. They send a galley to communicate the decree and order the Athenian commander Paches to carry it out. Yet the following day "brought repentance with it and reflection on the horrid cruelty of a decree which condemned a whole city to the fate merited only by the guilty." The assembly reconvenes to debate this change of heart, allowing us to witness not just the declarations of one over-whelmingly prestigious leader, but a full-scale debate that reveals all the fissures in public opinion that Pericles had tried to smooth over in his Funeral Oration. Pericles had claimed that Athens could be both generous in principle to its foes and Spartan-like as needed. In the debate over Mitylene, that equilibrium falls apart, with Cleon arguing for the Spartan side and Diodotus for the more generous side of the Athenian character.

Cleon, "the most violent man at Athens" and at this time politi-cally the most popular, tells the Athenians that they are too trusting—much the same criticism the Corinthians had leveled at their allies the Spartans. But the Athenians' trust in others, Cleon implies, is namby-pamby—it has no Spartan backbone. Cleon wants to impart more of Spartan ruthlessness to the easygoing Athenian outlook praised by Pericles. The Athenians must stick to their resolve about Mitylene, he argues, and have the entire population killed or enslaved. An unedu-cated honesty is better than an educated deceitfulness, he proclaims, echoing Archidamus's speech about Spartan probity while swiping at Pericles' praise of liberal cosmopolitan Athens as "the school of Greece." We pay too much attention to orators and clever speeches, he thunders away. We should be more laconic and firm of purpose.

Cleon echoes Archidamus's claim that people are roughly equal in their basic nature, and that they should not be overly educated if such education threatens to undermine their patriotism:

> Ordinary men usually manage public affairs better than their more gifted fellows. The latter are always wanting to appear wiser than the laws, and to overrule every proposition brought forward, as if there was no more important way for them to show their wisdom, and by such behavior they too often ruin their country, while those who mistrust their own cleverness are content to be less learned than the laws and less able to pick holes in the speech of a good speaker. These we ought to imitate instead of being led on by cleverness and intel-lectual rivalry.

Cleon puts one in mind of Joe McCarthy or George Wallace ranting about "pointy-headed innerleckshuls" and effete Ivy League "eggheads"—we need to be as tough as our Communist foes. At bottom, Cleon's position is that the Mitylenians are unjust because they hurt our interests, and therefore they must be punished. It is a more vulgar and unvarnished version of Pericles' final warning to the Athenians that they are a tyrant city whose allies are waiting to pounce upon any display of weakness. He is playing Joe McCarthy to Pericles' more polished Dean Acheson. Cleon continues:

> If you follow my advice you will do what is just toward the Mitylenians and at the same time expedient, while by a differ- ent decision you will not oblige them so much as pass sentence on yourself. For if they were right in rebelling, you must be wrong in ruling. However, if, right or wrong, you determine to rule, you must carry out your principle and punish the Mity- lenians as your interest requires, or else you must give up your empire and cultivate charity without taking any risks.

Cleon wants Athens to pursue its interests with the harshness and inflexibility he attributes to the Spartans. Once you make a decision, he tells the Athenians, you must carry it out no matter what. The cos- mopolitan openness to the world that Pericles had praised, his plebe- ian successor—a tanner by trade—disdains. He wants Athens to imi- tate the parochialism and xenophobia of the Spartan oligarchy with its distrust of outside opinion and diversity. The Athenians had very much reflected the Periclean outlook when they had argued at the prewar conference in Sparta that they did not claim to be just in their foreign policy, but that they were gentle and generous with others as much as possible. Cleon, reflecting the darker age that follows Pericles' passing, is saying: This flirtation with generosity is a luxury that we as an empire can no longer afford.

Cleon's speech is followed by that of Diodotus. Though we know nothing about him from history outside of Thucydides, Diodotus's speech patterns and arguments suggest he was a more genteel figure, from an aristocratic background; in that respect he would have resembled Pericles, a member of the influential Alcmaeonid clan. Diodotus argues that if the Athenians always resort to killing their rebels or enemies, they will force them to fight to the last man, out of pure desperation—an outcome that would hardly be in Athens's best interest. On purely pragmatic grounds, therefore, he argues that in ruling over other peoples the Athenians should alternate fear of death with hope for life:

> If you butcher the people of Mitylene, who had nothing to do with the revolt, and who, as soon as they got arms, of their own motion surrendered the town, first you will commit the crime of killing your benefactors and next you will play directly into the hands of the higher classes, who when they induce their cities to rise, will immediately have the people on their side, through your having announced in advance the same punishment for those who are guilty and for those who are not.

This milder policy happens to be more intrinsically just, but Diodotus claims to be defending it primarily on grounds of expediency. "The question is not justice, but how to make the Mitylenians useful to Athens."

Both speakers maintain that the pursuit of self-interest is inherently just, but their lines of reasoning are diametrically opposed: Cleon argues that treating the Mitylenians brutally is in the Athenians' self-interest, and therefore just, while Diodotus argues that treating them more justly is in the Athenians' self-interest. Diodotus is trying to restore the prudent middle ground of Pericles: Maintain the empire; schedule your conquests; do not treat your enemies with wanton cruelty where persuasion will succeed. But, in this darker time, Diodotus can no longer invoke the shining image of the liberal empire city that Pericles did, suggesting that simply feasting their eyes on her splendors would inspire every individual to serve the common interest. He takes the more candid and realistic position that just behavior is only incidentally pursued for its own sake—that self-interest must be its main justification. In this way he tries to preserve whatever remains of Athenian geniality under a rubric of unvarnished expedience.

There is one problem with Diodotus's argument: the Mitylenians *had* in fact fought to the last. That was why the verdict on them was so harsh to begin with. Yet there is a segment of the Athenian population that shares Diodotus's generosity. Their underlying geniality and fear of hubris is revealed by the speed of the two ships that were sent out after the first debate and during the second. The first ship, bearing the order to execute the Mitylenians, traveled as slowly as possible because the crew was so horrified by the decree. The second ship, bearing the reprieve, made the greatest possible speed:

> Another galley was at once sent off in haste, for fear that the first might reach Lesbos in the interval and the city be found destroyed, the first ship having about a day and a night's start. . . . Luckily they met with no contrary wind, and the first ship making no haste upon so horrid an errand, while the second ship pressed on in the manner described, the first ship arrived so little before them, that Paches had only just had time to read the decree, and to prepare to execute the sentence, when the second put into port and prevented the massacre.

Though Cleon may have been more clear-sighted about the stakes facing what even Pericles, at the end of the day, had openly labeled "a tyrant city," many Athenians still prefer the gentler approach to empire.

In sharp contrast with the Athenians' ambivalence toward a rebellious ally is Sparta's response to the behavior of Plataea, an ally of Athens. The Spartans offer the Plataeans their version of a fair trial:

> Upon their arrival, no charge was preferred. They simply called up the Plataeans and asked them whether they had done the Spartans and allies any service in the war then raging . . .

and upon their saying that they had not, took them out and slew them all without exception.

It was another instance of the Spartan code: united and conflict-free at home, harsh and unforgiving abroad. Their ruthless and wordless justice (that is, vengeance) is what Cleon wants the Athenians to emulate. Yet even the nature of the debate undercuts the comparison: in keeping with democratic politics, Cleon must give a lengthy speech before the assembly arguing that lengthy speeches aren't necessary. The Spartans remain perfectly unanimous all along. They need no debates. They are more public-spirited and far nastier.

The Human Equivalent of the Plague: Civil War in Corcyra

There follows Thucydides' famous description of the horrors of civil war—the passages that Hobbes and other modern students of statecraft found so instructive. Thucydides reveals vividly how civic life can degenerate, under the impact of war, from debate to bloodshed, insurrection, the confiscation of property, and mass political murder.

The outbreak of civil war in Corcyra returns us to the original brushfire war that mushroomed into the superpower conflict, which began with Corcyra's dispute with Corinth. As the war spreads throughout the Greek world, the oligarchies line up behind the Corinthians and Spartans, the democracies behind the Athenians. The war between the two governing principles of Athens and Sparta eats into them all, and engenders a war within each regime between these partisan factions. "[T]he whole Hellenic world was convulsed," Thucydides writes, "struggles being made everywhere by the popular chiefs to bring in the Athenians, and by the oligarchies to introduce the Spartans."

War subverts the internal order of each state and makes citizens begin to fight each other as if they were foreign foes. As in Iraq after the toppling of Saddam Hussein, ideological and religious hatreds that had previously been suppressed or managed now resurface, providing an excuse for personal vendettas, extortion, kidnapping, and sadism. The old ethical and religious prohibitions are rejected, places of worship defiled:

> The Corcyraeans were engaged in butchering those of their fellow-citizens whom they regarded as their enemies, and although the crime imputed was that of attempting to put down the democracy, some were slain also for private hatred, others by their debts because of the monies owed to them. Death thus raged in every shape, and, as usually happens at such times, there was no length to which violence did not go; sons were killed by their fathers, and suppliants were dragged from the altar or slain upon it, while some were even walled up in the temple of Dionysos and died there.

Thucydides' language makes it clear that he saw the civil war in Corcyra as a human equivalent of the plague that earlier ravaged Athens. He uses the same medical language and observes similar traits in describing it as he did with the plague:

> The sufferings which revolution entailed upon the cities were many and terrible, such as have occurred and will always occur, as long as the nature of mankind remains the same. . . . In peace and prosperity, states and individuals have better sentiments, better because they do not find themselves suddenly confronted with imperious necessities. But war takes away the easy supply of daily needs, and so proves a rough master, one that brings most men's characters down to a level with their fortunes. Revolution thus ran its course from city to city, and the places which it arrived at last, from having heard what had been done before, carried to a still greater excess the refinements of their inventions, as manifested in the cunning of their enterprises and the atrocity of their reprisals.

Civil war, to Thucydides, is the ultimate destroyer of the harmony between the individual and the common good, breaking up families and undermining religious faith. Just as during the plague, boldness, selfishness, and vice become the standard, while moderation and altruism are regarded as mad.

> Thus every form of iniquity took root in the Greek countries by reason of the troubles. The ancient simplicity into which honor so largely entered was laughed down and disappeared, and society became divided into camps in which no man trusted his fellow.

The connection between rationality and morality is utterly confounded, leading to a dichotomy between clever rogues and honest fools. Neutrals are simply destroyed. Pericles had worried that envy would undermine patriotism, and now his fears are realized; he had hoped that citizens would realize that only by helping one another could each individual be safe, but now that benign vision is swept away by murderous passion:

> In the confusion into which life was now thrown in the cities, human nature, always rebelling against the law and now its master, gladly showed itself ungoverned in passion, above respect for justice, and the enemy of all superiority, since revenge would not have been set above religion, and gain above justice, had it not been for the fatal power of envy. Indeed men too often take upon themselves in the prosecution of their revenge to set the example of doing away with those general laws to which all alike can look for salvation, instead of allowing them to subsist against the day of danger when their aid may be required.

The civil war spreads a contagion of moral darkness over all of Greece—even reaching back to Athens, where any notion of the common good dissolves under the clash of different factions jockeying for power. There are only partisans now. "War is a violent teacher," Thucydides concludes: It teaches us, as nothing else can, to submit to the necessity of preserving ourselves first, regardless of what happens to our fellow citizens.

Nemesis: The Melian Dialogue and the Sicilian Expedition

Athens's inexorable slide into disaster begins in a deceptively promising way, with a real prospect for a negotiated end to the war with Sparta. In 425 B.C., the Athenian fleet captures the island of Pylos, hard by the home territory of Sparta, and captures a Spartan force. The Spartans, in addition to wanting their fellow citizens back, are also keenly aware that the presence of Athenian forces so close to their heartland might incite the Helots to revolt, hoping that the armed representatives of the great democracy nearby will assist their effort to throw off their shackles. Anxious to have more troops at home for heightened internal security, the Spartans withdraw their forces from the outskirts of Athens, where they have been menacing the city with a land assault since the beginning of the war.

In their fear of internal subversion, and the uprising of their vastly more numerous class of slaves, the Spartans reveal the opposite of the unanimous ruthlessness they displayed in slaughtering the Plataeans. Their fear of rebellion at home is their Achilles' heel, the chain around their neck that yanks them roughly back whenever they overextend themselves. The Spartans had thought they could rely on their superiority as a land army to offset the naval power of Athens—that it would protect them from a land invasion. But Demosthenes' ability to combine naval and land force operations to capture Pylos demonstrates that the Spartans aren't as self-sufficient on land as they like to think. The Athenians, with their swift and agile ships, are able to appear suddenly on the Spartan coastline and aim directly at their oppressive internal class structure. The Athenians prove to have the versatility and flexibility Pericles had encouraged them to cultivate—and which the Spartans' allies lamented—showing that they can in fact mount a successful land battle as well as maintain naval supremacy, while the Spartans are unable to attack Athens by sea. Their naval ineptitude prevents the Spartans from recapturing Pylos, and they sue for peace over a mere handful of captured men. They are gentle toward their own—as drastically so as they are harsh toward outsiders and to their own class of slaves.

Sparta now sends a delegation to Athens with a formal proposal of peace, urging that both sides step back and be allowed to keep what they have. True to form, they believe that people everywhere prefer to keep what they have in safety rather than risk it all on a bold gamble in which they may lose everything—as exemplified by Archidamus in his original case for avoiding war, the Spartans tend to believe that fortune is treacherous and cannot be relied upon. Daring is much more likely to be disappointed than rewarded by unpredictable reversals of chance. War can always get out of hand, can always go further than you originally intended, and end up making everyone the loser. As their delegation now argues to the Athenian assembly:

> The prosperity which your city now has must not make you fancy that fortune will always be with you. Indeed, sensible men are prudent enough to treat their gains as precarious, just as they would also keep a clear head in adversity, and think that war, so far from staying within the limit to which a combatant may wish to confine it, will run the courses that its chances prescribe, and thus, not being puffed up by confidence in military success, they are less likely to come to grief, and most ready to make peace, if they can, while their fortune lasts.

The Spartans' argument for their peace proposal is the embodiment of their entire way of life and how it shapes their statesmanship. But it fundamentally misunderstands the Athenians, or at least their most radical war party—who want *more*, not just the untroubled enjoyment of the status quo. Would Pericles have favored making peace at this juncture? Based on what Thucydides tells us about him, he might well have, depending on the circumstances—perhaps as a breathing spell while Athens consolidated her gains and built up new resources. But this prudent middle course is more difficult now because the choice between war and peace has become more draconian, more open and divisive, in Athenian politics. Public opinion has become polarized as the war drags on with no final outcome in sight. The war party and the peace party each coalesce around the two representative statesmen of the post-Periclean era: Alcibiades, standing for war, and Nicias, standing for peace. Even now, Sicily looms as Athens's nemesis. For the Sicilians have been trying to make peace with Athens while the hostilities between them are not yet serious. But the side of Athens embodied by Alcibiades is intoxicated by its apparent invincibility and is eyeing Sicily ever more greedily:

> So thoroughly had the present prosperity persuaded the Athenians that nothing could withstand them, and that they could achieve what was possible and impracticable alike, with means ample or inadequate it mattered not. The secret of this was their extraordinary success in general, which made them confuse their strength with their hopes.

Henceforth, Athenian politics increasingly divides into two factions represented by Nicias and Alcibiades. The Periclean middle ground—calling for prudent expansion through the scheduling of conquests calibrated with a realistic assessment of resources—is driven apart into the extremes of an excessive desire for immediate peace and a limitless lust for further victory and imperial expansion. Both extremes are at odds with the Periclean legacy, for Pericles did not believe the empire could simply be relinquished or that Athens could return to the good old days before Marathon, when life was rustic and needs were simple. The empire was a tiger that must be ridden or it would turn around and devour its master. But the overconfidence of the war party about the upcoming struggle with Sicily—their inability to recognize the power of this prodigious foe—also departed from the prudence of Pericles, playing into Alcibiades' hands.

Thucydides gives us brief but revealing profiles of these two new leaders of Athens. His description of Nicias recalls Archidamus's account of the code of Sparta. Nicias does not embody the most harsh and violent side of the Spartans, the one revealed to outsiders and imitated by Cleon. Instead, Nicias mirrors their internal way of life—the pious side that lies low, relying on custom, and distrusting individual brilliance, daring, and innovation. Like Archidamus and the Spartans, Nicias wants the Athenians to keep what they have: If we aim for more, his position implies, fortune and the gods may strike us down like Oedipus. Let us quit while we are ahead and enjoy our present prosperity.

As Thucydides relates it:

> Nicias, the most fortunate general of his time, desired peace more ardently than ever. Nicias, while still happy and honored, wished to secure his good fortune, to obtain a present release from trouble for himself and his countryman, and hand down to posterity a name as an ever-successful statesman, and thought the way to do this was to keep out of danger and commit himself as little as possible to fortune, and that peace alone made this keeping out of danger possible.

Nicias tried to assume Pericles' mantle, echoing his argument that Athens had everything to gain by sitting tight and consolidating her gains without undertaking new expansion. Sparta may want peace now, he argued, but in time her resources will worsen compared with ours. Sparta will then realize that quickly resuming hostilities, and dealing a potential knockout blow, would be preferable to waiting until her material resources have declined even further. Thus, he reasons, it's in Athens's interest to bind Sparta to a peace treaty for as long as possible—until Athens's material advantages are insurmountable.

> The adjournment of the war could only increase [the Athenians'] own prestige and injure that of their rivals. The excellent state of their affairs making it their interest to preserve this prosperity as long as possible, while those of Sparta were so desperate that the sooner she could try her fortune again the better.

Alcibiades, by contrast, "thundered away more loudly than ever at the Spartans," calling for an instant resumption of all-out war. A scion of the powerful and long-established Alcmaeonid clan, and a nephew of Pericles, Alcibiades emerges as the new leader of the war party: "Foremost among these was Alcibiades, a man yet young in years for any other Greek city, but distinguished by the splendor of his ancestry." In some ways, Alcibiades was a realization of the Athens that Pericles had conjured in his Funeral Oration. He was a beautiful and charismatic youth whose hunger to serve the city for distinction, and to feast his eyes on her splendor, as his uncle had exhorted the Athenians, alternated with that love of high culture Pericles had also praised in his fellow citizens—notably through his intimate friendship with the philosopher Socrates, part of an elite circle of educated and prominent men. Indeed, in Plato's portrait of Alcibiades in his dialogue *The Symposium*, he is genuinely torn between the philosophic life and his political ambition, knowing in his heart that love of wisdom is the higher life, but unable to tear himself away from his love of fame and public prominence, which he can win only by wooing the democracy. If Pericles' middle-ground policies had prevailed, a balance between the love of honor and the love of the life of the mind might have been Athens's finest accomplishment, as crystallized in his magnificent nephew. In reality, however, Alcibiades abandons the life of the mind and gives himself over entirely to his lust for power and glory—and seduces the Athenians into embarking on their wildest adventure yet, the invasion of Sicily, which will spell their doom.

THESE DIFFERENT LEADERS, and divergent currents of Athenian opinion, lead us directly to the so-called Melian Dialogue, which has come down through history as the consummate statement of the creed that "might makes right." This idea has influenced a string of realpolitik thinkers throughout history, from Machiavelli and Hobbes to the "realist" school of international relations identified with Hans Morgenthau and Henry Kissinger. Such latter-day realists were not necessarily advocates of the wanton and limitless pursuit of imperial power through conquest. Rather, they held that every nation is steered by its own self-interest, without reference to any higher ethical authority or value system—and that, as "rational actors" who want to maximize those interests, states generally prefer to carve out a sphere of influence and respect the spheres of others rather than go to war, which entails the risk of defeat and human and economic devastation. On the other hand, there have been ruthless men—among them Kaiser Wilhelm II, Adolf Hitler, and Joseph Stalin—who took the maxim to mean that any nation that can get away with conquering others should go ahead and do so, because morality counts for nothing in the real world.

Yet the simple maxim "might makes right" is not, in truth, a fair expression of the actual argument Thucydides locates in the Melian Dialogue. The Athenian position he captures is more complex: "Of gods we believe, of men we know, that by a necessary law of nature they rule wherever they can." As we look into it further, we should always bear in mind that, as we have already seen, this represents only *one* view among the Athenians and their leaders.

The island of Melos is an ally of Sparta whom the Athenians attack and subdue. The Athenians send envoys to negotiate their surrender. But the Melian "few," the oligarchical ruling class, choose to talk to the Athenians alone rather than allow the common people to hear them—thus giving us access to a closed-door discussion between two elites. In such a setting, the two groups can speak more candidly than they might before their respective public audiences. Although Thucydides never claims to have solid eyewitness accounts of every event he relates, and freely admits to reconstructing certain events for which imperfect evidence exists in order to clarify what he thinks must be their meaning, the Melian Dialogue is by far the most artificial event in the whole book. There is no external evidence from other sources that it ever took place, and, of course, no one but the unnamed participants could have related it word for word.

The passage resembles a Platonic dialogue, in which figures from real life begin with their concrete political situation, and go on to debate the abstract meaning of justice and morality. The Melians say of themselves "we are at rest." Literally, this means they have no ambitions beyond preserving their isolated island's way of life, but allegorically it can also be read as a reference to the conversation itself—a haven for brief philosophical conversation while the turmoil of war is kept at bay. As Thucydides presents it, Melos is an island both literally and metaphorically, a place of temporary repose outside of the clash of foreign affairs; it is also the historian's vehicle for a more principled exploration of the moral questions raised by the Peloponnesian War—the only philosophical exchange in Thucydides' work between representatives of the two regime principles at war: democracy and oligarchy.

In asking the Athenians to end their occupation and leave them alone (although allies of Sparta, they have never actually joined the war against Athens), the Melians invoke the protection of the gods, the importance of justice, and the need for moderation. Respecting justice, they argue, provides protection for all regimes—powerful ones like Athens no less than minor ones like Melos. In fact, they say—perhaps unwittingly echoing an earlier warning by Pericles—if Athens's injustice to her subject peoples should provoke her downfall, the vengeance taken by the oppressed would be especially terrible:

> As we think, at any rate, it is expedient—we speak as we are obliged, since you enjoin us to let right alone and talk only of interest—that you should not destroy what is our common protection, the privilege of being allowed in danger to invoke what is fair and right, and even to profit by arguments not strictly valid if they can be got to pass current. And you are as much interested in this as any, as your fall would be a signal for the heaviest vengeance and an example for the world to meditate upon.

The safest course for a people is to concentrate on domestic affairs, the Melians argue—avoiding war and other foreign entanglements, which expose one to the reversals of fortune.

The Athenian generals, however, counter that all regimes must compete for power at each other's expense—that, for all practical purposes, there is no justice in international affairs.

For ourselves, we will not trouble you with specious pre-
tenses—either of how we have a right to our empire because
we overthrew the Persians, or are now attacking you because
of the wrong that you have done us—and make a long speech
which would not be believed; and in return we hope that you,
instead of thinking to influence us by saying that you did not
join the Spartans, although their colonists, or that you have
done us no wrong, will aim at what is feasible, holding in view
the real sentiments of us both, since you know as well as we do
that right, as the world goes, is only in question between equals
in power, while the strong do what they can and the weak
suffer what they must.

These words reflect a coarsening of the Athenian character in the
post-Periclean age. The Athenians no longer bother justifying their
empire as they did at the first congress in Sparta; they do not even
bother consulting the assembly at home to debate the fate of Melos,
as they did with Mitylene. Still, we must bear in mind that Nicias and
the peace party—the "silent majority" of Athenians who are troubled
by Athenian hubris and impiety—might be closer to the Melian view.
They are nowhere represented among these coolly predatory generals.

The generals' conclusion here is that there can be no lasting peace
in foreign affairs, nor is it possible for any state to absorb itself exclusively in its internal affairs. A nation must either rise or fall, compete
or die. ("World power or downfall!" as a high-ranking German general put it when his country provoked World War I.) A regime must
expand and fight or be overwhelmed by the immoderate ambitions
of other states. Even if one's own people want peace, they advise the
Melians, the ambition of other countries won't permit this inward-
looking stance. On the face of it, one might see the Athenian generals as simply expressing candidly what everyone believes in secret. In
this respect, they retain some of their disarming openness about their
ambitions, that characteristic disdain for preachy self-justification and
fake moralizing. Admit it, they seem to chide the Melians, you are
invoking justice and peace only because you are weak.

The Athenians have already won on Melos. They have no need to explain themselves. But they want this weaker people to see the world as it is, if only to make their subjection seem less painful and arbitrary. In their conduct abroad, then, the Athenian cynicism is still mixed with a certain generosity. If their worldview is correct, they need only have conquered the Melians, without wasting time on debate. But perhaps something in their egalitarian spirit makes them at least want the conquered to see their fate as inevitable, so that they can reconcile themselves to it. Yet one wonders if the Athenian generals had really thought through the implications of their position. What about Athens's *own* domestic affairs? Does the formula "one takes power where one can" work at home as well as abroad? Would they be prepared for one of their own number to treat fellow Athenians the way they propose to treat the Melians and other countries? This is the dilemma of trying to combine free government with imperialism, however generous and reasonably explained.

Another problem that the Athenians identify in the Melian position is that it cannot be applied universally. It is a recipe for isolationism—which is fine only as long as a nation has the power to repel aggressors. One case in point, as the Athenians remind the Melians, is Sparta. The Melians are relying on the Spartans to come to their aid in their present distress. But the Athenians caution them to see the Spartans as they really are. The Spartans, like the Melians, also prefer peace, moderation, and domestic affairs—and for that very reason they have not, and will not, come to the Melians' assistance. Their justice is for themselves alone; when dealing with other states, including their allies, all that matters is their own self-interest. Precisely because the Spartans share the Melians' value system, they don't *care* about anyone but their own people:

> The Spartans, when their own interests or their country's laws are in question, are the worthiest men alive. Of their conduct towards others much might be said, but no clearer idea of it could be given than by shortly saying that of all the men we know they are most conspicuous in considering what is

agreeable honorable, and what is expedient just. Such a way of thinking does not promise much for the safety which you now unreasonably count upon.

The Athenians' cynicism suggests further evidence of the "Spartanizing" of the imperialist party that was first evident in the rise of Cleon: We must be like our foes and do only what is best for ourselves, ignoring morality in international relations just as they do. Again, though, there's something liberal-minded in the way they express this openly—as opposed to the Spartans, who tend to cloak themselves in hypocritical claims of justice. The Athenians openly accept the world as it is, a clash of interests devoid of morality, and this allows them to be relatively generous to their subordinates. There is no need for gratuitous cruelty or violence, they say, as long as you give us what we want. As for being willing to live in peace and leave other states alone, unfortunately even that requires imperial strength.

So the Athenians here still show a trace of Periclean generosity, or at least a preference for an open and pragmatic settling of differences—though their hard core of cynicism has now lost any sense of nobility, or any real claim of justified predominance based on their role in saving Greece from the Persians. The Athenian generals claim that there is no inherent justice in international affairs, but that there *can* be a common interest when the weak are reconciled to the rule of the strong. The Melians reply: If you harm us, your allies will think you are unjust, and that will undermine your grip on them. In this, they echo Diodotus and the more moderate, peace-inclined faction in Athens—the faction that argues that you shouldn't gratuitously harm other peoples because they will only turn upon you, and that will harm your interests. But the Athenian generals reply: We rule through our strength, not based on claims of justice. It is precisely *because* we are strong that we can afford to give you a fair deal as our subjects.

In the second phase of the dialogue, the Melians abandon their claim that justice has any force in international relations. Instead they turn to fortune and divine providence, arguing that the gods will provide. Since we are weak and unjustly oppressed, they say, divine providence will bring the Spartans to our rescue. But they also count on the Spartans' shame over abandoning an ally—much as the Corinthians had tried in their efforts to win over Sparta at the start of the conflict. As Thucydides observed, however, Sparta voted for war only out of fear of Athens's growing power, not out of shame over leaving their allies in the lurch. Their support for the intrinsic justice of the war was purely rhetorical. So it's unlikely that shame alone will bring them to the aid of Melos, appearing to vindicate the Athenians' cynicism about honorable treatment of others as a motive in foreign policy. Sometimes, the Melians insist, fortune enables the weak to defeat the strong. Like Archidamus earlier, and Nicias more recently, the Melians believe that fortune and the reversals of fate can level differences in power, military technique, and daring.

> You may be sure that we are as well aware as you of the difficulty of contending against your power and fortune, unless the terms be equal. But we trust that the gods may grant us fortune as good as yours, since we are just men fighting against unjust, and that what we lack in power will be made up by the alliance of the Spartans, who are bound, if only for very shame, to come to the aid of their kindred. Our confidence, therefore, after all is not so utterly irrational.

To this the Athenians respond with what from a pious view of providence is a shocking position: If anything, they claim, fortune favors the strong, not the weak. There is no fairness built into the order of the world that compensates the weak. On the contrary: The gods care no more about justice than we do.

> When you speak of the favor of the gods, we may as fairly hope for that as yourselves, neither our pretensions nor our conduct being in any way contrary to what men believe of the gods, or practice among themselves. Of the gods we believe, and of men we know, that by a necessary law of nature they rule wherever they can.

This comes close to pure blasphemy. But, again, these generals don't necessarily represent the stratum of Athenian opinion that believed that the plague was a divine punishment for their hubris and their abandonment of the old religious customs. These generals are so cold-blooded that they don't even claim the gods are on their side. Ordinary Athenians more likely believed that Athens's cause was just and favored by the gods. For the members of this sophisticated military elite, however, the gods are simply indifferent: They care about neither justice nor the acts of man. As for the Spartans, they are out for themselves like everyone else. Wake up, they urge the Melians: We live in a cosmos of cold, calculating rationality. Conquer, or make the best deal you can.

The Melians protest once again that the Athenians intend to have their way whether it is just or unjust. The Athenians respond that they will talk about only what is expedient for both sides, what is in the best interest of the Melians and the Athenians in the present situation. As Cleon had argued earlier, justice is what is good for us. And the same goes for the Melians, the generals tell them: Justice is what is good for the Melians, and in this situation, that means giving into us in order to survive.

The Melians then try a last-ditch effort to defend justice in terms the Athenians will understand, arguing that one state should not oppress another if it doesn't want to incur that people's hatred. This echoes the argument Diodotus made over the fate of Mitylene: Justice toward others is also best for ourselves, for acting selfishly will only create too many enemies waiting to pounce if we falter. Pericles had cautioned the Athenians in like fashion, but unlike the Melians he didn't actually argue that they should follow some higher ethical code, only that they shouldn't get themselves into a position where they have too many enemies and too few resources. By the same token, he also warned the Athenians that they could not afford to let their empire go and live inwardly, as the Melians preach. His position was a middle ground now almost vanished from Athenian politics: moderation for the sake of expediency. Alcibiades and the generals on Melos stand for immoderate imperialism, Nicias and the peace party stand for an expedient isolationism.

The Athenian generals respond that they don't fear the desire of other strong nations for revenge, for strong nations don't care about justice, which is the source of the desire for revenge. Rather, they care only about their own interests. Only weak nations and allies, they claim, want to punish the strong when they are down. Yet that position assumes that powerful foes don't allow sentiments of revenge and hatred to guide their policy—that they are "rational actors" who use force only for their own maximum net gain.

As we'll learn in the final denouement of Athenian hubris, the Syracusans—who lead a rich and powerful alliance of Sicilian city-states on a par with that of Athens—disprove this theory when they slaughter the Athenian invaders horribly in the marble quarry on Sicily. The Syracusans' response to the Athenians' unprovoked aggression *is* hatred and a desire to punish them for their unjust invasion. States may act to maximize their material interests, but that doesn't always prevent them from indulging in revenge or feeling outraged by the injustice of a would-be oppressor. The side of Athens represented by the generals is riding for a fall. Their view is clear: People invoke justice only when they are weak, when they can repel a foe neither by force nor by offering it a concrete advantage in exchange for a peace agreement. The Melians have nothing to offer Athens. Athens, on the other hand, can offer the Melians survival.

THE SICILIAN EXPEDITION, the nemesis for Athens's hubris, follows directly upon the Melian Dialogue. It's a dramatic shift, fueled by the Athenians' lust for new dominions, overconfidence, and shocking ignorance about the size and resources of their chosen foe. The Athenians view Sicily as a rich little island ripe for the picking. In fact, it is more like a separate country with many rich cities, comparable to the Peloponnesian mainland. Mounting the invasion, thus, is tantamount to starting an entire second war before the first one has been successfully concluded.

As Thucydides relates:

The same winter the Athenians resolved to sail again to Sicily, with a greater armament than before, and, if possible, to conquer the island. Most of them being ignorant of its size and of the number of its inhabitants, and of the fact that they were undertaking a war not much inferior to that against the Peloponnesians. For the voyage round Sicily in a merchantmen is not far short of eight days, and yet large as the island is, there are only two miles of sea to prevent its being mainland.

The Athenians are about to get their comeuppance for the generals' position in the Melian Dialogue that "one takes power where one can." Yet, as Thucydides presents it, placing blame and responsibility for the disaster involves a delicate intertwining of pragmatism and ethics. Pericles might well not have undertaken the mission; it proves the most drastic possible illustration of his warning to the Athenians not to overextend their resources. But his view could only have been expedient, not moral or pacifistic. Had victory in the Peloponnesian War been secured, and Athenian resources sufficient, on what basis could he have opposed it? Moreover, Thucydides himself indicates that the expedition may have been feasible. The failure, he suggests, was rooted in Athenian domestic politics: After Pericles, no leader had found his own good to be in harmony with that of the city as a whole, instead leading the democracy based on his own selfish inclinations.

Pericles had argued that every Athenian should see the common good of Athens and his own good as identical. But by good, he too meant "having more," just as the Melians accuse the Athenian generals of in their dialogue. Pericles' moderation was pragmatic, not moral. Moral moderation would have argued for being content with what you have rather than tempting fortune. Pericles, by contrast, believed that serving Athens would reward you with all you could possibly want of prosperity and honor. His successors did not think this way. They put their own good ahead of what was expedient for Athens as a whole. But in a certain sense this was justifiable as an unintended corollary of the Periclean thesis. For, if having more is best, why not have more than your fellow citizens? Alcibiades was at first put in charge of the invasion because of his matchless military daring. But he was widely suspected of wanting to become the tyrant of Athens, a Persian-style despot. At the same time, if the city as a whole aims at having more, then wasn't Nicias effectively going against the common good by rejecting imperialism?

The death of the bellicose Cleon opens the way for a peace treaty with Sparta, which came to be known as the Peace of Nicias after its primary architect. Nicias hopes that the city will identify its interests with his own, given his moderate leanings, piety, and distrust of adventurism. But the most vocal part of the city rebels, whipped up by Alcibiades. This faction sees itself as being taken advantage of: Peace, to them, means no more profits, booty, or trade. Alcibiades is for *endless* expansion, setting a model for Alexander the Great and Julius Caesar; he is a founding member of the young Abraham Lincoln's tribe of the eagle. After Sicily falls, he boasts, we can go on to defeat Carthage and her rich trading empire:

> Most of the Athenians in the assembly spoke in favor of the expedition, although some spoke on the other side. By far the warmest advocate of the expedition, however, was Alcibiades, who wished to thwart Nicias both as his political opponent and also because of the attack he had made upon him in his speech, and who was, besides, exceedingly ambitious of a command by which he hoped to reduce Sicily and Carthage, and personally to gain in wealth and reputation by means of his success.

Alcibiades embodies an almost insane hubris. It's as though he is bent on implementing, quite literally, the doctrine of the generals in the Melian Dialogue that, wherever gods and men can rule, they must. No limit can be set on Athenian power, he tells the Athenians, for as soon as we stop expanding, others will overwhelm us. Constant expansion is necessary to prevent the city from being destroyed. The only way to stop is to live as austerely as the Spartan oligarchy:

We cannot fix the exact point at which our empire shall stop.
We have reached a position in which we must not be content with
retaining, but must scheme to extend it. For if we cease to rule
others, we are in danger of being ruled ourselves. Nor can you
look at inaction from the same point of view as others, unless you
are prepared to change your habits and make them like theirs.

Pericles had thought that maintaining an empire was compatible
with retaining the status quo. Though it's dangerous to let go of the
tiger's tail, he told the people, it's equally perilous to reach for another
tiger. To his nephew, however, there is no such middle ground: One
must conquer or be conquered, rule or be ruled. Life is all motion,
rest is only an illusion, a momentary interval between new waves of
destruction. There are no islands of peace, only the roaring ocean of
greed and glory.

Alcibiades' character was a fatal combination of brilliance and vice.
His personal vanity, luxurious scale of living, and desire to preserve
his charisma through generous gifts to the common people threatened
to bankrupt him. This gave him a selfish interest in inflaming the
Athenians to expand their conquests. Like his successor in the tribe of
the eagle, Julius Caesar, he was compelled to become the top dog, or
be dragged down by relentless creditors and outraged former partners.
In Thucydides' telling, he utterly subverts Athenian foreign policy,
diverting it from Pericles' prudent course to a bold and risky new
path that will save him from financial ruin and greatly increase his
wealth and prestige. In doing so, he trounces Pericles' hope that the
self-interest of a nation's citizens, and especially of its leading statesmen,
will coincide with what is prudent for Athens. Alcibiades' self-interest
can be furthered only by urging Athens to imprudent actions:

For the position he held among the citizens led him to indulge his tastes beyond what his real means would bear, both in
keeping horses and in the rest of his expenditure, and this had
not a little to do with the ruin of the Athenian state.

Worse still, the Athenians themselves were deeply conflicted about this charismatic young war leader. On one hand, swayed by his urging, they greedily eyed the rich prize of Sicily. On the other hand, they deeply distrusted him and feared that success in that war would embolden him to seize tyrannical power at home. It was widely suspected that he had defiled figurines of the Hermae, a god dear to the common people, during one of his drunken carousals with his rich young pals, and his enemies seized on this as a pretext to defy him. "They loudly proclaimed that the mutilation of the Hermae was part and parcel of a scheme to overthrow the democracy, and that nothing of this had been done without Alcibiades."

At the time, the city was gripped with a fear of plots to set up a tyranny, with Alcibiades the main suspect. In this paranoid mood, the assembly voted for measures that combined the worst of both worlds: They continued the imprudent imperialistic expansion of invading Sicily, while removing from its command the one man, Alcibiades, who might have brought it off. For even Thucydides, in the midst of his withering denunciation of Alcibiades, concedes that Alcibiades' conduct of the war was beyond criticism:

> Alarmed by the greatness of his licence in his own life and habits, and of the ambition which he showed in all things that he undertook, the mass of the people set him down as a pretender to the tyranny and became his enemies. And although his conduct of the war publically was as good as could be desired, individually his habits gave offense to everyone, and caused them to commit affairs to other hands, and thus before long to ruin the city.

It is the first instance of an age-old type: the military commander whose talents threaten to overwhelm his civilian masters, and we should pause for a moment to ponder it.

THUCYDIDES IS THE first historian of statesmanship to identify—in the recall of Alcibiades from the command of the Sicilian expedition—a possibly unresolvable and potentially hazardous contradiction between the requirements of victory abroad and of democratic self-government at home. Alcibiades' fractious relationship with the Athenian assembly, who want victory in Sicily but do not want him to be their master in Athens, is the first in a long list of similar pairings between civilian authorities and talented but insubordinate or overly zealous commanders with political ambitions, some of whom we considered earlier. Caesar and the Roman Senate; Napoleon and Talleyrand; McClellan and Lincoln; Patton and Eisenhower; MacArthur and Truman. In each case, a political leader needs the talent of a brilliant general to win the republic's wars or restore order (Caesar, Napoleon, McClellan, Patton, and MacArthur). In each case, the general in question will not submit to the civilian magistrate: Caesar and Napoleon wanted endless conquests. McClellan would not prosecute the war in the vigorous way Lincoln wanted and had ambitions to replace him as president. Patton and MacArthur both wanted to wage war in a way thought too risky by their superiors. Eisenhower was also a general, of course, but had no extensive combat record of his own and functioned much like a politician and diplomat as supreme allied commander in World War II.

Patton and MacArthur perhaps most closely resemble Alcibiades' conflict with his civilian masters. And the same irony first uncovered by Thucydides is present in their cases as well, namely, that the insubordinate commander both really *did* pose a threat to civilian authority and most likely really *would* have achieved military victory for his country. For although Truman had no choice but to sack MacArthur when he publicly urged carrying the Korean War into China, it is beyond question that MacArthur's daring outflanking movement had earlier broken the resistance of the North Korean military, even as it risked drawing in China. In Patton's case, Eisenhower relieved him of command after he recommended that the Red Army be driven back out of central Europe with the help of the recently defeated German Wehrmacht. It was dubious advice and threatened the alliance with Russia. Yet a case can be made that Patton saw the Soviet threat more clearly than his superiors.

. . . .

LET'S RETURN TO Thucydides' narrative of the debate over the Sicilian expedition. For his part, Nicias absolutely opposes the expedition he is now assigned to command:

> Nicias, who had been chosen to the command against his will, and who thought that the state was not well advised, but upon a slight and specious pretext was aspiring to the conquest of the whole of Sicily, a great matter to achieve, came forward in the hope of diverting the Athenians from the enterprise.

Nicias hopes the Athenians will not want to make the huge preparations necessary to defeat Sicily. It turns out, he tells the assembly, that the war party had underestimated the size and strength of Sicily; furthermore, he says, reports of a huge hoard of treasure within the island's temples are inaccurate. Sicily is too strong to attack, and has no significant wealth to plunder. He also cautions that the Spartans have been set back only temporarily: They may well rebound and break the peace treaty, especially if they sense that Athens is tied down in Sicily, attacking the city directly over land or trying to subvert her allies by promoting oligarchical coups. They should focus on delivering a knockout blow to their main adversary, not open war on another front:

> Instead of being puffed up by the misfortunes of your adversaries, you ought to think of breaking their spirit before giving yourselves up to confidence, and to understand that the one thought awakened in the Spartans by their disgrace is how they may even now, if possible, overthrow us and repair their dishonor, inasmuch as military reputation is their oldest and most important study. Our struggle, therefore, if we are wise, will not be for Sicily, but how to defend ourselves most effectually against the oligarchical machinations of Sparta.

The speech, however, backfires. His cautions only convince the Athenians that they have the prudent advice they need in order to succeed. As Thucydides relates:

> Nicias thought he would either disgust the Athenians by the magnitude of the undertaking, or, if obliged to sail on the expedition, would do so in the safest way possible. The Athenians, however, far from having their taste for the voyage taken away by the burdensomeness of the preparations, became more eager for it than ever. And just the contrary took place of what Nicias had thought, as it was held that he had given good advice, and that the expedition would therefore be the safest in the world.

In this way, Nicias plays right into Alcibiades' hands, serving Alcibiades' canny argument that he and Nicias would together comprise the qualities of great Pericles—the older man's prudence and caution would balance the boldness and impetuosity of the younger.

> Do not be afraid of my youth, but while I am still in its flower, and Nicias appears fortunate, avail yourselves to the utmost of the services of us both.

Nicias relies on divine providence and the favor of fortune. He represents the strongest influence within Athenian domestic politics of the worldview associated with the Spartans and Melians. He believes we must act justly and piously because the world upholds these values. And, like the Melians, he is destroyed: Fortune leaves him in the lurch. Nicias has a history of being moderate at the wrong time in a way that backfires and actually plays into the hands of the war party. A very cautious commander, he had once been blamed for not destroying or extracting the surrender of a Spartan contingent trapped on the island of Pylos when he had the chance, instead timidly besieging them, just as later he would doom the Athenian army on Sicily by not withdrawing in time. He had resigned his commission on Pylos and let Cleon take it over, hoping that Cleon, who had no military experience, would be defeated, thereby discrediting the war party. Instead Cleon won a stunning victory, and the ambitions of the war party were emboldened. Nicias's miscalculation on that occasion foreshadows his even greater misstep with Alcibiades, when his prudent reservations about the war only bolster Alcibiades' claim that they have taken every precaution. A move meant to promote moderation ends up bolstering imperialism.

In the final irony, the man who least wanted the expedition is placed in command of it. Nicias favors a gingerly approach to the invasion, but he is afraid the Athenians will reproach him again for being too cautious. Accordingly, although he knows the Athenian force is in a precarious position with the Syracusans nearby, he does not withdraw his men. His moderation, which is admired on the domestic front, goes against what Athens wants abroad. They want a moderate ruler, but not a moderate general. However, increasingly worried by the precarious situation they are in, he changes his mind and prepares to withdraw. But he then delays *again* out of piety because of an eclipse of the moon—and misses his last chance for escape. He is in agreement with the still-pious average Athenian that they should wait and perform the proper ritual—and it leads to their destruction.

All was at last ready, and they were on the point of sailing away, when an eclipse of the moon took place. Most of the Athenians, deeply impressed by this occurrence, now urged the generals to wait, and Nicias, who was somewhat over-addicted to divination and other practices of that kind, refused from that moment even to take the question of departure into consideration, until they had waited the thrice nine days prescribed by the soothsayers.

This incident reveals that the majority of men in the fleet and army, although bent on conquering Sicily, come from that same silent majority at home who fear that the plague was brought on by human impiety. Now, at just the wrong moment, they seek to practice abroad the decency they practice at home—the decency that makes them suspect Alcibiades and admire Nicias, who shares their attachment to pious custom. The democracy is hopelessly conflicted about what it most wants.

It finally begins to dawn on the Athenians that they've more than met their match in the Sicilians, whom Alcibiades had dismissed in the assembly as "rabble."

> The Syracusans had now gained a decisive victory at sea, and deep, in consequence, was the despondency of the Athenians, and great their disappointment, and greater still their regret for having come on the expedition.

For the first time, the Athenians are encountering a foe as resolute and dynamic as themselves, a bitter comeuppance. None of the Athenians' proven techniques work here as they had before; they prove unable to defeat the Syracusan alliance head-on. Moreover, Athens has no power to weaken the Sicilians indirectly by subverting their ruling oligarchies and winning the people over to a democratic regime like their own, because the Syracusans are already democratic. Finally, and most crushing of all, the Athenians are defeated at sea, where they believed they would always prevail:

> These were the only cities they had yet encountered, similar to their own in character, under democracies like themselves, which had ships and forces and were of considerable magnitude. They had been unable to divide and bring them over by holding out the prospect of change in their governments, or to crush them by their great superiority in force, but had failed in most of their attempts, and being already in perplexity, had now been defeated at sea, where defeat could never have been expected, and were thus plunged deeper in embarrassment than ever.

The fate of the Athenian force is horrible indeed. Nicias is put to the sword—"a man who, of all the Greeks in my time, least deserved such a fate," says Thucydides in pronouncing his epitaph, "seeing that the whole course of his life had been regulated with strict virtue." Still, his end might seem to vindicate the view of the generals on Melos that fortune does not favor the pious any more than the impious. By delaying the Athenians' escape in order to make sacrifices to the gods, Nicias relied on providence—and was betrayed by her. The rest of the Athenians are left to die in agony through exposure and starvation in an enormous quarry. The moans and putrefaction of the dying men roll off the pages of Thucydides down through the centuries, reminding us of the horrors of many wars, murder pits, and death camps down to this very day. And, once again, Thucydides' meticulous description of the stages of slow death reminds us of his earlier description of the plague and the civil war, for, in human affairs, imperialistic hubris is the moral equivalent of a fatal disease:

> The prisoners in the quarries were harshly treated by the Syracusans. Crowded in a narrow hole, without any roof to cover them, the heat of the sun and the stifling closeness of the air tormented them during the day, and then the nights, which came on autumnal and chilly, made them ill by the violence of the change. Besides, as they had to do everything in the same place for want of room, and the bodies of those who died of their wounds or from the variation in the temperature, or from similar causes, were left heaped together one upon another, intolerable stenches arose, while hunger and thirst never ceased to afflict them, each man during eight months having only half a pint of water and a pint of corn given him daily. In short, no single suffering to be apprehended by men thrust into such a place was spared them.

Thucydides pronounces his grim epitaph in which the wheel of destiny has raised the Syracusans high and brought Athens low:

> The victory of Syracuse was the greatest Greek achievement of any in this war, or, in my opinion, in Greek history, at

once the most glorious to the victors and the most calamitous to the conquered. The Athenians were beaten at all points and altogether; all that they suffered was great; they were destroyed with a total destruction, their fleet, their army—everything was destroyed, and few out of many returned home.

But was the calamity inevitable, beyond any influence by human action? Not necessarily. Alcibiades, unlike Nicias, would never have been prevented by piety from taking the right measures. His shamelessness about the gods, which made him feared at home as an aspiring tyrant, would have served the pious Athenians well in the expeditionary force. The invasion of Sicily is ruined by the poorly timed entry of domestic politics into foreign affairs: When the majority at home are swept by a wave of piety, the majority of the Athenian forces on Sicily follow suit, to disastrous results. Although Alcibiades was the best available commander for the invasion, Athens fears him as a ruler and dooms the expedition by recalling him. Like Nicias, he too must violate the common good, not through too much moderation but through its complete absence. Knowing he may face capital charges if he goes home after being stripped of his command, Alcibiades flees abroad, first to Sparta and then to Persia. He gives the Spartans advice on how to conduct the war. But the Spartan king Agis, jealous of his prominence, seeks his death and drives him to the Persians. With consummate cynicism, he advises a leading satrap of the Great King to let the two sides in the Peloponnesian War wear each other out. But since Sparta at this point has the upper hand, owing to the disaster in Sicily, by dissuading Persia from siding with Sparta and tipping the scales, he is indirectly still helping Athens. He is still loyal in his way, and also hoping for a comeback in Athens.

After the terrible news of the defeat in Sicily reaches home, Athens is gripped by an unprecedented paranoia—a swift change of heart, the act of a guilty conscience wracked by terror at what their former subjects may do to them now that they have been crushed in their latest, most arrogant exploit. The Athenians suddenly *want* to exercise moral moderation, to keep what they have, to avoid expansion. They entrust more power to the elders, as Nicias had advised. In turn the Spartans, sensing their advantage, grow more confident. They stop talking about how they are fighting with Athens for the sake of liberty for the other cities, and begin simply issuing orders, and many new allies flock to them. In this connection, Thucydides offers one of his rare direct judgments: Sparta, he writes, is the only major regime he knows of that was able to be moderate in prosperity and not embark on excessive expansion.

The success of Sparta appears to refute the Athenian generals' thesis on Melos that one always takes power where one can. For Sparta, expansionism is not inevitable. On the other hand, the slave class of Helots has a lot to do with retarding the Spartans' ambitions abroad. They rightly fear the destabilizing effects of war on their class system; in fact, democracies may be more prone to imperialism than such conservative regimes. Freedom at home tempts one to spread freedom abroad even while enriching oneself.

As for Athens, she needs an oligarchy now, a conservative government to correspond to her chastened mood. Athens sees the need to become more like Sparta internally so as to quench its destructive thirst for foreign expansion. (The more so because Alcibiades is still intriguing to get back in their good books.) The Athenian democratic majority can no longer rule itself because a Nicias leads to disaster abroad while they fear an Alcibiades at home. The oligarchy is a middle-class regime, combining the "center" between rich and poor (as Thucydides puts it), a halfway house between democracy and tyranny. It is, he pronounces, the best government Athens had during his lifetime—but it lasts only six months. As Thucydides' history ends, the glory and grandeur of Athens fade from view in a twilight of anxiety and uncertainty.

WHAT, THEN, ARE the lessons of this first democratic empire and its leaders? They are stark indeed.

The Athenian generals on Melos represent the most daring, innovative, and sophisticated side of Athens. They recall the cool tech-

nocrats who ran the Vietnam War, men who had a visceral disdain for
the kind of moralizing about godless communism that may well have
been necessary to defend the war in public. But there was another side
to Athens—a silent majority of those attached to the old ways of life
from before the rise to empire. The uprooting of the ancestral villages
and shrines to build the city's fortifications and enclose the population within them remind these Athenians of their forsaken ancestors,
religion, and traditions of moderation. Even as the empire grows, this
contingent of average Athenians remain concerned about the gods;
the rumors of Alcibiades' impiety bolster their suspicion that he aimed
to become their tyrant. Nicias represents this silent majority, and he
entertains the same fears and suspicions about Alcibiades.

As the Sicilian expedition goes from bad to worse, culminating
in the ghastly death of the Athenian force in the quarry, Athens is
increasingly gripped by a paranoia about tyrants and hidden plots to
overthrow the democratic government. A moderate man like Nicias
is afraid that acting on his moderation will get him in trouble with
the most vocal imperialists back home, who want tyranny over other
peoples but not over themselves. The Athenians elevate Nicias to the
command and recall Alcibiades because they do not want tyranny
over themselves. But Nicias is afraid that if he behaves too moderately,
the "tyrant city," as Pericles had frankly described it, will be angry at
his military timidity. Then, when he does act moderately, he takes
the wrong measure. He prefers a private death that is honorable (put
to the sword by the enemy) to a public death that is disgraceful (tried
before a roaring mob in the agora). We have now traveled the furthest
possible distance from Pericles' hope that a public death in the service
of Athens would always be preferable to a private death, and always
more honorable.

The Athenian "few," the military elitists who debate the meaning of life with the Melian "few" on their island, may well not have
expressed themselves so candidly when speaking at home to the Athenian "many." They think the gods are indifferent to justice, but the
Athenians as a whole are outraged by the desecration of the Hermae,
and in book eight we learn that they had consulted oracles about the

course of the war. The generals on Melos represent the sophisticated new Athens at its extreme, the side that Alcibiades belongs to and comes to lead. But the Athenian generals do not think through the domestic consequences of what they propose for international relations: If you must acquire power and "have more" wherever you can, why not have power over your own people? Athenians feared Alcibiades for this very reason: they understood or felt this logic intuitively.

The Athenians want power over others, but they are afraid that the one man with enough daring to achieve this power abroad will seize power over them as well. They want to tyrannize others without being tyrannized themselves. Whereas Nicias lacks the daring to carry off the invasion of Sicily, Thucydides tells us that Alcibiades' conduct of the war up until his recall "was as good as could be desired." The demands of freedom from tyranny in domestic politics contradict the measures required to achieve tyranny abroad. This is the true link between the Melian Dialogue and the Sicilian expedition: The expedition is an extreme realization of the bold adventurism that the Athenian generals on Melos epitomize. It fails because that policy subverts democratic political freedom, and causes the Athenians to remove the one man who could have won it.

Back to the Future: Where Do We Go from Here?

As noted, in *The Symposium* Plato portrays Alcibiades as torn between his attraction to the philosophic self-reflection of Socrates and the lust for honor that led him to woo the Athenian masses and inflame their desires for power and riches acquired through imperial expansion. Alcibiades' Socratic leanings did not prevail over his passion for imperial politics. But beginning with Plato himself, in his image of the chariot of the soul, and continuing through classical writings, including Cicero's *Dream of Scipio* and down to the civic humanism of the Renaissance, history has seen numerous attempts to resolve this conflict in favor of the intellect and to codify the correct balance between the life of the mind and public service that Alcibiades should have achieved. That balance, as we've already seen, has served as a standard throughout the Western history of statesmanship down to the present day—in the person of former warriors such as John McCain, who ascended from extraordinary service to their country on the battlefield to the higher moral and intellectual courage required to exercise responsibility as a leader. This attempt to codify sound statesmanship also led to the distinction between the servant of the republic and its usurper—the distinction with which Lincoln wrestles in the Lyceum speech between the man who seeks honor through saving the republic and the one who, denied a constructive outlet, seeks a criminal glory by enslaving it.

Perhaps in part because the defects of Alcibiades' character seemed to mirror the failings of democracy itself, history in effect decided that it was impossible to maintain a purely democratic empire as Athens had attempted—or, indeed, any kind of democracy—without degenerating into mob rule and demagoguery. Democracy therefore went into a deep freeze, disappearing from the West until the American Founding Fathers recalled both the glory and the vices of Athens and swore that America would not make the same mistakes. After the decline of Athens, the small neighborly Greek *polis* or city-state gave way to a multinational cosmopolitan empire—the kind first attempted by Alexander the Great and put on a firmer footing by Rome. Alexander tried to spread through his conquests a synthesis of the old Homeric code of sacrifice to the common good epitomized by Sparta and the cultivation of the arts and learning epitomized by Athens, leading to a multinational meritocracy of those able and willing to embrace this aristocratic ethos.

In Rome's case, the rise from a republic of laws to a world empire replayed the problem of Alcibiades and some of the other tensions between freedom and imperialism first diagnosed by Thucydides. Gnaius Pompey and Julius Caesar, ostensibly serving Rome only by acquiring new territories abroad, were also dynasts bent on attaining unique power and prestige for themselves and their factions at home. Although officially mere servants of the Senate, by their conquests abroad they procured vast off-the-record fortunes, client states, and private armies, which they could then deploy to have their way back in Rome. While Caesar in this way followed in Alcibiades' footsteps, courting the passions of the plebeians for more land and booty and thus undermining the authority of the Senate and his own aristocratic class, his foe Marcus Brutus, descendant of the man who had founded the Roman republic, played a role analogous to that of Nicias, trying to defend the old traditions at the expense of greater prosperity and opportunity for outstanding new talent.

As the republic lurched into civil war and dynastic strife based on this contradiction between republican government at home and empire abroad, Cicero reached into a more virtuous past to propound Scipio as the model of an ideal statesman who would subordinate personal ambition to the common good. But Cicero was a dreadful failure as a political player, continually manipulated by cold-blooded barracudas like Pompey and Caesar who used him at will, then threw him aside. Even Caesar's heir, the nineteen-year-old Octavius, took advantage of Cicero's idealistic delusion that he would educate this young prince in the ways of virtuous statecraft, acting as a more successful Socrates to a reformed Alcibiades. Resolving the contradiction of the republic between liberty at home and empire abroad by creating a world monarchy headed by himself, Octavius waded through an ocean of blood from his long string of putsches, broken pacts, and political murders, and emerged as the living god Augustus (aided by some of the best spin doctors in history, Vergil among them). He grafted the outward shell of Roman republican constitutional forms onto what was in fact a benevolent multinational despotism like that of the Great King of Persia. Unscrupulous and hypocritical as he was, Augustus bequeathed the most successful recipe for stable government for a thousand years—revived several times by Christian monarchs, and finally reinhabited by Napoleon as the splendid vehicle for his campaign to spread democratic ideals to conquered Europe. Yet the republican spirit lived on, and even the liberal-minded entertained grave reservations about Napoleon's creation of a liberal empire by force of arms. America, which saw itself in some ways as a revival of the early Roman republic before its subversion by demagogues like Caesar, remained a beacon for the hope that liberty and equality could

be combined with civic virtue and the common good. The American
founders regarded the example of Caesar opprobrious; it was Scipio,
Cato, and Brutus they took as their models.

All of which leads back to Theodore Roosevelt's intriguing observation about reading Thucydides during his evening hours in the
White House. Roosevelt described Thucydides' tone as "unmoral,"
comparing him to Tolstoy in this regard. This may seem an odd comparison, but on reflection it makes sense—especially when one con-
siders that TR always saw politics in moral terms, refusing to distinguish between his ambition to serve and a commitment to justice and
decency. For it is true that both Thucydides and Tolstoy do take a
very broad-minded and impartial view of their characters, watching
at a distance as they reflect and diverge from their time and circumstances. While Tolstoy diagnoses the differences between Pierre Bezukhov and Prince Andre Bolkonsky, or between Anna Karenina and
the husband she deserts for an adulterous affair, he never pronounces
an absolute moral judgment upon them. Thucydides, too, has a certain noble but bleak and distant objectivity when surveying the wide
canvas of the Peloponnesian War. Armed with his insight into the
permanently recurring types of human nature, he limns their psyches,
sets them into motion in the great clash of freedom and empire, and
watches the permutations, the self-delusions, the willful sophistries,
and the grandeur as they unfold. Examples of unqualified heroism,
or unqualified villainy, are difficult, though not impossible, to find in
his pages.

And in this judgment, TR reveals that Thucydides' account of
democracy and empire, while deeply instructive, is not a perfect parallel for the American experience in all respects. For America, unlike
Athens, has always seen its mission as providing freedom and prosperity not only for its own people, or even merely for itself and its
allies, but as fulfilling a universal ethical obligation to promote liberty
throughout the world. This mission reflected a blend of modern egalitarian principles derived from the Enlightenment with the underlying
Judeo-Christian view that all men are equal in the sight of God. That
American belief cuts against the current of cynicism in the Athenians

as Thucydides presents them and their inconsistent attempts to promote freedom both at home and for others.

It goes without saying that, if one surveys America's many wars—against the Spanish empire in the New World, twice against Germany, against North Korea and North Vietnam, twice against Saddam Hussein—that the motives of some have been mixed, a blend, depending on one's evaluation, of a genuine commitment to advancing freedom with crass ambitions for material gain and political advantage. But the overall intention was almost always sincere in its aim to promote freedom in the world. Looking back at Thucydides' utterly pragmatic assessment of the tensions between democracy and empire, one that is almost entirely lacking anything analogous to modern democratic and Abrahamic aspirations to promote justice and human dignity for their own sake everywhere, we see both how very different we are from ancient Athens but also how, in at least some underlying ways, we are the same.

TR is right that Thucydides omits the moral dimension that we are accustomed to identifying with modern American democracy so as to set it apart from the Athenian precedent. Alfred Beveridge's stirring prediction—that the American world republic would regulate the affairs of all peoples for their own good—was the keynote address at the convention that nominated TR in 1900, and there is not a word in it to which Roosevelt would not have shouted "Bully!" But we, too, have often been wracked by the Thucydidean dilemma of how to reconcile global economic and military might with a binding ethical standard for international affairs, and with the protection of rights at home. To this extent, Thucydides' lessons—and the instructive value of his examples of greatness and frailty in leaders—live on.

Thucydides was the first historian of statesmanship to see that a great democracy will inevitably be drawn into foreign conflicts, not only because of the desire for commercial prosperity and the temptation to acquire new allies by persuasion or force, but because of a more or less sincere desire to extend the benefits of freedom to other peoples, especially when other peoples ask for it. For exactly the same reasons, more than two thousand years later, as we await our second twenty-first-century president, America will *inevitably* act the role of a superpower in the world, regardless of who is commander in chief. Pat Buchanan and past isolationists notwithstanding, America can never be an isolationist country because everyone who advocates it always has a favored exception: except for famine in Darfur, nuclear weapons in North Korea, human rights in Myanmar, the Israeli-Palestinian conflict, and so on. Only if America ignored every plea for justice in the internal affairs of other countries with ruthless consistency, turning a deaf ear to other peoples' pleas for relief from external aggression and internal tyranny, and pursued relations for no other reason than cold-bloodedly enhancing American prosperity and security regardless of the suffering of others, would it be possible to withdraw from international entanglements, including the periodic risk of war. And, as we have seen throughout this book, while avoiding foreign entanglements is a strong American preference going back to Jefferson, equally strong is the belief crystallized by Lincoln that America is mankind's last best hope.

Nothing would have been easier, for example, than for America to have done a deal with Saddam Hussein. He was open for business as he felt the squeeze of the oil sanctions, and, if an economic motive did exist in the decision about invading, it was not on the part of the Bush administration, but the governments of France and Germany, whose economies had enormous contracts pending with Saddam Hussein's regime. America could easily make peace with dictators, do profitable business with them, and ignore their victims—and has sometimes done so. But then the very people who most loudly decry American exceptionalism and superpower bullying abroad would be just as voluble about American indifference to injustice and suffering around the world. The next American president will inherit this paradox, first uncovered by Thucydides and reexplored by the founders, Lincoln, and his greatest successors, from the moment one of them enters the Oval Office. The new president will only be able to calibrate the degree and intensity of America's overseas involvements, not withdraw from them.

Thucydides foresees at the very beginning of democracy in the

West the fundamental tensions and contradictions that have informed it throughout, down to the present, and await the new president of the world's one unquestionable superpower. That tension between freedom at home and imperial might abroad also embraces the tension between the satisfactions we enjoy as individuals and the wealth that flows home to us from the exercise of global power. Like the Athenians when Pericles gave them a timely warning that they were a "tyrant city" in the eyes of their allies, we can sometimes be haunted by the sense that our affluence is based on the exploitation of other peoples. The tension is further complicated by the noble impulse to extend our own democratic freedoms to other peoples through the often paradoxical means of using overwhelming armed might to free them from their own masters or, more controversially, from their own non-Western cultures and values, such that attempting to give them their freedom can sometimes look like cultural imperialism and contempt for the traditions of the intended beneficiaries.

Paradoxes such as these both bedeviled and ennobled Athens's rise to empire and her statesmanship, the same blend of idealism and materialism, of conquering others to both liberate and profit from them, often provoking a backlash of resentment among those who have been liberated. We saw a similar set of paradoxes when JFK took the torch passed by Churchill and the waning British Empire and promised that America would bear any burden to extend freedom around the world. The resulting war in Vietnam undermined two of his successors for—as victory remained elusive—dissenters at home feared the imperial powers of the presidency to undermine their liberties through illegal surveillance and the suppression of dissent. Ronald Reagan built up America's military arsenal in a way that provoked fear in the tottering Soviet empire and worries at home, real if exaggerated, that America intended to provoke a final superpower Armageddon. Bill Clinton reasserted the Democrats' claim to a more centrist foreign policy but, worried that Americans would not accept heavy casualties, waged an air war in Kosovo that some viewed as too extreme and others as too timid.

Finally, George W. Bush achieved two rapid military victories in response to 9/11, shattering the earthly outpost of jihadist extremism's grim utopian blueprint in Afghanistan and toppling Saddam Hussein, long-standing regional troublemaker, mass murderer, and comforter of terrorists. The early euphoria of victory gave way to profound disillusionment that military conquest alone could not eradicate residual opposition to foreign invaders and, above all, the internecine conflict unleashed in Iraq by the overthrow of Saddam Hussein and the brutal social peace he had imposed. American forces died in large numbers, while Americans at home were troubled both by the appearance of huge profits made by corporations close to the Bush administration and that the civil liberties of war prisoners and Americans themselves were in danger of a presidency gorged on its own military power, leaving the president with the lowest approval ratings since Truman and his legislative program paralyzed. His aspiring successors were shaped by the same dilemmas, and their responses were touchstones for their own characters and visions of statecraft. McCain had to pledge to win in Iraq while disavowing his president's methods. Obama wanted to end it, and paid a price for seeming imprudent and unrealistic. Hillary Clinton could not break free of her husband's comparatively hawkish legacy nor her own misgivings about an overly hasty withdrawal, and paid a price as well.

Indeed, the old struggle between hawks and doves, between age and youth, that we first see in the competition between Alcibiades and Nicias as they compete for the fallen mantle of Pericles, himself under a cloud in his final years, comes back to life in today's political battles as they have in every generation from Lincoln's tribe of the eagle, Churchill's burning desire to serve, and JFK's Periclean idealism about the spread of freedom through empire and making America a beacon of culture and learning. As always, as the historical kaleidoscope shifts, the enduring elements realign in altered patterns. In the most recent presidential contest, we once again saw a young man and an old warrior vie for the democracy's leadership in the wake of an outgoing leader who had initially enjoyed universal popularity and approval but whose popularity plummeted and reputation was under a cloud by the end of his tenure. This time, however, it was not the young hothead and hawk Alcibiades versus the peace-loving and dovish general, but something more like the opposite—a charismatic young man who believed in world peace through dialogue against an old soldier known for his hot temper and his cavalier remark that if need be we would stay in Iraq for a hundred years. The more things change, the more they do and do not remain the same.

The new president will inherit these same quandaries that once beset Pericles, Alcibiades, and Nicias, as they later beset Lincoln, Churchill, FDR, and the cold war presidents. If the new president tries to withdraw from the world, that will look like a selfish unwillingness to use might abroad to help others—abandoning Israel, the Palestinians, the fledgling democracy in Iraq, afraid to go up against Iran and North Korea, allowing China to hold sway over Southeast Asia. If, on the other hand, he asserts American power in one or more of these hot spots, the familiar charges will arise about American exceptionalism and arrogance, mixed motives of idealism and profit seeking, and the threat posed to freedom at home by an overeager commander in chief. Reading Thucydides, as Theodore Roosevelt once did, would not be a bad place for the new president to start in preparing himself.

CONCLUSION

The Ten Secrets
of Leadership

According to Anselm's proof of the existence of God, since we can conceive of a perfect being—and since we could not conceive of a perfect being that did not also exist in reality, because a merely imagined perfection would fall short of a being that was perfect both in our imagination and in reality—we therefore know that God exists. Needless to say, many have been dissatisfied with the medieval scholar's proof. As one modern logician witheringly replied, imagining that you have won the lottery will not put any money in your wallet.

If Anselm's proof does not work to assure us of the existence of a perfectly just and wise divinity, it's even less likely that a version of this argument will convince us that the perfect leader ever can or will exist. We can conceive of one. But does that mean that he or she is real? Yet we continue looking, because it is human nature to hope for a better world, if not now then for our children and the future.

Pericles understood this when he urged his fellow Athenians to rise above mere prosperity and cultivate art, learning, and culture, so as to become a beacon of learning for all Greeks. Lincoln understood it when he urged Americans to persevere with the Civil War not only for their own sake, but because their country was the last best hope for the whole human race. It inspired JFK's summons to Americans to bear any burden for freedom anywhere in the world, and, most recently, Barack Obama's encouragement of "the audacity to hope" in a period when the country's energies were flagging and its dreams on hold.

We can imagine what the ideal leader would be like. Since ancient times, great thinkers, historians, and artists have given us a series of shining portraits. Such a leader will be courageous if need be on the battlefield or under other tests of physical adversity. That physical courage will be the underpinning for an even more important courage of character and mind, the capacity to act on what is right and to fashion, at turns boldly, at turns cautiously, whatever means are needed to bring about what is right, to the degree possible under the circumstances, persuading the citizenry through an appeal both reasoned and uplifting.

Such a leader will be capable of resisting the sway of majority opinion, but open to the public's views and not intolerant of dissent. He will have, or at least aspire to cultivate, a sound character in which reason and passion are prudently balanced, and a mind honed both by an immersion in real-world experience and a study of great statesmen, thinkers, and historians who stimulate us to reflect on how the past can provide lessons for the present, but also how it may not, or not in precisely the same way. He will be capable of inspiring his fellow citizens to rise above their narrow everyday concerns to a higher level, but also capable of sympathizing with their difficulties, worries, and limitations. He will be compassionate for the suffering of others at home and abroad, but will not let compassion paralyze the sometimes grim necessities of waging war for the sake of justice, peace, or the common good.

Every great leader, and even some of the flawed ones, discussed in this book have embodied some of these qualities. But has any one such leader embodied all of them? Probably not. Certainly none of the greats—Pericles, Scipio, Napoleon, Lincoln, Churchill, FDR— was universally thought to have done so, and, in their more reflective moments, most were aware of how far short of the mark they fell. The difficulty of identifying a perfect leader goes back to Aristotle, whose own reflections were shaped by the history of the world's first democracy. Perfection, Aristotle writes, is available in certain theoretical spheres like mathematics, and every competent student can be led to understand why a mathematical proof is correct. It's not a matter of opinion. But the practical realm of politics is inherently a realm of conflicting opinions, a clash between justice and self-interest, immersed in an eddy of shifting, contingent circumstances. In that realm, a consensus that a leader has been flawless is rarely if ever possible, and when success is achieved one day, circumstances may so alter the next that it will be discredited. As we have seen, the Athenians' near unanimous respect for Pericles' leadership was severely undermined by the unpredictable cataclysm of the plague. One day he appeared responsible for all their successes, the next for all their problems. Many recent American presidents have lived through the same fall from popular highs to lows, and, like Richard Nixon and George W. Bush as their presidencies wound down, ruefully found themselves more popular in other countries than at home. All in all, a statesman is less like a geometrician and more like the pilot of a ship who tacks and trims as necessary to tap the power of the waves and winds without the ship and its passengers sinking.

At the beginning of this book, I somewhat lightheartedly compared the most recent crop of candidates to the perfection of the fictional TV president Jed Bartlett. I returned to this theme at the end of Part One in suggesting a presidential algorithm of both good and bad leaders made up of the qualities we traced in the generations of leadership from World War II and the cold war now passing from the scene. In conclusion, and hopefully illuminated by the rest of this book, we come back to the same issue: Where is that perfection to be found, if not in whole then in part? The three parts of this book give us a sense of what the best kind of leadership looks like, along with some flesh-and-blood examples of leaders who really do embody at least some aspects of perfection, as well as those who fall severely short.

After considering the world closest to us and the challenges of war and peace in our time; the origins of American statecraft; the problematic place of honor and ambition and the temptation to tyranny; and then Athens, the original democratic empire, with its dilemmas over the exercise of power abroad while maintaining freedom at home—

after reviewing all this, one is readily struck by many time-tested parallels, both positive and negative, with the leaders of our own epoch. Take the importance of battlefield courage as a psychological baseline for civic courage. It has always been understood that not every leader will have combat experience, but that there are other ways of showing bravery. President Reagan never saw combat. As he disarmingly put it in declining France's offer to award him the Cross of the Legion of Honor, "all I did in the war was fly a desk." But in taking a bullet from a would-be assassin, he displayed courage and grace under the threat of death, assimilating late in life some of the qualities of bravery in combat. George W. Bush's military record has often been questioned. But by flying into a still unstable Baghdad for a surprise Thanksgiving dinner with the troops in 2003, he at least symbolically shared the dangers of the soldiers he commanded. As for negative parallels with the past, contempt for public opinion of the kind Pericles always strove to avoid was crystallized in the reaction of Vice President Cheney to the widespread unpopularity of a foreign policy he was instrumental in shaping: "So?"

John McCain comes close to embodying at least some aspects of an ideal of statecraft reaching back to Cicero's Scipio Africanus. Scipio always endeavored to be a virtuous statesman and avoided the temptations of the Alcibiadean demagogue and adventurer. He was a war hero and a statesman, and devoted above all to the life of the mind. McCain was certainly a war hero, and that courage under fire certainly sustained his moral courage in taking stands against his own party on issues like campaign finance. Whether he has cultivated the life of the mind is less certain. His opponent Obama embodies the grace and charisma of youth, the same beauty of soul some Athenians saw in Pericles and, more ambivalently, Alcibiades. Like Pericles, Lincoln, and Churchill before him, Barack Obama certainly understands the importance of uplifting rhetoric in a democracy. While McCain is an old-fashioned patriot, Obama senses and embodies the fresh appeal of the values of American democracy in the global age. What remains to be seen is whether his belief in the magic of inspiring words is moored in a prudent grasp of the realities of American power in the world and the willingness to use it if need be. Pericles could also inspire people to rise above themselves, as could Lincoln and FDR. But they also knew that sometimes evil had to be opposed by force, and that dialogue will not work with those who hate you in principle.

So while we may not be any closer to our own Anselm's proof that a perfect statesman can exist, we are in a position at the end of this book to extract some lessons from the long gallery of great and flawed leadership stretching from Thucydides' Athens through the reappearance of democracy in America and America's dilemmas of democracy and empire during the long struggle with totalitarianism and the succeeding war on terror. From Pericles to the next American president, statesmanship remains all about peace with honor, about an aspiration to justice backed with the might to defend it, and whether superpower status necessarily corrupts the soul of a self-governing people.

We have covered a broad canvas and a lot of territory in this book: ancient and modern statesmanship, great leadership in America and elsewhere. Much in the past is different, but much remains the same. In looking for the soul of a leader today, character still counts above all else. Surveying that whole odyssey, starting from the saga of the American presidency of recent generations, going further into its roots by exploring the epic mission of Lincoln and the surrounding dilemmas of the role of greatness in modern times, and finally, returning to the roots of democratic statesmanship at the dawn of the West, can we arrive at some maxims that might apply across the board today?

In conclusion, I want to suggest ten lessons on the meaning of political greatness that range throughout the preceding three parts of this book and plumb the depths of history in order to illuminate the recent past, the present, and the challenges to come. Taken together, while they may not add up to a recipe for the perfect leader, they at least show how the moral, psychological, and intellectual resources we inherit from the traditions of the West, its experiences and its reflections on statecraft from ancient times onward, can give us a compass for the challenges America's next generation of leaders will inevitably face.

1. Character trumps brains—or at least formal education.

Neither Winston Churchill nor Abraham Lincoln received a formal university education, and their names live on among the greatest leaders of this or any age. Richard Nixon and Jimmy Carter possessed among the most disciplined minds of any American president, and both had troubled presidencies. Ronald Reagan was often derided for his lack of intellectual depth and apparent laziness, but these qualities often worked to his advantage. When he slept through the American air fight over Libya, some were shocked that he did not get involved, but others took solace in this evidence that the modern presidency was something a normal man could handle without tearing himself apart. Although of course some of America's most distinguished presidents have also been accomplished intellectuals—think of Woodrow Wilson—it does seem true that a leader with little formal education can rise to the first rank as a statesman, while a sterling educational pedigree does not guarantee such an outcome.

2. Inspiring rhetoric is necessary—but only in moderation.

Napoleon once said: "A leader is a dealer in hope." To inspire hope, a leader needs to be a rhetorician. Everyone wishes that George W. Bush had been capable of speaking more memorably about 9/11 or the invasion of Iraq—especially those who listened carefully to the speeches of Bush's far more eloquent partner Tony Blair. But too much beautiful speechifying can lead to overkill: for example, Reagan's speech about the space shuttle disaster ("let slip the surly bonds of earth") or Bill Clinton's tendency to rhapsodize about pretty much everything. If your rhetoric is beautiful on every occasion, large or small, people will begin to tune out. And when an extraordinary challenge does come along, you may already have exhausted your supply of superlatives on lesser matters. FDR consciously used a very plain speaking style in most of his speeches, reserving his most memorable turns of phrase for those grave occasions when he wanted to make sure listeners were paying attention. Everyone remembers Roosevelt's classic exhortation "we have nothing to fear but fear itself"—in part because it stood apart from FDR's usual, more pedestrian style. Moreover, sometimes public speech must sacrifice edification for bluntness. As an admiring editorialist wrote of Theodore Roosevelt: "He called thieves thieves, regardless of their millions. . . . He told the plain unvarnished truth as his indignant eyes saw it." Sometimes being pithy is more impressive than being inspiring: When Lincoln expressed his moral indignation in eight simple words, "If slavery is not wrong, nothing is wrong," he summed up his entire career. Leaders must also realize that words are not all-powerful against reality. During the 2008 primaries, when Senator Clinton criticized Barack Obama for valuing words over deeds, he rightly responded that inspiring oratory in a democracy was indispensable to motivating citizens. But she also had a point. The ability of leaders like Jefferson, Lincoln, and Martin Luther King Jr. to inspire with words was matched by years of hard slogging, and the occasional compromise, to win over opponents or the undecided.

3. Moral conviction is necessary—but only in moderation.

As Machiavelli says, a man who tries to be good at all times will necessarily come to ruin in a world where most people are not good. On a personal level, President Jimmy Carter was a very decent man. But this made him naïve about Soviet intentions, a weakness that helped pave the way for the bitter comeuppance of the Soviet invasion of Afghanistan. Carter saw the world purely in American terms, believing that everyone should aspire to universal human rights—but he failed to realize that many regimes in the world exceed on a daily basis what the United States is capable of only at its very worst when it comes to abusing its citizens or those of other countries. Once again, Lincoln proves the point: In his time, many abolitionists would settle for nothing less than the immediate and complete eradication of slavery, and therefore ended up getting nothing. Yet Lincoln, whom they despised as a compromiser, achieved it for them in the long run. Sometimes choosing the lesser evil ends up doing the most good. We saw how Lincoln was plagued by the notion that people thought he might support the Know-Nothings because he did not oppose them publicly. But to attack the Know-Nothings would have risked alienating the same fervent Protestantism that provided the backbone of abolitionism. Lincoln needed their churches as allies in combating the worst evil—not mere discrimination against newcomers, deplorable as that was, but the actual enslavement of Americans who had been here from the beginning.

On the other hand, no rule is infallible, and sometimes a stance of uncompromising moral conviction does earn the greatest admiration for a leader. The sincerity of Marcus Brutus in opposing the ambitions of Julius Caesar on behalf of the republic earned him respect even from staunch Caesar allies like Mark Antony, who said that he alone of Caesar's assassins was not motivated by personal gain or envy. By contrast, Cicero's maneuvering between one dynast and another earned him contempt as an opportunist and, finally, a horrible death on the orders of Antony, who had not forgotten an earlier insult (Cicero's tongue, the organ of his famed loquacity, was mutilated by Antony's furious wife).

4. A leader embodies the times.

This is a part of what we mean by charisma: When a leader finds his moment, we feel we already know him: He is like us, he faces what we face. As John Morley remarked about Theodore Roosevelt: "Roosevelt is not an American, you know. He is America." The biographer John W. Bennett said of TR, not entirely approvingly: "Many of our people are boastful and self-assertive. Roosevelt is their ideal. Fulmination, bluster, clamorousness, appeal to some of us. Roosevelt satisfies us."

When I was teaching in the Midwest, I often heard my students say about President Reagan: "He's like me. He's even more like my dad." Reagan always did better with the public than with the pundits. Likewise, Bill Clinton somehow fit the 1990s, with its brash optimism and exuberance, its mixing of classes in a new hybrid of money and talent. Churchill was an English bulldog, Eisenhower the calm and steady manager of the Pax Americana, Franklin Roosevelt the charismatic aristocrat who rolled the dice to save capitalism by turning against the plutocrats and borrowing ideas from social democracy.

Political historians will spend years reexamining the historic Democratic presidential race of 2008, which pitted the charismatic young African-American senator Barack Obama against the divisive but resilient former First Lady Hillary Clinton. For all her campaign's strengths and weaknesses, one of the cleverest decisions her strategists made was to encourage her being known simply by her first name, "Hillary." Subliminally, this says: You know this woman. You have for a long time now. You know who and what she is, even if you don't entirely like her. Hillary Clinton had certainly been through every-thing boomers had been through: She embodied the uneasy combi-nation of career ambition and motherhood, the challenges of a shaky marriage to a philandering male-menopausal husband. The capacity of leaders like Hillary—whose appeal proved surprisingly enduring as the campaign dragged on—to embody the times is perhaps the most mysterious element of success. The number of human qualities that can mesh with the zeitgeist is infinite; sometimes they mirror it pas-sively, while at other times they defy the status quo, defining—even demanding—a new avenue for the nation.

5. A leader must have two or three main goals, and not try to do too much.

Ronald Reagan's broad agenda of restoring American military su-premacy abroad and stimulating entrepreneurialism at home contrasted favorably with the impression left by his predecessor, Jimmy Carter, whose leadership style seemed purposeless and micromanagerial (in-cluding, notoriously, keeping the schedule for the White House tennis court). Bill Clinton wanted to restore the Democratic Party as the party of fiscal responsibility at home and as not flinching from the use of mili-tary force abroad. Despite many fits and starts, he delivered on both.

A corollary of this rule is: Do your big thinking *before* you begin running. Don't wait until the race itself or, worse still, until win-ning office to figure out what you stand for. A common thread running through the careers of successful leaders is that their main aims had years, even decades, to incubate. By the time they gained high office, they had the luxury of changing tactics as needed, because the strategic goal was firmly fixed. This is true of Lincoln with respect to slavery, and of Churchill with respect to the Nazi threat. Margaret Thatcher quietly honed her pro-market views while serving in the cabinet of Ted Heath, a centrist who did not share her leanings at all. Biding her time as a low-profile cabinet minister, assembling a kitchen cabinet of intellectuals and advisors who would accompany her to 10 Downing, she was already fully convinced of what she wanted to do when the opportunity opened up for her to become leader of the Conservative Party. Ronald Reagan had nurtured his faith in the free enterprise system and his loathing for Communism for years, back to his leadership of the Screen Actors Guild in the 1940s. As he told his first national security advisor, Richard Allen, in their very first chat, "Here's my idea of our relations with Russia. We're going to win, and they're going to lose." As a five-term governor of Arkansas and a major participant in the center-right Democratic Leadership Council, Bill Clinton was able to articulate his conviction that Democrats must cease appearing to be the enemies of capitalism and shed their pacifist image, such that when he began his run for the presidency, he already knew what he stood for. By contrast, political races are strewn with the corpses of campaigns by people who made themselves up as they went along, such as John Kerry and Al Gore.

6. Time will run out.

Again and again, we see great leaders fall just short of the Promised Land of their main aim in politics, cut down by premature death or disease, or simply worn out and distracted by years of labor. Pericles died from exposure to the plague before he had a chance to dissuade the Athenians from rashly undertaking more foreign expansion than they could possibly sustain. His premature passing allowed unscrupulous adventurers like Alcibiades to corrupt the Athenian people with dreams of endless imperial gain. Winston Churchill was, by some accounts, too exhausted by the end of World War II to focus as sharply as he should have on Stalin's lies and plans to occupy central Europe. Roosevelt died tragically on the very eve of the triumph of his policies. Because time will run out—because leaders exhaust themselves, fall ill, grow weak and die—something major will always be left undone. And that can be bad or good: The premature death of the Soviet premier Yuri Andropov, last of the old guard and a hardliner bent on restoring Stalinist ideological rigor, left a power vacuum that brought Mikhail Gorbachev and a new generation to power unexpectedly quickly, leading to the end of the Soviet empire. Mortality is something no focus group or spin doctor can overcome.

7. History will choose its leaders.

When the conditions discussed above come together, history itself will create an energy and identify itself with the right leader. In any successful political race, that magic moment always comes—the "big mo," the big transformation when a candidate mysteriously melds with the zeitgeist, seems to walk with history and lead a charmed life. You must learn to anticipate that wave, be ready to ride it without being dumped by it. And remember that, having picked you up and swept you invincibly along for some years, that wave can just as suddenly dump you. Tony Blair, the embodiment of "Cool Britannia" who for so long could do no wrong, ended his third term with the sharks of his own party circling and the public deserting him in droves. Almost no great leader leaves office with a fraction of the popularity with which he assumes it, unless prematurely by death.

8. The great leader wants power badly—but not too badly.

As we have seen throughout this book, political power and high office can fill an inner emptiness—but they can just as surely undo even a great leader, and certainly lesser ones, when their attractions inevitably grow sour or retirement looms. Churchill's depression, his childhood feelings of rejection, haunted him all his life, breeding in him a ferocious hunger for success, a desire to be loved by the public. Yet it's doubtful whether his achievements, so glorious to others, brought him lasting inner peace or happiness. One may have to be content with having done one's duty. Toward the end of his life, he shocked his young granddaughter by telling her that everything he had accomplished had been a failure. Richard Nixon wanted nothing more than the presidency, or so he believed. Yet as soon as he achieved it the satisfaction vanished, and his darker side returned undiminished—his paranoia, his bitterness over perceived past slights, his fear that people looked down on him—until he destroyed the very prize he had fought so hard to win. Being *seen* to want power too badly can also alienate your supporters. Toward the end of the 2008 Democratic primaries, Bill Clinton said the nomination would go to whoever "wants it the most." But by appearing to want it at any cost, Hillary's ambition and perseverance, previously sources of admiration for her, began to look as if she was willing to tear her party apart rather than lose. Remember—other lives are conceivable. There are other ways of being happy, very possibly better ones.

9. Greatness can turn out to be villainy.

Charisma can conceal a dark side. No one ever expects the emergence of new tyrants; they seem like part of a distant, more barbaric past. But they are always with us. It seemed impossible that Germany, the world's best educated and most cultured nation, would embrace someone like Hitler. You can't always spot these people in advance. As late as 1935, Winston Churchill, the most intransigent foe of Nazi Germany in British politics, could not entirely make up his mind about whether Hitler was an unmitigated disaster or might yet prove a beneficial leader for Germany, restoring the pride of a great people after the searing humiliation of Versailles and the Depression.

And the last and hardest lesson:

10. The great leader must be prepared to ignore all of the above.

When in doubt, the great leader must be bold and stick to his guns—

must lead, not follow. As Emerson put it, moral force gives a man both fearlessness and tranquillity. Sticking to your guns means not being afraid to reverse yourself and change your policies if your inner compass convinces you a change is needed. People admire an honest effort even if it turns out to be flawed. They take comfort from a leader who cares enough to try something big. Jimmy Carter's speech about America's "moral malaise" sounded like a man both bewildered by the challenges of his job and somehow peevishly blaming his own fellow citizens for his difficulties. It paved the way for Ronald Reagan, who radiated confidence in both himself and the country. Or think of Margaret Thatcher: "the lady's not for turning." She made herself the object of intense unpopularity, even hatred, but her reforms rescued Britain from sliding into the economy of a third-world country. Tony Blair was unflinching on Britain's support for the war in Iraq because he was convinced it was the right thing for his country, just as earlier he had been unflinching in not reversing Thatcher's pro-market economic stance; he was determined to drag the Labour Party back to the center of British politics.

Does sticking to your guns always work? No. It's impossible to know ahead of time whether you will succeed or fail. The only certain thing in life—and therefore in political life—is uncertainty.

Acknowledgments

Thanks are due to my editor, Cal Morgan, for another fruitful collaboration, and to my agent, Chris Calhoun. I am also indebted to friends and colleagues who read earlier versions of the book. Chief among them are Norman Doidge and Andrew Stark, whose critical insights about the entire manuscript were of great help. Thanks also to Charles Fairbanks, Michael Moses, Barry Strauss, Peter Ahrensdorf, Joan Fairbanks, Robert Sibley, Gary Clewley, and Conrad Black for advice about specific themes and people. I owe Robin Roger a special thank-you for making me aware of Anthony Storr's *Churchill's Black Dog*. As always, my wife, Jacqueline Etherington Newell, was my best critic and ally.

I should also mention my two erstwhile students Matthew Post and Alex Duff for their valuable work as research assistants. I am grateful as well to my students in political science and the College of the Humanities at Carleton University for giving me the opportunity to try out parts of the argument on them. An earlier version of the introduction was presented as a public lecture at the University of Notre Dame, and I thank Catherine Zuckert and Michael Zuckert, along with their students, for their stimulating comments and their hospitality.

This book is dedicated to the memory of my late father, Waller Newell, and to my two beautiful new relatives, Edie Newell and Lukas Sealey Oddie.

Index